Phew. 21,
66,
70.
183

Sartre and the Sacred

Sartre and the Sacred

Thomas M. King

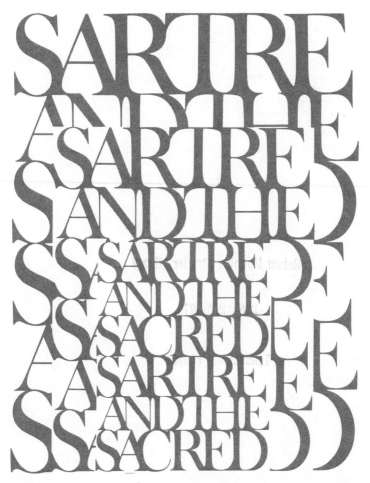

The University of Chicago Press
Chicago and London

The University of Chicago Press,
Chicago 60637
The University of Chicago Press, Ltd.,
London
© 1974 by the University of Chicago

All rights reserved. Published 1974.
Printed in the
United States of America

International Standard Book
Number: 0-226-43612-8
Library of Congress Catalog
Card Number: 73-87304

THOMAS M. KING, S.J., is assistant
professor of theology at Georgetown
University.
[1974]

Contents

v

Abbreviations
for the Works
of Sartre
Cited in the Text

Alexander. New York: Berkley Medallion, 1956.

IF   *L'Idiot de la famille.* 2 volumes. Paris: Gallimard, 1971.

KV   *Kierkegaard Vivant.* A collection of essays on Kierkegaard, one of them by Sartre. Paris: Gallimard, 1966.

LPE   *Literary and Philosophical Essays,* translated by Annette Michelson. New York: Macmillan, Collier Books, 1962.

N   *Nausea,* translated by Lloyd Alexander. New York: New Directions, 1969.

NE   *No Exit* and three other plays (*The Flies, Dirty Hands, The Respectful Prostitute*). *No Exit* and *The Flies* translated by Stuart Gilbert, *Dirty Hands* and *The Respectful Prostitute* by Lionel Abel. New York: Random House, Vintage Book, 1949.

PI   *The Psychology of the Imagination,* translator not indicated. New York: Citadel Press, 3d edition, 1965.

R   *The Reprieve,* translated by Eric Sutton. New York: Bantam Modern Classics, 1968.

S1   *Situations, I.* Paris: Gallimard, 1947. This is a collection of articles written by Sartre between 1938 and 1945. Many are translated in *LPE.*

S2   *Situations, II.* Paris: Gallimard, 1948. This is a collection of articles written by Sartre between 1945 and 1947. Most of this volume is translated as *WL.*

S3   *Situations, III.* Paris: Gallimard, 1949. This is a collection of articles written by Sartre between 1944 and 1948. Some are translated in *LPE.*

S4   *Situations,* translated by Benita Eisler. New York: Fawcett Crest Book, 1966. This is the translation of most of *Situations, IV;* all references are to the translation.

SM   *Search for a Method,* translated by Hazel Barnes. New York: Random House, Vintage Books, 1963.

TE   *The Transcendence of the Ego,* translated by Forrest Williams and Robert Kirkpatrick. New York: Farrar, Straus and Giroux, 1957.

TM   *Les Temps Modernes.* A review edited by Sartre. Paris.

TS   *Troubled Sleep,* translated by Gerard Hopkins. New York: Bantam Modern Classics, 1968.

W	*The Words,* translated by Bernard Frechtman, New York; Fawcett Crest Book, 1966.

WL	*What is Literature?* translated by Bernard Frechtman. New York: Harper and Row, 1965.

Introduction

Many psychologists have spoken of a basic human drive and some have tried to identify it. Freud called it the sexual libido and Adler the will to power. Sartre objects to these and other similar identifications as being incompatible with the structure of consciousness; he proposes his own: "To be man means to reach toward being God. Or if you prefer, man fundamentally is the desire to be God" (BN,694). But for Sartre God turns out to be impossible, and man is left with a theological "complex" and ultimate frustration. Though God is impossible, the divine ideal is basic to being human, hence man has theological intuitions and religious experiences in abundance. In the writings of Sartre an endless assortment of people and things are touched with religious feeling and are said to be sacred: the dead, children, racial prejudice, adventure stories, the theater, mother love, and the occupational hazards of the professional thief. The writings of Sartre are left with an overriding theological character that often seems to be unaffected by the atheism that he professes. Sartre is occupied with Good and Evil, Being and Nothingness, guilt, salvation, total despair, and blazing hierophanies; in short, the same themes that have always occupied mystics, saints, yogis, and other less-classified holy men.

This is not to say that Sartre agrees with the yogis and saints. He does not. He is resolutely opposed to them; but in his opposition he witnesses how deeply he has been affected by their way of thinking and their values. I was familiar with the mystical tradition before I began reading Sartre, otherwise I would have missed the point of many of his cryptic allusions. I have come to believe that much of Sartre's thought can be understood only in the context of the spiritual tradition that he endlessly renounces. I also believe that Sartre's brilliance has something to offer that tradition. I have organized a study of Sartre around theological themes, and in the process I have come to believe that this is the natural basis for understanding his achievement. Sartre has suggested as much himself (*W*,156-57). The work that follows is primarily an objective exposition of Sartre's thought. In the body of the chapters I generally have refrained from giving my own evaluation, but at the conclusion of each chapter I express some reservations or try to situate Sartre within the traditions of various spiritual masters.

The chapters that follow are not equally difficult or equally original, but their sequence is important. The first chapter should be easy to read; it introduces the material and illustrates basic Sartrean themes with examples. The second chapter is more abstract; it tries to sum up *Being and Nothingness* and is necessarily difficult. The third chapter takes the Sartrean definition of God and uses it to understand various encounters with the numinous. The fourth chapter shows Sartre at his phenomenological best; it follows in detail his careful analysis of self-knowledge and his critique of the search for one's identity. Chapters five and six stand together as a pair; they contrast two opposing mentalities (the religious and the spiritual), and Sartre turns out to be opposed to both of them. The final chapter tries to pull the many Sartrean themes together into a comprehensive picture. The literary career of Sartre has spanned forty years; during this time many significant changes can be found in his thought. These are indicated as the study advances, but their full extent is probably not evident until the final chapter. The sequence that appears to underlie his growth is one that is familiar to those who have studied the religious tradition.

The present work has developed out of the doctoral dissertation that I defended at the University of Strasbourg. Wherever there are English translations available, I have referred to them; and wherever possible I have referred to the paperback editions. I am particularly grateful to my thesis director, Reverend Robert Javelet; his encouragement and his practical advice were invaluable.

1

Moses Dictating the New Law

The Predestined Life

Contemporary psychologists consider the first years of childhood the key to an understanding of the adult psyche; Sartre is no exception. But Sartre is probably unique in tracing the psychological importance of childhood to the child's concern with the great philosophical questions. The child is said to experience anguish and his anguish is metaphysical; he asks fundamental questions which imply religious answers, so to interpret the mind of the child Sartre writes in religious terms.

The Anguish of the Child

A child first becomes conscious in a world that has already been structured by his parents: all of the objects that he sees have been designed for use and embody an accepted value; these include the child himself. Before he was born the social standing of his parents has shaped the hopes they would have for him; he is given a place and a predetermined role. Adults see the child as one more object that they are to put in order. They speak of him as "he" or even as "it" long before the child has learned to say "I." Gradually the child comes to know himself in the third person with the value adults have provided; perhaps he even refers to himself as "he."

Grownups never weary of taking stock of their belongings, this is called regarding. The child is part of the lot, between two stools or under the table. He comes to know himself through their regard, and his happiness lies in being part of the stock. To Be is to belong to someone (G,6).

The child is part of a structured world. He is given a name and told what to do. Like the other objects about him, he too has a proper place. 'We had our first existence as absolute objects' (S4,238).

The child is given a role to play, and in this role his parents have given the child a place in their own quarrels, regrets and ambitions, for the child is an object that they can maneuver. But when his parents were young they too were maneuvered. They were "pigeonholed" into a social role, and they respond by pigeonholing their children in return (IF,20). Thus the social struggles of one period determine the destinies of generations to come. The child discovers his destiny from his parents; they communicate it to him in the way they speak and smile, but especially in the way they look at the child. Through the judgment that is contained in their looks the child comes to find his "nature" —except that his nature is not really his, it has been manufactured by others and given to him. The child finds that he is a "Jew" or an "aristocrat" or something else. But he was not born that way. If he has a nature it is because adults have given him one, and he will become deformed by the role it requires him to play. Sartre compares all parents to the members of primitive societies who believe that a dead relative is incarnated in a newborn child. Believing that the child is the reincarnation of an uncle who has died, they treat the child as someone else. The child begins to go along with the idea, he becomes someone else, he adopts the character of his dead uncle. To his parents it seems that a dead man has been reincarnated, but in reality—a child has died (S4,238). According to Sartre, every man bears this burden from the past; he has been forced by society to reincarnate at least one dead man.

A child might come to believe that he is his own uncle, or to believe that he is a born aristocrat, or to believe that he is a pariah by his very nature. But he is none of these, he is born free. It is just that he has been tricked into seeing himself as an object. After the trick has been played, all that is required of him is to accept his proper place and live out the role that he has been assigned. He becomes a person possessed. He is in the possession of an image that others have given him. Perhaps even in his old age he still will be acting out the role that some adult gave him years before.

Usually it is the parents who determine Good and Evil for the child; their judgments establish his universe of truth and value. Since it is they who have established the True and the Good, the child sees his parents as divinities. Before the gaze of these divinities the child's aim is simple: he must please the gods. But then comes the experience of growing up. The child begins to find his own individuality, and he loses faith in the gods. He finds his freedom, and in this discovery realizes that there is no necessity that really applies to him. He is no longer an absolute object, he has discovered subjectivity. This discovery is disturbing, for with it the child becomes aware that Good and Evil are no longer given to him. His subjectivity is without norm or character. He has no identity. Nothing justifies his existence, he is superfluous. Why is he here? Where is he going? What is he made for? The anxieties of childhood are metaphysical. Separated from the sacred world of fixed values, the child finds his existence gratuitous; he does not fit in anywhere, he is *de trop*. He has memories of a world where values were established, but now he has come into his freedom; he has been cast out of paradise and cannot return. The child may desire the sacred universe where Good and Evil are objectively determined, but where is the authority who can provide it? The child is involved in an identity crisis; he knows he must choose for himself who he is and must invent for himself his own Good and Evil. He may try to forget the dreadful freedom and blindly submit to some authority outside of himself, or he might invent himself. In either case he has become aware of his freedom, and there is no real turning back.

Moses Dictating the New Law

The Sacred World of Childhood

Sartre has written several psychological studies of children; the first is a 1937 short story, *The Childhood of a Leader*. The story begins when the leader, Lucien, is a very young child; he is puzzled by vague suspicions that his parents are only playing roles. But to Lucien's eyes there is something sacred about the activities of adults: the ordinary commands of his parents are experienced as if they were sacramental formulas, they convey "haloes of religious obligations." When grownups are gathered together, he finds it beautiful, like being at Mass.

One of Lucien's cousins accuses him of being stuck-up. He reflects to see if the word really applies to him. He tries to determine his own character, but reflection tells him nothing. He finally makes something appear in his head that is like a bit of cloud.

Lucien made desperate efforts to *look* at this bit of cloud and he suddenly felt as though he were falling into it head first, he found himself in the mist and became mist himself, he was no more than a damp white warmth which smelled of linen. He wanted to tear himself from this mist and come back but it came with him....Then suddenly he told himself "I am..." and there was a slight click: he had awakened from his long somnolence. It was not pleasant....In place of his stupor so sweet to him and which lost itself in its own folds, there was now a small, wide-awake perplexity which wondered "Who am I?"....There was this fog rolling back on itself, indefinite. "I!" He looked into the distance; the word rang in his head and then perhaps it was possible to make out something, like the top of a pyramid whose side vanished far off into the fog. Lucien shuddered and his hands trembled. "Now I have it!" he thought, "now I have it! I was sure of it: *I don't exist!*"....He closed his eyes and let himself drift: existence is an illusion because I *know* I don't exist, all I have to do is plug my ears and not think about anything and I'll become nothingness" (*Int.,* 100–101).

Lucien presents his doubts to a teacher, who quotes Descartes' "cogito ergo sum" and assures Lucien that one cannot doubt his own existence. Eventually Lucien comes to accept that he does exist, but he still cannot understand why, for he feels useless and arbitrary:

His existence was a scandal and the responsibilities he would assume later would barely be enough to justify it. "After all, I didn't ask to be born," he said...fundamentally, he had not stopped being embarrassed with his life, with this voluminous, useless gift, and he had carried it in his arms without knowing what to do with it or where to set it down. "I have spent my time regretting I was born" (*Int.*, 134).

As Lucien grows older his character begins to take on definition: he becomes anti-Semitic. Anti-Semitism evokes respect among his friends, and adults show their approval. When the anger of anti-Semitism arises within him, Lucien is no longer amorphous, he becomes somebody important. He no longer feels he is the same "me" and hardly recognizes this new inner-self.

Sartre ends the story as Lucien is sitting in a café, reflecting on the transformation that has been happening within himself. Through the transformation he suddenly finds his "nature": he is someone who can't stand Jews. The mist that had formed his consciousness is replaced by an inner firmness that feels like a steel blade. Lucien decides that he had been looking for himself in the wrong place. "'First maxim,' Lucien said, 'Not to try and see inside yourself; there is no mistake more dangerous.' The real Lucien—he now knew—had to be sought in the eyes of others." He is filled with sacred awe. He recalls the religious respect he once had for his parents. Then, in imagination, he sees his own muscular back, he sees himself as only others can see him. Then he sees himself in a religious setting that is beyond the anguish of existing.

Quietly, cautiously, he raised his hand to his forehead, like a lighted candle, then drew into himself for an instant, thoughtful and holy, and the words came of themselves. "I have rights!"...rights were beyond existence, like mathematical objects and religious dogma. And now Lucien was just that: an enormous bouquet of responsibilities and rights. He had believed that he existed by chance for a long time, but it was due to a lack of sufficient thought. His place in the sun was marked...."I exist," he thought, "because I have the right to exist." And, perhaps for the first time, he had a flashing, glorious vision of his destiny! (*Int.*, 158).

This early work sketches the main outlines of Sartre's understanding of both consciousness and the sacred. The young Lucien in the presence of adults feels he is in a sacred world; it is their world, not his. He tries to look into himself, but sees only cloudy indefinition. He feels ashamed because his existence seems to be a scandal that cannot be justified. He is finally delivered from this confusion through his anti-Semitism. In an inner transformation that seems to be part of a religious rite, Lucien sees himself as one who cannot stand Jews. He has become an object in his own eyes and sees his own back. He resolves to know his own self through the judgments of others. He is now an adult, ready to take his place in the adult world. Passing through this "identity crisis" is a sacred experience; now his contingent existence assumes the necessity found in mathematics or "religious dogma." The scandal of his existence is past, he has found what he was pre-destined to be.

Sartre again presented a childhood experience of *délaissement* in his biographical study of Jean Genet. Genet was a foundling child who was placed in the care of Morvan peasants. He was a well-behaved boy, smaller than his playmates but more intelli-gent. Genet accepts fully the ethics of his foster parents, he is good. "This Good is simple: one has parents whom one worships, one does one's homework in their presence, and before going to bed one says one's prayers" (*G*,6). To this religious soul, adults are seen as gods. Genet is told he is good and he believes it. Still, he feels a vague uneasiness although he cannot describe his malaise. Sartre attributes much of this malaise to Genet's status as an adopted child.

Genet watches adults with admiration and awe, and in his efforts to identify with them he imitates their gestures. Adults possess objects and use them freely; they are their possessions. Genet tries to imitate the actions of adults, but this he cannot do for the child possesses nothing. He appropriates things. He does not really seek the object appropriated, he seeks to be like others because others are just and good. At times a vague anguish comes over the child. When no one is around he relieves his anguish by stealing. But though he steals, he still considers himself well-be-haved and virtuous, for there is only one life that counts: the life one leads in the presence of adults.

One day when Genet is about ten years old, he is playing in the kitchen. Suddenly he becomes aware of his inner solitude, and he is seized with anxiety. To get relief he will appropriate. But this time someone is watching. An adult voice calls out, "You're a thief!" This moment divides Genet's life into two parts: before and after. Sartre refers to the incident as a "sacred drama" or as a "liturgical drama" (*G*,1). In this moment the unreflecting act of a child has been objectified, and an unreflecting child has been fixed as an object. Genet learns what he is objectively: he is a thief. His act is petrified and eternalized by the gaze of the Just. He is a thief and will be a thief forever. Before this moment, Genet lived in the sweet confusion of the immediate, unaware that he was a person. After it—all is in order, he has been provided with a nature and a soul. It is the nature and the soul of a thief. Later Genet will write, "Guilt first gives rise to individuality." The gaze of adults has transformed his mindless innocence into an eternal essence. He is caught in the act of apprehending and cannot deny the evidence. He apprehended only to imitate the gestures of adults, but suddenly an adult looked at the matter differently. Then Genet himself sees the matter differently. He sees himself as others see him; he is an object and that object is a thief. Genet decides against himself. He gives the judgments of society priority over his own consciousness. What is most real to him is no longer his own consciousness but what someone else has told him. Consciousness is sacrificed to the principle of authority, and Genet is convinced in his own heart that he is someone other than his own self. That someone other is the person adults see and he cannot. From this point on, his life will be only the history of his attempts to perceive this other. For him, to live is to watch himself live; duality becomes the permanent structure of his consciousness.

Genet was called a thief and thus received his sacred nature. As an adult Genet is accused again and again. He steals and goes to prison many times. But for Genet stealing became not so much a way to make a living as a religious ceremony, for it recalls the sacred moment. "By virtue of this ceremony Genet symbolically gives himself his thief's nature. It is a repetition of the crisis and of the rite of passage, a death followed by resurrection" (*G*,69). Genet has mystic intuitions, but they all center around that moment of anguish when he received his nature. The drab time of his daily life is "shot through with the blazing hierophanies which restore to him his original passion, as Holy Week restores to us that of Christ" (*G*,5).

Sartre uses the language of mysticism to describe a painful incident in the life of a child. But Genet describes the incident in the same language. What has happened is that the vacant consciousness of a child sees itself as others see it. The child becomes possessed by the judgment of an adult, his mind is divided. Genet sees himself as an object; like Lucien, he finds the experience filled with religious significance. A nature has been conferred. A sacred drama has taken place, a god has decided who he is. With mystical fervor Genet embraces his destiny. He is a thief.

Sartre presented another analysis of childhood *délaissement* in his study of Charles Baudelaire. Baudelaire's father died when Charles was very young. The child became totally devoted to his mother. Sartre describes the relation of mother and child in religious terms:

The mother was an idol, the child *consecrated* by her affection for him. Far from feeling that his existence was vague, aimless, superfluous, he thought of himself as *son by divine right*. He was always living in her which meant that he had found a sanctuary. He himself was nothing and did not want to be anything but an emanation of the divinity, a little thought which was always present in her mind. It was precisely because he was completely absorbed in a being who appeared to be a necessary being, to exist as of right, that he was shielded from any feeling of disquiet, that he melted into the absolute and was *justified* (*B*,16–17).

However, the situation changes abruptly. Baudelaire's mother remarries and the young Baudelaire is sent away. Suddenly the sacred relationship is over. The bliss that he had known draws back like a tide. In shame he discovers that he is alone and has been given existence for no purpose. He has lost his justification. Sartre generalizes on the experience: "Each of us was able to observe in childhood the fortuitous and shattering advent of self-consciousness" (*B*,19). To explain Baudelaire's anxiety, Sartre refers to several literary descriptions of a similar type. He quotes at length a passage from the novel *A High Wind in Jamaica*. Because Sartre regards the passage as the best literary account of a child's coming to subjectivity, it is worth examining. The passage tells of a young girl named Emily. One day while playing on the deck of a ship, she is struck by the thought that she is she.

What agency had so ordered it that out of all the people in the world who she might have been, she was this particular one, this Emily: born in such-and-such a year out of all the years in Time ....Had she chosen herself, or had God done it?....Wasn't she perhaps God, herself?....now she got such a sudden feeling of being a distinct person that they [her family] seemed as separate from her as the ship itself....A sudden terror struck her: did anyone know? (Know, I mean, that she was someone in particular, Emily —perhaps even God—not just any little girl) (*B*,19).

Sartre observes that this experience is frightening and one that does not pay. Most people try to forget it. But there are some people who decide to practice a certain type of asceticism by which they choose to make this experience of otherness their whole life. They come into the presence of pure self-consciousness and choose to live this empty experience in opposition to the rest of society. Sartre terms the choice metaphysical pride, the pride of the Stoics. By this act the individual sets himself up as an absolute beyond human society and beyond reason. Such a choice is made in desperation; in the end it leads nowhere. This otherness is something that every man has, but when someone chooses it in opposition to society, he makes it the symbol of what he considers a deeper individuality that is uniquely his. This is how Sartre understands the fundamental choice of Baudelaire. Baudelaire is the man who could not forget himself; he is always spying on his own consciousness, he wants to find his unique nature. Since his consciousness is always aware that it is spying on itself, his actions become false, "like a child playing under the eyes of grown-up people" (*B*,23).

Everyone who saw Baudelaire was impressed by his singularity. Baudelaire tries to regard his own singularity, but he finds nothing. He was seeking his nature, that is to say, his character and his being, but all he could find was a long, monotonous series of psychic states. Baudelaire cannot determine what his character is: is he spiritual? vulgar? intelligent? He cannot determine. He watches himself closely, but he lacks the distance necessary to see; to see himself he must be two. Reflex consciousness watches reflected consciousness, yet he knows the two are one. Baudelaire wants to possess himself, but one can only possess a thing. His desire is to be something, to be immutable like a stone or a statue. But his consciousness knows itself as totally gratuitous. It can find nothing meaningful except that which it arbitrarily decides to consider meaningful. It is lucid, proud, and bored. Baudelaire must either stagnate in indifference or invent good and evil for himself. He has no other choice. Sartre considers this the lot of every man. There are no values given to man, because there is no God to give them. The child must invent his own values or have none. This is why the child is forlorn, he has discovered the gratuitousness of being human.

Baudelaire seeks someone to deliver him from his anguish. He begins to write shocking poetry, he sins in public. He tries to horrify the gods, and this horror will be his consecration. What he is seeking is a stern judge who will condemn him, for a condemned man has a character that is fixed and stable. Baudelaire has love affairs with harsh women who scold and berate him, for then he is delivered from the sense of gratuitousness. He writes: "In politics the true saint is the one who whips and kills the people for their own good." Baudelaire seeks a divinity who will make his guilt an absolute, for the man who is damned at least has an established place in a hierarchic universe. He refuses to resolve what Sartre terms the "theological complex"—the complex that assimilates one's parents to divinities. His original choice was not to choose his own good, and his problem was that he could find no one to choose it for him.

Baudelaire's character is different than Genet's. Genet had a sentence imposed on him and he took that sentence to heart, thereby fixing a duality at the base of his consciousness. Baudelaire seeks a similar duality, for then he could see himself as an object. But duality eludes him, he can find no judge to determine his character, there is no one to establish good and evil. He calls out, "I am Satan." But Sartre objects that Satan is nothing other than the disobedient child who does evil in the framework of established good. Since Baudelaire desires such a good, his theological complex has not been resolved. Baudelaire has been called the *poète maudit,* as if a curse had given him his destiny.

But, according to Sartre, Baudelaire was the man who never could find what his destiny was and at the same time was unwilling to invent his own life.

When the attitudes of childhood endure in the mind of the adult, Freud speaks of the person having an Oedipus complex that has not been resolved. Sartre objects to the Oedipus complex and proposes in its place the theological complex. Like Freud he would see the complex as the mentality of the child continued into the adult years, but unlike Freud Sartre describes the mentality of the child in theological rather than sexual terms:

> The child takes his parents for gods. Their actions like their judgments are absolute. They are the incarnation of universal Reason, law, the meaning and purpose of the world. When the eye of these divine beings is turned on him, their look is enough to justify him at once to the very roots of his existence. It confers on him a definite, sacred character. Since they are infallible, it follows that they *see* him as he really *is*. There is no room in his mind for hesitation or doubt. True, all that he sees of himself is the vague succession of his moods, but the gods have made themselves the guardians of his eternal essence. He knows that it exists; even though he can have no direct experience of it, he realizes that his *truth* does not consist in what he can know of himself, but that it is hidden in the large, terrible yet gentle eyes which are turned towards him. He is a real essence among other real essences; he has *his* place in the world — an absolute place in an absolute world (*B*,52).

In coming to self-consciousness the child is not cast from a paradise of pleasure, rather he is cast from his place in the absolute. He longs to return to his "*true* essence," but he cannot — he is free.

The Vocation of Sartre and the House of Flaubert

In 1963 Sartre published *Les Mots*; it is the story of his own childhood, and much that he has written about other authors is seen to reflect his own experience. Jean-Paul Sartre was born in Paris in 1905. When he was less than a year old his father died and he and his twenty-year-old mother returned to Alsace to live with her parents. Sartre's grandfather was a somewhat pompous literary gentleman who doted playfully on the young Jean-Paul. An aura of the sacred hovered about the man: the book that he had written seemed to be a holy object, and his reading room was as solemn as a temple. Grandfather himself was regarded as a "patriarch," a "Moses," a "priest." Sartre assures us that his grandfather so resembled God the Father that he was often mistaken for him!

To find value in the games that he played, Sartre felt that he needed an adult audience. When adults were watching him he would perform dutifully; he felt himself to be an object, a potted plant. When adults were not watching he would act out dramatic deeds of heroism before an imaginary audience. "My truth, my character, and my name were in the hands of adults. I had learned to see myself through their eyes" (*W,* 52).

Still, all is not well: he experiences a *défaut d'être* which he cannot understand or cease to perceive. His mother tells him that her little boy is happy. He believes her and does not think about his *délaissement*; since adults do not see it there is no word for it. When he is alone he tries to take refuge in solitary truth, but he reports "I had no truth. All I found in myself was an astonished insipidness" (*W,* 69). When he is with others he seems to know who he is, but when he is alone he seems to be no one at all. Adults speak of a well-ordered world, but in this well-ordered world he can find no place for himself. He counts for nothing and feels shame before his unjustified presence. The pebbles, the chestnut trees, his grandparents—all of them are beings, but the young Sartre is nothing. He is a transparency without inertia, depths, or impenetrability (*W,* 57). This is what is behind his desire to play before adults: by imposture he can escape his anxiety. But his acts become gestures, and he becomes a fake child surrounded by stage props.

As he grows older he begins to suspect that he is not the only actor. Adults are playing the same game; before one another they are acting out roles given them years before. They too are impostures. Adults have been discredited, and this leaves him only more deeply forlorn. He has no reason for being and now he can find no one to give him one.

I needed a Supreme Court, a decree restoring my rights to me. But where were the magistrates? My natural judges had fallen into discredit through their hamming; I objected to them, but I saw no others (*W,* 58).

He tells us that he needed a God, he needed a Creator; but he was told only about the fashionable God in whom his family believed "as a matter of discretion." "I was serving without zeal the Idol of the Pharisees, and the official doctrine put me off seeking my own faith" (*W,*61).

One day when Sartre was eight years old, a friend of his mother, the lady whom Sartre considered his best audience, announced with conviction that Jean-Paul would become an author. Upon hearing this, Sartre's grandfather decides that the time has come to have a serious talk with the boy concerning the future. To discourage Jean-Paul he describes the hard life of an author and suggests that he consider teaching as a second profession. His grandfather speaks without the buffoonery that he usually adopts when talking with the boy.

For the first time, I was dealing with the patriarch. He seemed forbidding and all the more venerable in that he had forgotten to adore me. He was Moses dictating the new law. My law. He had mentioned my vocation only in order to point out its disadvantages. I concluded that he took it for granted (*W,*98).
...a misunderstanding at the age of eight caused me to believe that my venerable grandfather ordered me to write. Nothing else was necessary for me to feel charged with a mission (*IF,*1,598).

In this experience Sartre found the mandate that he had been seeking. Between the ages of nine and eleven he felt this mandate become his character; it was given to him by adults.

Nothing could confirm or deny my mandate, which was based on the principle of authority, on the unquestionable goodness of grown-ups. Sealed and beyond reach, it remained inside me but belonged to me so little that I had never been able, even for an instant, to have doubts about it and could neither dissolve nor assimilate it (*W,*130).

Sartre tells us that he did not choose his vocation, but that others imposed it upon him: "The grown-ups, who were installed in my soul, pointed to my star; I didn't see it, but I saw their fingers pointing; I believed in the adults who claimed to believe in me" (*W,*129). As a child he received the vocation of an author; he resembles the young Genet, who was given the vocation of the thief. Like Genet, Sartre did not really choose his vocation, it seemed to be imposed on him. As Genet made stealing a religious rite, Sartre would consider writing a sacred duty: "the sacred was deposited in *belles-lettres.*" "I decided to write for God with the purpose of saving my neighbors" (*W*,112). "I thought I was devoting myself to literature, whereas I was actually taking Holy Orders" (*W*,157). In becoming an author he claims that only a superficial modification of the faith was involved.

Sartre writes his autobiography in a somewhat playful style. When he tells of his "vocation" he presents it as coming from "Moses," but at the same time he implies that he knew better all along; he was conspiring with adults in order to sustain his belief and conceal his own anxiety. This is what Sartre will come to call "bad faith"; he would see a similar conspiring in any "vocation."

For many years Sartre has been working on a study of Gustave Flaubert; in 1971 he published two volumes (2,136 pages) on the first part of Flaubert's life, *l'Idiot de la famille.* The childhood of Flaubert is studied in detail, Sartre using incidents from it to present his own reflections. The work is permeated with references to the religious character of childhood with Flaubert's father referred to as Lord, Creator, Jehovah, the All-Powerful, or as Feudal Lord, Patriarch, Moses, and so on. The work resembles Sartre's earlier studies of childhood, but it is more nuanced and introduces several new themes that are significant; it also presents the childhood of Gustave's older brother, Achille.

The father of Achille and Gustave came from a peasant family, but because of his determination to get ahead he was able to become the leading doctor of Rouen. Dr. Flaubert became established among the rising bourgeoisie and soon began to consider himself the founder of the House of Flaubert; he planned that his sons would succeed him as doctors and thus continue his noble lineage. Sartre observes that when parents have plans, their children have destinies; this applies particularly to the bourgeoisie. Flaubert would take his oldest son, Achille, to the hospital and show him around with pride; Achille was given a destiny: he would be the continuation of the person of the father (*IF*,110). Dr. Flaubert was a scientist and an atheist, so Achille dutifully became a "prefabricated atheist." But Sartre explains that atheism does not eliminate religion. Rather, Achille is "protected against Christianity by a cult that is more ancient and meticulous: he is the most faithful adept of the domestic religion" (*IF*,114). To explain the domestic religion Sartre adopts many phrases from Trinitarian theology: Achille will do the Father's will; he is the Son and the Father is in him; he is the perfect image of the Father. This is the religion of Achille: he assimilates the being of the Father into himself. The House of Flaubert has become his destiny. His life has become the repetition of the life of his Father, "the eternal return and its sacred pomps." The eyes of his fellow citizens assure him that he is "the best possible incarnation of the eponymous hero." As a practicing physician he will claim to favor scientific progress as his father had done—but there is a difference: Achille is not a scientist; he lives by authority and not by evidence. Inwardly he rejects any new development in medical practice, for it separates him from his God (*IF*,129). Still, Sartre will allow that Achille was probably not unhappy in playing the role of "his own Creator."

Nine years after the birth of Achille, Gustave is born. His mother is disappointed as she had wanted a girl. Dr. Flaubert is busy at the hospital, but from time to time he dotes on Gustave and the boy responds with all his heart: "When the child perceives himself so pure, so vast and so calm that he believes that he is on the point of abolishing himself, the All-Powerful does not disdain to mirror himself in his vacuity" (*IF*,510). The child travels about town with his father and sees how the people of Rouen admire their eminent physician; the boy is thrilled.

The little boy believed himself drawn out of nothingness for the express purpose of chanting the glory of his Creator, and the daily ceremony of adoration seems to him constitutive of his being as creature; he does not altogether deceive himself: Dr. Flaubert, a patriarchal bourgeois, does not lower himself to solicit love, but he would be very astounded if someone did not adore him (*IF*,675).

Gustave is a quiet and obedient child; he would refer to this period as his Golden Age. But when his mother tries to teach her obedient son to read, she finds that Gustave cannot even understand what he is supposed to do. His mother finally explains to her husband the difficulty she has been having with the boy, and Dr. Flaubert decides that the time has come for a serious talk with his son. Sartre speculates on the content of the conversation and sees Dr. Flaubert showing Gustave how the House of Flaubert is destined to become a great lineage. He points out that in spite of the greatness of his heritage Gustave has plainly shown that he is *insufficient*. At that moment "an object is born; insufficiency" (*IF,*371). Gustave is compared with his diligent brother and the difference is obvious: he is "inferior." This is the Fall. He is cast out of Paradise, and the Golden Age is over. By the time Gustave is seven, a sovereign judge has discovered his particularity and has designated him to be it (*IF,*189). He is a member of the great Flaubert family, but what kind of a member? The family idiot.

He has been given a double reality: the greatness of the House of Flaubert and his own personal insufficiency. It is this double reality that he will try to live: he will see great opportunities presented to him, but endlessly he will see that he is insufficient for the task. He will be a mixture of genius and sterility, but through it all his basic self-understanding will remain: "Je suis un grand homme manqué." He will devise magnificent projects (these will be "the familial truth of his being," "the Flaubert patrimony") but he will not undertake them because his empirical character must be "a deviation, a weakening, a de-substantialization, in a word, a betrayal of that superb and demanding Ego that the Flauberts have given him" (*IF,*571). He will identify himself with Satan, the angel of light created for a great destiny but subsequently cursed for a fault that he cannot recall. Behind his misfortunes he will see his father, "the terrible Jehovah who drew him forth from the mire so that there could be a man on earth who would commit original sin" (*IF,*284).

After he finishes his baccalaureate, Gustave unwillingly begins the study of law. But late one night, at the age of twenty-two, he is driving home in a gig next to his brother. Suddenly, out of the darkness, a carriage appears, coming towards them; Gustave's horse bolts in fright and Gustave falls over limp. He remains conscious, but for ten minutes Achille believes Gustave is dead. Gustave slowly revives and is brought back to the family home for a period of recovery. Sartre interprets this nervous collapse as part of Gustave's plan. It is his choice of passivity as a way of life; "since the cadaver or idiot represent *irresponsibility in the family* his nervous affliction is a way of *living* this irresponsibility" (*IF,*1,867). Before his collapse he had written numerous tales of doomed men, ape-men and robots, men who were passive before an overriding fate; Sartre sees these tales as "spititual exercises" written in preparation for Flaubert's own passivity. The passivity is seen as an effort to return to the Golden Age when he had rested passively in the arms of his father; then he did not have to work to merit love, he only had to show his open wounds (IF,2,084).

When Gustave is young, his family tends carefully to his physical needs, he is well nourished and protected. But his father is occupied with his work and his mother gives him only perfunctory attention. He hears adults speaking, but since no one really cares what he has to say, he remains passive in an active world of discourse (IF,50). He realizes that he is signified by what the adults are saying, but he is not encouraged to speak himself. Thus, language is not reciprocal, "the naming ceremony is for adults"; he is always the object expressed by language, but rarely the subject using language to express. He wanders through his house like a domestic animal, sensing that he is spoken about, but not expected to comprehend and respond. His own feelings float through his mind as vague intuitions, but no one cares what he thinks so his intuitions never enter language and seem to be very unrelated to the sentences he hears. His mind becomes a receptacle for the judgments of adults, but he makes no judgments of his own. Evidence has been discredited and his unique basis for knowing is hearsay; his norm for truth is hierarchic, it is measured by the importance of the speaker. He does not *see* what he says, he *believes* it. He had an authoritarian father and an indifferent mother; he was deprived of the reciprocity of human relationships and so is condemned to belief. The forlorn child adopts as his motto: "I see nothing, I can see nothing; the criterion of truth is that it be affirmed by others and be engraved on me by them" (IF,172). Language fascinates him, but he does not use it to express his own intuitions. He repeats the impressive sentences he has heard and then pretends to feel what he has expressed. In short, he becomes a little actor. But Sartre would have it that all bourgeois children are actors, for their upbringing is fundamentally the same: their physical needs are well tended, but there is nothing for them to do—except please others by the way they perform. Gustave comes to believe that reality is equivalent with having his performance accepted.

An actor accepts lines from another and tries to experience the line as he says it; but it is the line that evokes the feeling and not the feeling that evokes the line. An actor declaims a sentence, he does not affirm it. He speaks it only for the effect it will have on himself and his audience. The actor is said to believe his line; belief is then defined as the imported affirmation that rests in the speaker without ever becoming his affirmation (*IF*,172). Gustave and his friends begin putting on plays in the billiard room. Language is used to play a role, to please others, to amuse them, to shock them, to produce a reaction—not to communicate. The role that he adopts will use his mouth to say "I" but for the most part the "I" is only an imported term. Acting suits him well for he seems to be made of a "diaphanous and protean substance which can imitate everything because it never is anything" (*IF*,678). Endless voices seem to be speaking within him; he repeats the phrases for the strange, exotic sound of the words, but none of the voices are his. In order that a voice be his own, he will have to make a judgment based on the immediate evidence, but this is what he cannot do. He lacks the fundamental human act, the affirmative judgment (*IF*,159).[1] For Gustave all truths are revealed and he responds to them in faith. Problems arise, for he is able to believe all things but unable to judge anything; he can reach no conclusion. When he is nineteen he writes: "There is neither a true nor false idea. One begins by adopting things enthusiastically, then one reflects, one doubts, and one rests there" (*IF*,646).

Sartre interprets Flaubert's nervous collapse in religious terms: it is a rite of passage. The "I" had always been weak, now it fades completely. The death is followed by a resurrection, and out of the corpse will arise Gustave as "he," a second narrator who will speak of himself in the third person. Like a child, he speaks of himself as an object. Gustave writes:

He who lives now and who is me only contemplates the other who is dead. I have had two very distinct existences: the exterior events [fainting, etc.] are only the symbol of the end of the first and the birth of the second; all of that is mathematical (*IF*, 1,799).

At the age of twenty-two he has gone through a rite of passage;

---

1. The judgment must be affirmative, as the negative judgment does not implicate the speaker; this matter is treated in the final chapter.

he refers to a "He...who is me"; his life is over but an object remains. Flaubert sees the experience as a death and a transfiguration, describing the bliss he has come to know as "a type of sanctity which perhaps is higher than the other as it is more disinterested" (*IF*,585). He believes his experience resembles that of St. Theresa; he writes several plays about St. Anthony the hermit. He signs his letters "St. Polycarp" — at first it is only a joke, but his friends will fete him on St. Polycarp's day. Sartre goes along with it all, calling him St. Flaubert (*IF*,1,920). It was just this type of transfiguration that Sartre had found in the life of Jean Genet. Genet became fascinated with sanctity, so Sartre had called his earlier study, *St. Genet, Actor and Martyr.* Gustave is also considered a saint for he lives in the third person: the "I" has been martyred and only the actor remains.

Sartre is well known for his radical position on the totality of human freedom; it can, then, be somewhat surprising to read in his autobiography, "I had not chosen my vocation; it had been imposed on me by others." He writes that he still feels obliged by the mandate that he was given by his grandfather years ago. He tells that when he is in bad humor it occurs to him that he has written night and day, covered pages with ink, and cast a stack of unwanted books on the market in the foolish hope of pleasing a grandfather who has been dead many years. If this does not sound like the radical Sartrean freedom that is proposed in *The Flies,* it is at least the man Sartre himself, the genial author of *The Words,* musing on his weakness. Some of Sartre's critics have argued that he has changed his position on human freedom in becoming far more aware of the limitations of the human situation, and certainly Sartre has become increasingly cognizant of the limiting effects of the whole social environment (*IF*,117–18). This difference can be seen if one compares his study of Baudelaire with his recent study of Flaubert. The earlier study lacks the detailed consideration of its subject's family and times that is integral to the later work. But for Sartre freedom is absolute, or it is not at all. Man is deeply influenced by his family and environment, but he freely chooses how he will relate to this influence.

In coming to self-consciousness the child is not cast from a paradise of pleasure, he is cast from his place in the Absolute. He longs to return to his "true essence" but he cannot — he is free. A subjectivity has no truth and no assigned place. This is the problem that makes the growing child forlorn: it is a metaphysical problem, for it concerns the reason for his existence; it is a theological problem, for only an all-knowing mind could justify the child's physical presence. The child may accept the judgment of another as the truth of his life and thus be delivered from his anguish, but he must pay for this decision by living with a divided mind.

The theological complex is the result of a choice whereby another's consciousness is preferred to one's own. It is this choice that establishes the sacred world. Every object that is associated with the judgment of the foreign consciousness appears hallowed with a religious value. If the other is preferred absolutely, the person becomes a "saint" and perhaps will begin to speak of himself in the third person.

Sartre is often bitter in his opposition to sanctity. His comments are usually in the context of the nonconventional sanctity of Genet and Flaubert, but what he is criticizing is not far from the more orthodox religious traditions. For example, in a study of Hinduism, Huston Smith recommends that the aspirant try thinking

of one's finite self in the third person. Walking down the street, the yogi, instead of thinking "I am doing this" should say to himself, "There goes Jones down Fifth Avenue." He should even try to visualize himself as seen from a distance (*The Religions of Man*, p.38).

Smith finds this transformation to the third person implied in the famous phrase that runs through the *Upanishads*: "That art thou." The one who meditates on the phrase eventually comes to see himself as a "that." The same shift is found in Western spirituality when St. Paul tells of his own mystical experience in the third person: "I know a man in Christ who...was caught up to the third heaven" (2 Cor.,12). In a similar way Ignatius and Theresa sometimes spoke of their mystical experiences as if they had happened to another. It is to the moment when consciousness is objectified into another that Sartre would trace the phenomenon of the sacred. How this basic shift of consciousness is involved in specific religious phenomena is the subject of this book. But first, the notion of Sartrean consciousness.

2

This Refusal
to Be Substance

The Conscious Life

Simone de Beauvoir tells of an evening in the early thirties when she was with Sartre and Raymond Aron in the Bec de Gaz, a café on the rue Montparnasse. They ordered the speciality of the house, apricot cocktails. At that time Aron had been studying the phenomenology of Husserl, and in the course of the conversation he pointed to his glass and said to Sartre:

"You see, my dear fellow, if you are a phenomenologist, you can talk about this cocktail and make philosophy out of it!"

De Beauvoir adds:

Sartre turned pale with emotion at this. Here was just the thing he had been longing to achieve for years — to describe objects just as he saw and touched them, and extract philosophy from the process (*The Prime of Life*, p.112).

Sartre began reading about Husserl in great excitement and

in the following year, 1933-34, went to the French Institute in Berlin to study phenomenology.

Being and Nothingness

The term "phenomenology" goes back to Kant's distinction between the phenomenon and the noumenon. The phenomenon is the appearance that reality makes to consciousness, while the noumenon is the reality itself that could be said to lie behind the phenomenon. Husserl objected to this positing of a reality behind the appearance, saying that it is to the phenomenon itself that one must look to find the essence of that which is. Husserl judged it of no importance whether the appearance he was studying had an actual existence apart from being known. He felt that since knowledge and meaning had nothing to gain from the actual existence of the world, we might as well forget it.

Edmund Husserl (1859-1938) was a mathematician who later turned to philosophy. In philosophy he wanted to have the same clarity and certainty that he had had in mathematics, so he used a similar method. A mathematician can analyze what is implicit in the notion of a perfect circle without being concerned with whether a perfect circle really exists. Using this method in philosophy, Husserl set aside the problem of existence. He did not affirm it or deny it, he left it in parentheses and moved on. The philosopher should concern himself with what appears to consciousness; he must give an exact and careful description of what appears; truth lies in what appears and not behind it.

A fundamental axiom of phenomenology is that every consciousness is consciousness *of* something. Consciousness always has an object, it is never "by itself"; it always refers to something which is known. Whether the object is a truth of mathematics, the tree that is before me, or an imaginary beast, makes no difference. Whatever the object may be, it is not consciousness and it is not "in" consciousness. Consciousness is other than its object, but at the same time its whole being is an orientation to its object. This is what is meant by the intentionality of consciousness. Intentionality is the essential structure of consciousness (*In.*, 144).

In January 1939 Sartre published an article in which he tried to introduce intentionality to a French audience. He begins by saying that the error common to both realists and idealists is that they make knowing some kind of eating. Sartre sees the French idealists treating consciousness as if it were a spider digesting objects and turning them into its own proper substance. Against this understanding Sartre presents the intentionality of Husserl, where objects remain objects and do not dissolve into consciousness. The tree is out there in the heat and the dust; it cannot enter into consciousness as it is not of the same nature as consciousness. Rejecting the digestive image of knowing (*connaître*) Sartre reluctantly proposes another: to know is to explode towards (*c'est s'éclater vers*). With this new understanding of consciousness Sartre felt that

consciousness purified itself, it is bright as a great wind, there is nothing in it except a movement to flee itself, a sliding beyond itself; if by the impossible you would enter "in" a consciousness, you would be seized by a whirlwind and be cast out, next to the tree, in the dust; for consciousness has no "within," it is nothing but the outside of itself and it is this absolute flight, this refusal to be substance which constitutes it as consciousness (*S1*,33).

Consciousness is out of itself; if it should try to recapture itself or coincide with itself and rest closed on itself, it would annihilate itself. It is this necessity of consciousness to exist as consciousness of something other than itself, this total fleeing of self, that Sartre presents as intentionality.

Husserl had set aside the question of the existence of the object as a problem without real value. Sartre does not dismiss the problem so easily but argues for the real being of the phenomenon. He considers the matter in his major philosophical work, *Being and Nothingness*, published in 1943. He begins by approving of the phenomenological approach which reduces the existent to the series of appearances which manifest it. As phenomenologist he denies the noumenon; there is no reverse side to the phenomenon, no "true interior" behind the appearances. An electric current is nothing but the actions that manifest it, and the apricot cocktail would be nothing but a light color, a fragrance, and a sweet taste. These are the appearances and that is all there is. The "being" is nothing but the well-connected series of its manifestations. The actual number of these manifestations is always limited, but the possible number of manifestations is infinite (*BN*,iv). Each appearance is an aspect of the object. The object can never appear as a whole.

The essence of an appearance is an appearing (*BN*,lvii), and no noumenon is involved. One can ask, then, whether the being of the appearance is only the actual appearing itself. Sartre sees this position as being the same as the extreme idealist position of Berkeley, where *esse est percipi* and beyond the *percipi* there is nothing. Sartre is resolutely opposed to idealism; he sees this idealism implicit in Husserl and breaks with him by arguing for a being that cannot be identified with the *percipi*. He begins his argument with the starting point of phenomenology: all consciousness is consciousness of something. He argues that to be conscious of something is to be confronted with a concrete, full presence that is not consciousness (*BN*,lxxii). If the table I know were identified with my knowing, it would be consciousness and disappear as a table (*BN*,lxviii). Consciousness is always supported by a being which is not itself (*BN*,lxxiii). Therefore the nature of consciousness requires something beyond consciousness. Sartre's argument is stated very briefly and many commentators have not found it convincing.[1] Whatever may be the value of his argument, Sartre holds for a being which is beyond consciousness. Sartre terms this being the being in-itself, while consciousness is termed being for-itself. These are two absolutely separated regions of being (*deux regions d'être absolument tranchées*) (*BN*,lxxvi). This amounts to saying again that consciousness is distinct from its object.

Perhaps the principal characteristic of being in-itself is its total self-identity. Sartre presents this self-identity descriptively: It is wholly within itself, without the slightest suspicion of duality. The in-itself is full of itself and no more total plenitude can be

1. Roger Troisfontaines, in *Le choix de Jean-Paul Sartre* asks how one can postulate an in-itself that is beyond all relation even though it can be known only through its relations (p.40). Kurt Reinhardt, in *The Existentialist Revolt*, sees the entire Sartrean structure resting on "the *arbitrary postulate* of an absolute and massive 'being-in-itself' " (pp. 165-66). Klaus Hartmann, in *Sartre's Ontology*, gives the most thorough treatment of the point and sees a *petitio principii* involved; he finds Sartre's argument to be based on a preconceived ontology (p.16ff.). Wilfrid Desan, in *The Tragic Finale*, would find Sartre's proof inadequate, but would add that the overall coherence of Sartre's thought should weigh as some evidence for evaluating this aspect of his thought (pp.145-48; see also p.208). Francis Jeanson, in *Le problème morale et la pensée de Sartre*, defends Sartre (pp.145-48).

imagined. There is not the slightest emptiness in being, not the tiniest crack through which nothingness might creep in (*BN*,90–91). It is an infinite compression with an infinite density. Being in-itself has no potentiality, it is all act.

In itself it is what it is—in the absolute plenitude of its identity. The cloud is not "potential rain," it is, in itself, a certain quantity of water vapor, which at a given temperature and under a given pressure is strictly what it is. The in-itself is actuality (*BN*,120).

The cloud is "potential rain" only to the human consciousness that sees it that way. In itself it is just what it is. The in-itself is uncreated, but it cannot be said to create itself because *causa sui* suggests a lack of perfect self-identity; a slight separation is implied between the self which causes and the self which is caused. Since it is not caused by itself or by another, the in-itself is said to be absurd. Even to say that the in-itself is itself, is not accurate; it is beyond self, it is identity. Being in-itself cannot act, as it is glued (*empaté*) to itself (*BN*,lxxvii); it is opaque and massive (*BN*, lxxviii). It is beyond time, because time implies distinction. It undergoes no transition and no becoming, it simply is what it is. In it there is no negativity; this would imply a lack of perfect identity (*BN*,lxxix). "Uncreated, without reason for being, without any connection with another being, being-in-itself is *de trop* for eternity" (*BN*,lxxix).

The in-itself recalls the being of Parmenides, the being that Plato seemed to refer to when he wrote that "motion and life and soul and mind are really not present to absolute being, that it neither lives nor thinks, but awful and holy, devoid of mind, is fixed and immovable (*Soph.*,249). Plato responded to the challenge of Parmenides and proposed the opposing principles of the same and the other. One region of being is total self-identity and the other is total otherness. Sartre offers the same two regions of being (*BN*,756), but what is unique in Sartre is that he identifies this otherness with human consciousness. Consciousness is always other than itself. As other than itself, consciousness (or being for-itself) is defined paradoxically as that which is what it is not and is not what it is. Or as Sartre will explain, the for-itself does not coincide with itself (*BN*,91). The principle of identity does not apply to the for-itself (*BN*,90). If such an object would seem

This Refusal to Be Substance

impossible, it could be said that as an object it is impossible; but it is not an object, it is subjectivity, it is consciousness. Consciousness is always different than its object, it is different than any object, its whole being consists in being different, it is different than itself. It is an explosion. The for-itself is outside itself in the in-itself; this requires that it be defined by the in-itself which it is not. Since it must be defined by what it is not, it is said to be other than what it is. *But, of course.*

Sartre rejects the theories of knowledge that present knowledge as a union of two substances: the substance knowing and the substance known. If each were a substance complete and self-contained, there would be no true relationships between them. But consciousness is essentially a relationship, so it cannot be a substance. Consciousness is essentially other than itself so that in itself consciousness is nothing. It is real but still it is nothing. The result is that everything is on the side of the in-itself, and nothing is on the side of the for-itself. The title of Sartre's study, *Being and Nothingness,* refers to the in-itself and the for-itself, to the object and consciousness. The in-itself is full, concrete, and whole being; the for-itself is nothing but the emptiness in which the in-itself is detached (*BN,*215).

Sartre presents consciousness as nothingness and develops this understanding descriptively when he considers fascination. In fascination the subject feels his nothingness before the all-engaging object.

In fascination, which represents the immediate fact of *knowing,* the knower is absolutely nothing but a pure negation; he does not find or recover himself anywhere—he *is not.* The only qualification which he can support is that he *is not* precisely this particular fascinating object. In fascination there is nothing more than a gigantic object in a desert world. Yet the fascinated intuition is in no way a *fusion* with the object. In fact the condition necessary for the existence of fascination is that the object be raised in absolute relief on a background of emptiness; that is, I am precisely the immediate negation of the object and nothing but that (*BN,*216).

This extreme realism is extended to other human attitudes, hate, love, fear, and sympathy.

It is that things suddenly reveal themselves to us as hateful, sympathetic, horrible, lovable. It is a *property* of this Japanese mask to be terrible, an inexhaustible, irreducible property which constitutes its nature — and not the sum of our reactions to a piece of sculptured wood (*S1*,34).

In this passage Sartre speaks of "things suddenly revealing themselves"; that is how he understands consciousness. The emphasis is entirely on the object. Consciousness is the object revealing itself. It is not a property of a knowing subject; there is no knowing subject. A knowing subject would reintroduce all of the difficulties involved in taking knowledge as an internal relation between two substances. Consciousness is better understood as a subjectless revelation of things: "man is the means by which things manifest themselves" (*S2*,89).

Although there is no subject of consciousness, Sartre does speak of an Ego; but the Ego is an *object* of consciousness. The Ego is treated at length in chapter 4 below. Here it can be noted that both one's own body and one's Ego are known as objects. Consciousness itself is empty, everything is outside of it. "In a sense, it is a *nothing,* since all physical, psycho-physical and psychic objects, all truths, all values are outside it; since my *me* has itself ceased to be any part of it" (*TE*,93). The result is that there is no longer any *"vie intérieure"* (*TE*,93; *S1*,34). There cannot be, consciousness has no interior. Consciousness is a great wind, "there is nothing in it except a movement to flee itself." Since even the Ego is outside consciousness, we do not "find ourselves" in a retreat from the world but "on the highway, in the city, in the middle of the crowd." We are delivered from the interior life, as "all is outside, even ourselves; outside in the world among others" (*S1*,34).

Consciousness is always other and it must continually *make itself* other; if it were *established* in otherness it would not be other but simply itself, part of the "given" (*BN*,757). Since consciousness makes itself other, Sartre speaks of it as an absolute (*TE*,96; *BN*,757). It is absolute, but since its whole being is a refusal to be substance it is a nonsubstantial absolute. Consciousness is sheer spontaneity and ultimately is the source of any action in the world. Physical objects have motion only by inertia.[2] "A

2. Limiting the movements of relative existence to inertia may sound extreme,

relative existence [anything other than consciousness] can only be passive, since the least activity would free it from the relative and would constitute it as absolute" (*TE*,66).

Consciousness is called the absolute, and it is also referred to by other terms that have been traditionally reserved for God. Consciousness is cause of itself or *causa sui* (*TE*,82). It is a tireless creation of existence (*TE*,99). Its essence implies its existence (*TE*,84). But though consciousness is *causa sui*, it is not God. It is nothingness, and therefore it is not the cause of its own being but cause only of its own nothingness (*BN*,109).

Sartre refers to the for-itself in terms traditionally reserved for God, but the same is true when he speaks of the in-itself: the in-itself is beyond time, it is perfectly one, it is uncaused, it does not change, it is all act and full positivity. But neither the in-itself nor the for-itself is God. It might be said that each one has half the qualities of God but not the remainder. God would be the synthesis of the in-itself and the for-itself, but this synthesis is impossible (*BN*,110); there is no synthesis because their absolute qualities mutually oppose. One is changeless and the other is ceaseless change, one is uncaused and the other is *causa sui*, one is absolute immanence and the other is absolute transcendence, one is identity and the other is otherness, one is substance and the other is the refusal to be substance, one is being and the other is nothingness.[3]

The Anguish of Freedom

Sartre begins his study of consciousness by considering a consciousness that is asking a question. A question hesitates between a

---

but a similar principle lies behind the scholastic understanding of divine concurrence. Whenever a creature engages in an activity it passes from potency to act. Since the act was not actually present before the activity began, it must have proceeded from a being where the act was actually present. This being is God, or the Absolute, who moves the relative creature from potency to act.

3. Sartre's atheism is probably his best-known position. It has been argued abundantly and therefore it is not argued here. James Collins, in *The Existentialists*, refers to it as a "postulatory atheism" and an "emotional a priori" (p.70). Though Sartre argues to his atheism in *Being and Nothingness* he presents it as a personal experience of his childhood in *The Words*. Régis Jolivet, in *The Theology of the Absurd*, considers the opposites of which Sartre speaks, and sees

positive and a negative reply; the object about which the question is posed can be revealed as not existing at all. Every question presents something of a negative withdrawal in relation to the determined world that is simply given. In being in-itself there is no question; whatever is, simply is. The causal series of objects can produce only being, but a questioning consciousness is an indetermination. Consciousness is thus apart from the causal series.[4] In order to question, the questioner must be disengaged from being.

Being can generate only being and if man is inclosed in this process of generation, only being will come out of him. If we are to assume that man is able to question this process—*i. e.*, to make it the object of interrogation—he must be able to hold it up to view as a totality. He must be able to put himself *outside* of being (*BN*,29).

To pose a question (an indetermination), consciousness must withdraw from the determined. And Sartre finds such a withdrawal always present in consciousness. Consciousness is always an uncertainty, and in this uncertainty man is other than the world that is fully determined. If consciousness were determined, it would be part of the opaque solidity of the in-itself. By introducing the question, uncertainty, ignorance—in brief, nothingness—into being, consciousness is free and apart from blind necessity.

Consciousness can directly experience its own freedom and this experience is the experience of anguish.[5] In anguish I see myself as unpredictable. Sartre distinguishes between anguish and fear. Fear is before beings in the world, whereas anguish is anguish before myself.

---

them resolved in the ultimate mystery of God (pp.31ff.). This approach will be considered at the end of the present chapter. Desan, in *The Tragic Finale*, sees an inconsistency in that Sartre argues for the real existence of the transphenomenal in-itself as the condition of phenomenal perception, but does not similarly see a Supreme Being as a condition of thinking (p.178). Norman Greene, in *Jean-Paul Sartre, The Existentialist Ethic*, points out that since Sartre maintains that metaphysics deals with a realm beyond experience where certainty is impossible, he should be classified as an agnostic rather than an atheist (p.62).

4. Sartre would not really allow causality to the in-itself either, as causality involves duality.

5. Elsewhere the recognition of freedom by itself is said to be joy (*WL*,52), at other times it seems to be boredom (*B*,28ff.).

A situation provokes fear if there is a possibility of my life being changed from without; my being provokes anguish to the extent that I distrust myself and my own reactions in that situation (*BN*,35).

As an example Sartre considers a man who is walking along a narrow path over a steep precipice where there is no guard rail. The man might have fear that he will slip on a stone and fall into the abyss or he might have fear that the earth will give way under his feet. These are threats that come to him from the universal order of determinism; they cause fear. But the same man can have a different experience: he can experience that type of anguish that is called vertigo. The man feels anguish lest he might throw himself into the abyss. His anguish is before his own freedom. He would like to determine his conduct in advance, he would like to insure that he will not leap, but he cannot. He has motives for not leaping, but the motives do not really seem to bind him. His freedom extends beyond all reasoning, and it is that freedom that he knows. He feels horror at the prospect of leaping, but he knows that even this horror cannot determine him not to leap. When nothing compels me, I feel vertigo: I can save my life or take it, I can love someone or suddenly rise up and kill him. I escape causality, I am free. The decisive conduct will emerge from a self which I am not yet. In anguish I see that reasons will not control what I might do.

One can thus have anguish before his future self, but one can also have anguish before his past (*BN*,39). The gambler who has resolved not to gamble any longer stands before the gaming table and suddenly perceives the total inefficacy of his past resolution. He thinks of the resolution, but it appears distant and ineffective. In anguish he sees that the resolution that he made with such earnestness in the past does not determine his present conduct. For the resolution to have effect he must continually determine himself *now* not to gamble. Human freedom presents man with the constantly renewed obligation to form his character. At any moment he could change and be radically other. The virtuous man is in anguish before the sudden evil he might begin at any moment. His true self is not something given to him from which his acts proceed, it is something that by his acts he must create. The resolution not to gamble does not determine him not to gamble, but his nongambling determines that the resolution continues to exist. The virtuous man does not act virtuously because he has a virtuous nature; rather, his free virtuous acts lead one to speak *afterwards* of a virtuous nature. But at any moment the man might radically change and commit nonvirtuous acts; then one could speak of his evil nature or of an evil streak in his nature. But the truth is that his freedom comes first and his freedom determines his "nature." This is what Sartre means by his famous line that existence precedes essence (*EH*,12,22; *BN*,30, 537,573). Since a man's essence is a summation of his acts, it refers only to his past. "Essence is all that human reality apprehends in itself as *having been*" (*BN*,42). The nongambling man is one who *has* not gambled recently, or for the past several years, but this says nothing about his future. This is the nature of man's anguish; he sees his essence suspended in his present freedom (*BN*,30).

Since anguish is an apprehension of our freedom, the basic way to flee the anguish is to deny the freedom and adopt some form of psychological determinism (*BN*,48). Psychological determinism would see blind forces within man that determine his consciousness. In order to avoid responsibility, people want to say that they become angry because of uncontrollable passions or because of their temperament. Or they want to say they are cowardly because of heredity or because of their environment. But there is no angry temperament or cowardly temperament given to man. A man is angry or cowardly because he has chosen to be that way. Man is responsible for his passions. That which a man claims as his character is really a *vow*. When a man says that he is not easy to please, what he is doing is entering into a free engagement with the ill temper that he intends to maintain (*BN*,675). Sartre will not allow any form of psychological determinism. He argues that a man comes to know of his own freedom in a direct, immediate intuition—this experience was seen to be anguish. Thus, freedom is known directly from within, but psychological determinism is not known in a direct intuition at all. Psychological determinism is a philosophical theory that is adopted when the mind looks at itself from the outside. It is accepted as a "satisfying hypothesis" or as a postulate said to be necessary to develop a scientific psychology. Fundamentally, psychological determinism is an excuse. It is an attempt to see oneself as an object and thus dispel the anguish that is present in the immediate consciousness of freedom. But the anguish cannot be dispelled, because we *are* anguish (*BN*,52).

Sometimes I avoid thinking of my anguish; but in order not to think of it I must know it—precisely in order to know what not to think of. This means that an awareness of anguish and a flight from anguish can exist together in the unity of a single consciousness (*BN*,53). It means I can lie to myself. Ordinarily a lie depends on a duality of consciousness: the deceiver and the deceived. When I lie to myself this duality does not exist, there is a single consciousness. Sartre calls this condition bad faith. Bad faith is involved when a man conceals the truth from himself; but in order to conceal the truth from himself he must know the truth very exactly in order to know what must be concealed (*BN*,59). Freud was aware that a man can deceive himself, and to explain this self-deception introduced the duality of Ego and Id: the Ego is deceived by the Id. Sartre finds this duality unacceptable. He rejects it by considering an observation Freud made to the effect that a neurotic patient often shows resistance at the very moment the doctor approaches the true cause of the neurosis. At this critical time the patient often becomes defiant, refuses to speak, or even terminates the treatment altogether. Sartre observes that if the Ego (or consciousness) were simply the deceived it would not act this way, for it would not even suspect that a solution is approaching. The conscious and violent reaction of the patient shows that he is indeed conscious of what he is supposed to be unconscious of. He is conscious of it and at the same time consciously trying to refuse to be conscious of it. Sartre thus denies the Freudian duality. Consciousness is not only the deceived, it is also the deceiver. If consciousness resists and becomes obstinate it is only in fear that its self-deception will be revealed *to itself*. This enigmatic condition is bad faith, and Sartre proposes that bad faith is fundamentally possible because consciousness is what it is not and is not what it is. Consciousness is fleeing itself, it is an otherness that cannot be itself.

In introspection I try to determine what I am. I try to pass beyond self-deception and be really sincere. I even admit my base qualities; I say I am a coward, and so on. But I am not a coward in the way that a wall is white. At any moment I can change and be other; to be a coward I must continually allow myself to be a coward. I say that I am sad, but I am not sad in the way that a stone is a stone. I cannot even rest tranquilly in my feeling of sorrow but must continually make myself sad from beginning to end. I am sad, but I am never simply what I am. I must work at it. I am told to be a man or I am told to be more human, but these commands make sense only if I can somehow avoid being these things. I am told to conform to my nature, but how can anything do other than conform to its nature? A man can try to be what he is, but then he is using the principle of identity as an ideal or as a normative principle and not as the absolute law of his being. The principle of identity can serve as a *norm* for consciousness only because consciousness is not itself, it is always other than what it is. This is not true of the in-itself. The in-itself is identical with itself; only the in-itself is sincerely what it is.

A soldier stands at attention with his eyes fixed ten paces before him. He tries to make himself a soldier-thing. But a thing is what he is not. The waiter in the café tries to be just a waiter but his manner is a little too precise, he bends forward a little too eagerly. His walk tries to imitate the inflexible stiffness of an automaton. He only plays at being a café waiter, he tries to fit his freedom into a role. What he is trying to realize is the café-waiter as a being in-itself, but he transcends the role on every side. He is a waiter, but he is more, he is a waiter in the mode of being what he is not (*BN*,73). In sincerity I can try to be a soldier or a waiter, I can try to be just happy or just sad or just any other thing, but it does not work for I am not a thing. I am other. Sincerity does not work, for sincerity is aware of missing its goal inevitably, it misses its goal by its very nature (*BN*,81). Sincerity is also assumed in bad faith (*BN*,79,82). Good faith, bad faith, and sincerity are all found to be wanting. Consciousness is endlessly other and "man is never anything but an imposture."

Human Values

Sartre has no sympathy with a laicized form of morality that was proposed by a number of French professors towards the end of the last century. These professors wanted to do away with God quietly, and then afterwards discover again the moral values of honesty and human progress (*EH*,21ff.; *S1*,153). They regarded God as a costly hypothesis and felt that without God man could find moral norms that would let him know not to beat his wife, that he should raise a family, and the like. Sartre objects that, if there is no God to establish values, then there are no established values. The professors wanted to find laws for which there is no legistator, and Sartre finds this inconsistent. He sees his own existentialism as only an attempt to form a coherent atheism (*EH*,56). Dostoevski had written, "If God does not exist then everything is permitted," and Sartre assumes this as his starting point. Man is free and everything is permitted to him. But freedom is not just a cause for rejoicing, it is anguish. Man is free, alone, and abandoned. "Indeed, everything is permissible if God does not exist, and as a result man is forlorn, because neither within him nor without does he find anything to cling to" (*EH*,22). Within himself man finds nothing fixed; any "nature" that he has he must create for himself. Beyond himself there is no sign in the universe, for there is no one to put it there. Man is abandoned, for he has life but has been given nothing to live for. Since man has been given no values, he must invent values for himself — but then it is difficult to take such values seriously. When a man invents his own values, his life appears useless and arbitrary. Sartre observes that if a man wants to feel useful he must consider himself to be the means to an end beyond himself that he does not question. This is to live in a theological world. Yet once a man has tasted to the point of nausea the aimless consciousness that must invent the laws that it itself must obey, personal usefulness loses all significance and life appears as a game (*B*,30-32). If life is only a game where each man chooses his own rules, one can always ask if it is worth the effort to play. One feels incapacitated and paralyzed by a reflective lucidity from which there is no hope of deliverance. "For a thoughtful person every enterprise is absurd." This is the state of man without God. Sartre sees that this state resembles the mental illness that Pierre Janet had described and called psychasthenia. Sartre explains that these psychasthenics have often had metaphysical intuitions that the normal man tries to hide from himself (*B*,32). The nature of this malady is that the person suffering it cannot take anything seriously, for he sees only too well that the only values in his life are the values that he himself has put there.

Our daily activities may not seem to be pervaded with a sense of anguish, but they may be only ways of trying to conceal the truth that underlies them. In *Nausea* Roquentin watches the people gathered in a café and concludes: "Each one of them has his little personal difficulty which keeps him from noticing that he exists" (*N*,111). Under a long series of rituals I try to conceal my anguish; still it underlies whatever I do. The alarm clock rings. I get up. Getting up is reassuring, for it helps me to avoid facing the fact that I am free and life is something of a game. The serious man apprehends values as coming to him from the objective world; he "sees his obligations." He sees values given to him in the traffic signs that he obeys, in the tax forms that he fills out. The alarm clock and the traffic signs obeyed, the tax forms filled out, they are but "so many guard rails against anguish" (*BN*,47). We try to hide from ourselves that at each moment the value of things depends on the value that we give to them (*BN*,538). In hiding the arbitrary character of all values, we hide our own freedom. We see ourselves as already made. The small choices that we make refer back to something else, but this something else is also a choice.

All these trivial passive expectations of the real, all these commonplace, everyday values, derive their meaning from an original projection of myself which stands as my choice of myself in the world (*BN*,47).

When I hear the alarm ringing in the morning, I get up. Getting up is one small act by which I reaffirm and live out my basic choice.

I may wish to join a party, to write a book or to marry — but in such a case what is usually called my will is probably a manifestation of a prior and more spontaneous decision (*EH*,28–29).

Even a person's gestures can reveal this original decision. In seeing the gestures of another, we sense that they reveal something very basic about him, his way of being. For Sartre a man's being is his choice. Each act and each gesture has its meaning in this basic choice, but for the basic choice itself there is no reason. Should a man try to give the ultimate reason for his acts, he would eventually refer back to the basic choice of himself that he had made. But since it is this choice that gives reason and value to his life, there can be no reason for the choice itself. The world offers reasons for an action only if we question it with a goal already in mind (*BN*,548). All values depend on this goal. Not every sick person finds his illness regrettable; to some people illness fits in quite well with their purpose. The large rock on the road is not an obstacle in itself. It becomes an obstacle only if I want to get to the other side; the road is "too steep" only in terms of my interest in climbing it. Each of these objects presents itself as having value only in relation to the fundamental value I have chosen. Before this choice, there is no value. After my choice, the road, the rock, and the illness are seen as having meaning. They constitute my world. My world reflects me, for its values are organized around the project I have chosen. Because a man's choice creates his world, Sartre sees each man responsible for himself and the world in which he lives: "I carry the weight of the world by myself alone without anything or any person being able to lighten it" (*BN*,680).

Chapter 1 of this work told of children experiencing metaphysical anxiety. Salvation involved a religious experience in which an external value was assigned to them. Sartre would see any acceptance of external value as an act of bad faith, for it dissimulates the total gratuity of one's own free choice. In his trilogy *Les chemins de la liberté*, Sartre presents a man progressively trying to attain his own freedom. Mathieu has been feeling the emptiness of his life when a friend invites him to join the Communist Party. Mathieu reflects:

Join the party, inject a meaning into life, choose to be a man, to act and to believe. That would be salvation.

When Mathieu puts off making a decision until "later on," his friend Brunet replies:

"Later on? If you're counting on an inner inspiration to make up your mind, you may have to wait a long time. Do you imagine that I was convinced when I joined the Communist Party? A conviction has to be created." Mathieu smiled sadly, "I know that.

Go down on your knees and you will believe. I dare say you are right. But I want to believe first." "Naturally," ejaculated Brunet, "You're all the same, you intellectuals..." (*AR*,134-37).[6]

The fundamental choice is the unique foundation of value, and nothing, absolutely nothing, justifies one in adopting this or that particular scale of values (*BN*,46). The things I use are justified by the service that they render to me. But as the being by whom values exist, I have no value. I am the lawgiver, and as such there is no law that I can appeal to for my own justification. In the Communist Party Mathieu would have had values given to him, and to have values given to one is salvation. Yet it is no use. Mathieu realizes that it is only in first choosing the Party as value that the Party's values are given to him. Since it is his freedom that must first choose the Party, it is still his freedom and will always be his freedom that will be the ultimate source of his values, and since he is free there is no salvation. Even Brunet, the Party member who has made the choice and who "believes," still has anguish. At any moment he might reverse his choice and the belief would be gone. He has anguish at what he might do, anguish lest he become radically other. He is under the spell of a given value and has anguish lest he be exorcised.

Existential Psychoanalysis

Sartre presents consciousness ontologically as the nonsubstantial absolute. Using this ontological definition as his basis, he proceeds with an analysis of the subjective experience of anguish. It could be said that ontology underlies Sartre's psychology. He suggests a similar type of psychoanalysis, one where the final discoveries of ontology might serve as first principles: existential psychoanalysis (*BN*,704-5).

Sartre objects to an assumption that he finds to be common among empirical psychologists: this assumption would take man to be an assemblage of irreducible desires. Under this assumption one would consider a particular psychological analysis to be complete when the investigator had established a man's elemental drives, somewhat as the chemist would consider his analysis complete when he had determined the elements in a chemical

6. Elsewhere, Sartre will urge all workingmen to join the Communist Party.

This Refusal to Be Substance

compound. Sartre cites a psychological study of Flaubert to illustrate the method he rejects. Flaubert is presented as a man with a "need for violent action," a man with "intense feeling" and "grandiose ambition," and so on. Each of these drives is offered as if it were an irreducible fact that allowed no further analysis or comprehension. Sartre sees no justification for this supposed irreducibility other than the investigator's inability or refusal to push his analysis any further. Sartre's own ontology of consciousness will not allow him to see man directed by irreducible drives or allow that irreducible drives inhabit consciousness like so many little substances. Drives are of consciousness; as such, they are comprehensible and free, as is consciousness. This collection of empirical drives is a man; the man is responsible for what he does, there is then a unity and a unity that is freely assumed. If the unity were not freely assumed, it would not be of consciousness. The unity that Sartre seeks is the unity of an original choice, and fundamentally this choice is always an expression of the desire to be. Consciousness, which is the lack of being, desires to appropriate what it lacks. Consciousness desires being, this is the only desire that presents itself as irreducible beyond any question. But in desiring being, consciousness does not desire to be the contingent, absurd in-itself of which it is the negation. Consciousness wants to acquire the being, the density, and the impermeability of the in-itself while at the same time *remaining conscious* (*BN*, 109–10,693). Consciousness is the desire to be the in-itself-for-itself, and the in-itself-for-itself is the impossible synthesis that Sartre has presented as God. Man is defined as the desire to be God, a definition that will be developed in the following chapter.

The fundamental desire for being characterizes all men. This desire acquires its specific character through a man's basic choice. In this choice a man decides to acquire being in a particular way. Sartre proposes a method for deciphering a person's empirical behavior in order to discover the character of this ultimate choice. The method proposed is not greatly different from that proposed by Freud to uncover the complex. Sartre compares the fundamental choice that he proposes with the complex spoken of by psychoanalysts, and finds they have many similarities. But in using the word *choice* and not the word *complex*, Sartre is emphasizing that man's character has been freely assumed and is freely maintained.

Since man is a unified totality and not a collection, man expresses himself as a totality in even his most superficial behavior. His tastes, his mannerisms, his gestures, his every act express his choice. If a man has a taste for literature, this is not just one more among the many tastes that he happens to have, it is rather a manifestation of the way he has chosen to gain being. A taste for sweetness or a revulsion before what is slimy are not irreducible givens; each quality suggests an aspect of being, each taste symbolizes the whole Weltanschauung of the man (*BN*,735). Most people are aware that in some way their tastes give a deep expression of what they are, but still they cannot express the underlying choice in words. The method by which one can render this basic choice explicit is existential psychoanalysis.

Simone de Beauvoir told how Sartre had turned pale with emotion when he was told that if he were a phenomenologist he could make philosophy out of an apricot cocktail. Sartre makes such a philosophy when he analyzes tastes and gestures. He analyzes the ontological quest expressed in such ordinary activities as skiing, smoking, and scientific research.

One symbolism that Sartre develops on many occasions is that of stone. It can serve to illustrate his method. Sartre finds a fascination with stone in many authors and proposes a lapidary to analyze the many references to stone found in the works of Rimbaud (*BN*,737). Stone symbolizes the in-itself: it is massive, dense, impenetrable, and simply there. It possesses being with the solidity that the for-itself lacks. Stone has an interior, but man has not (*S1*,291). The passions and feelings that man has can never be felt strongly enough; they are always deficient and insubstantial—as is all consciousness. Man longs for feelings that will overcome his hesitations and give him the determinism and the solidity of stone. "Stone virtues, stone vices—how restful!" (*R*,152). Stone characterizes the materialist who sees himself determined by blind forces; his thought is thickened and coagulated by the world. The materialist takes life seriously: "he has given to himself the type of existence of the rock, the consistency, the inertia, the opacity of being-in-the-midst-of-the-world" (*BN*,711). He is hiding from himself the consciousness of his freedom. According to Sartre, Marx proposed the original doctrine of serious man when he asserted the primacy of the object over the subject (*BN*,711). Stone could be said to symbolize serious man. But symbols cannot be interpreted univocally; they must be understood in the entire context of a man's gestures, tastes, and acts. Stone can symbolize the actual mentality of a man, or stone can symbolize the mentality he longs to assume but cannot.

When Sartre uses symbolism in his novels, he often develops its philosophical meaning. Mathieu (*Les chemins de la liberté*) has been mobilized and is to leave Paris the following day to oppose the advancing German armies. He walks alone through the deserted streets and senses his desolation as he crosses the Pont Neuf:

He reached out his hands and slid them slowly over the stone parapet, it was wrinkled and furrowed, like a petrified sponge, and still warm from the afternoon sun. There it lay, vast and massive, enclosing in itself the crushed silence, the compressed shadows that are the inside of objects. There it lay: a plenitude. He longed to clutch to that stone and melt into it, to fill himself with its opaqueness and repose. But it could not help him: it was outside, and forever (*R*,280).

Mathieu has made an ordinary gesture with his hand, but the gesture contains a depth of meaning: Mathieu has tried to grasp being. It does not work. Consciousness is totally lucid only because it is totally empty; consciousness illuminates the world, but in that is its exile. Mathieu reflects:

I am nothing; I possess nothing. As inseparable from the world as light, and yet exiled, gliding like light over the surface of stones and water, but nothing can ever grasp me or absorb me. Outside the world, outside the past, outside myself: freedom is exile, and I am condemned to be free (*R*,281).

Sartre maintains that man can practice existential psychoanalysis on himself and believes that many have already done so. Mathieu has slowly gone through the process. He searched for his liberty for a long time, and when he came to find it "there was neither thunder nor joy." He found nothing but a vacant liberty, and in that liberty is his exile.

The in-itself and the for-itself occur in an ontological sequence. The in-itself is absolute plenitude and, as such, comes first; because the for-itself is a negation of the plenitude it comes after what it negates, for a denial must be subsequent to an affirmation; thus, nothingness comes after being. Because it is the denial of plenitude the for-itself is an emptiness. It strives to overcome its emptiness, but it does not want to return to the inertia of the original plenitude that it denies; it wants to remain for-itself and, as such, attain to being in-itself.

The for-itself arises as the nihilation of the in-itself and this nihilation is defined as the project toward the in-itself. Between the nihilated in-itself and the projected in-itself the for-itself is nothingness (*BN*,693).

The nihilated in-itself is the first phase of the process, the nihilating for-itself the second; the projected in-itself is the third phase — God, the object of all desire. For Sartre this third phase would involve the fullness and substantiality of a body, and the emptiness and agility of spirit; the solidity of stone and the transparency of consciousness. According to Sartre it is this double character that renders the third phase impossible. Ontologically there are only two phases: Being and Nothingness. It is in terms of this double ontological structure plus the ideal but impossible third phase that Sartre presents his studies of human experience.

Several references to the religious tradition will show the religious significance of the Sartrean structure. Various gnostic and Neoplatonic sects spoke of all creation as having fallen from an original Pleroma (the divine Fullness): now all creation is filled with a longing for the great return when the original Pleroma will be reachieved. The parallel with Sartre is obvious. For Sartre, however, this longing is not to return to the original Pleroma but a longing to achieve a different Pleroma which is also an emptiness. There is a closer parallel when Teilhard de Chardin refers to a three-phase sequence in which the terms "fullness," "void," and "God," occur in the same order as Sartre would have them: "The void (which draws God) can be created only at the heart of a preexisting fullness" (Quoted in Rideau, *Teilhard de Chardin*, p.523 — the parenthesis is Teilhard's). Similar elements are again presented in sequence in a Taoist treatise on meditation: *The*

Secret of the Golden Flower, a work that tells of an inner development that passes through three stages:

> When one begins to apply this magic it is as if, in the middle of being, there were non-being. When in the course of time the work is completed, and beyond the body there is a body, it is as if in the middle of non-being, there were being (*SGF*,31).

First there is being, then nonbeing, and finally the being that appears in the midst of nonbeing; that is, beyond the original body there is a body. It is with this third phase that Sartre would take issue. The third phase involves a being, a body, beyond nonbeing; Sartre would stop with the nonbeing. In the same Taoist text the body in the middle of nonbeing is sometimes referred to as the "spirit body." The text explains that the light of the mind crystallizes into spirit-body, and heaven is where this new corporeality is begotten (*SGF*,22–23). It is to this third phase, the being in the middle of nonbeing, the corporeality of spirit, to which Sartre objects. For Sartre, spirit (light, consciousness, and so on) is exiled from body and substantiality—this is its basic frustration; yet the Taoist text affirms the reality of the third phase, in which spirit crystallizes as body. This reference to a spirit-body beyond the physical body is not limited to Taoism. St. Paul also spoke of a spiritual body beyond the physical: "It is sown a physical body, it is raised a spiritual body [*soma pneumatikon*]. If there is a physical body there is also a spiritual body" (1 Cor. 15:44). Hindu yogis have spoken of a series of spirit-bodies beyond consciousness. This reference to a second body is one of the key concepts in spiritist literature. Various names are used: the astral body, the Beta body, the energy body, and so on. This second body is the corporeality of spirit and a vivid example of what Sartre means by the ideal of in-itself-for-itself. It is consciousness as a substance—what the atheism of Sartre denies.

In the passage quoted a few pages above, Mathieu was standing on the Pont Neuf desiring to identify with the stone. But his desires were in vain, for consciousness is exile. The union of consciousness and stone is used frequently by Sartre to symbolize the in-itself-for-itself. Such a symbolism could also be seen in a number of spiritual references to stone. Jung in his study of the alchemists has shown the importance of the philosopher's stone, an ideal stone that is described as the synthesis of stone and spirit (Jung, *Psychology and Alchemy*, p.284). The same symbolism could be seen in the many scriptural references to God as "my rock," or the reference to Christ as the "living stone"; it is also proposed that Christians can become "living stones" (1 Peter 2:4). Sartre sees the synthesis symbolized in many literary references to the diamond: Breton speaks of an "inner diamond which will no more be the soul of ice than the soul of fire." Genet sees himself ultimately forming "a kind of diamond rightly called solitaire," and Gerard Manley Hopkins reminds himself that he is "immortal diamond." Because the diamond suggests the double ideal of in-itself-for-itself, Sartre calls the diamond "the quintessence of being." The perfect diamond is perfectly transparent and luminous, and also perfectly solid and indestructible; thus it can symbolize both perfect consciousness and perfect substance. The ultimate goal of Buddhahood is sometimes spoken of as a diamond, a stage achieved with the appearance of the *vajra*, the diamond body within. The diamond is given a similar meaning in much Hindu literature. In the West St. Theresa would write, "I began to think of the soul as if it were a castle made of a single diamond" (*The Interior Castle*, p.28). The last book of the Bible uses a related image to describe the ultimate phase of creation: the New Jerusalem will have a "radiance like a rare jewel, like a jasper, clear as crystal," "pure as gold, clear as glass."

Simone de Beauvoir says that Sartre studied the mystics during the early thirties. Among the mystics there are many parallels for the opposition and the synthesis of which Sartre speaks. The mystics treat of radical opposites—fullness and emptiness, *Todo y Nada*, All and Nothing—but opposites that are in some way resolved. Among Christians the terminology of fullness and emptiness goes back to St. Paul, who saw Christ as the fullness of God (Col. 1:19) and also refers to the divine kenosis, or self-emptying of Christ ("Christ emptied himself taking on the form of a servant" [Phil. 2:8]). The Pauline reference to kenosis has been given widely different meanings in the history of Christian spirituality. Thomas Merton finds in the kenosis an expression of the contemplative ideal:

In this mystery we encounter the full Christian expression of the dialectic of fullness and emptiness, *todo y nada*, void and infinity, which appears at the heart of all the great traditional forms of contemplative wisdom (*Mystics & Zen Masters*,p.212).

It is in terms of these same oppositions that Sartre writes of the contemplative life—but unlike Merton Sartre would never speak of contemplative wisdom.

3

Relaxation of the Bonds of Being

The Contemplative Life

When Descartes made his famous analysis of the *cogito*, he judged that he was an imperfect being because he apprehended himself as a being that doubted. He found that to judge himself an imperfect being meant that he had at least an implicit knowledge of what was meant by a perfect Being. He apprehended a cleavage between the being that he found himself to be and the perfect Being of which he could conceive. Using this cleavage, Descartes proceeded to his second proof for the existence of God (*BN*,97).

Sartre also begins with a *cogito*; he also perceives that his consciousness is imperfect before the ideal of a Being that is perfect. He speaks of the ideal of the perfect Being as "haunting" his consciousness. But Sartre does not proceed to demonstrate the existence of this Being. This perfect Being is the in-itself-for-itself. As in-itself it is perfect self-identity and self-possession, while at the same time as for-itself it escapes itself to be its own cause. It is both substance and consciousness, it is God. For Sartre God is present to human consciousness as an ideal, much as God was present to the consciousness of Descartes. But the difference is that for Sartre such a being remains an ideal and cannot exist.

The Desire to Be God

Since the in-itself-for-itself is the ideal of perfect Being, it can be said that God is the ideal that every man desires to be. God is first "perceived" by man as that which identifies him (*BN*,694). It is with an awareness of this ideal being that every man makes his basic choice; the choice explicitates the way that the individual man will try to attain the ideal. All of a man's actions express this choice. Since the choice is made before the ideal of the perfect Being, it can be said that the ideal of God underlies every human activity. Thus the problem of God is not a peripheral problem for Sartrean man; "everything within me demands God and that I cannot forget" (*S1*,154). It is the core problem that every man must resolve, and does resolve, in his own individual way.

The problem of God is a human problem which concerns the rapport between men. It is a total problem to which each man brings a solution by his entire life, and the solution which one brings to it reflects the attitude one has chosen towards other men and towards oneself (*S4*,52). Thus my freedom is a choice of being God and all my acts, all my projects translate this choice and reflect it in a thousand and one ways (*BN*,734).

In explaining man's fundamental project, Sartre sums it up as "man is the being whose project is to be God" (*BN*,694). He continues by saying that, if man has a pre-ontological conception of the being of God, it is not the wonders of nature or the powers of society that have given him that comprehension. Rather, God is the value and the supreme end of consciousness, God is the limit in terms of which man makes known to himself what he is. God even enters in to what may be called Sartre's definition of man: "To be man means to reach toward being God. Or if you prefer, man fundamentally is the desire to be God" (*BN*,694).

All men desire to be God, yet Sartre acknowledges that they differ notably in the way they choose to realize this ideal. The choice of the materialist will have one character and the choice of the Catharist another. The materialist affirms that his acts are determined purely by the laws of matter. He hopes that by this belief his consciousness might take on the solidity and the inertia that are proper to matter. Consciousness would then become a substance, and consciousness rendered substantial would be God. The choice of the Catharist is the opposite: he tries to free himself of all materiality. He is distressed by his need for food and would like to purify himself of all that comes from the "world." Free of all matter, he wants to derive only from himself, for he who derives only from himself is *Causa-sui* and *Causa-sui* is God.

Each particular project of being-God is hightly nuanced and is reflected in many attitudes such as the attitude one has towards private property, towards knowledge, and towards other people. Sartre offers a phenomenological analysis of ownership which can serve to illustrate how he would find the desire to be God reflected in what is ordinarily considered a secular experience. Ownership seems to affect objects in their depths. Possession can seem to change a house or a room so that, even after the death of the owner, we can still speak of the house as "possessed." Objects that are mine seem to be fundamentally different from those that belong to others. My pen can seem to be so much a part of me that I do not distinguish it from my act of writing. When the objects that I use begin to show the small marks of my use, they become part of me. I begin to see myself in the familiar objects that I have gathered. The self that I see in my possessions is before me as an object, I can grasp it. My subjectivity is objectified. Taken together with the object, I seem to form an in-itself-for-itself. Sartre concludes:

The dyad, for-itself possessing and in-itself possessed, is the same as that being which is in order to possess itself and whose possession is its own creation — God (*BN*, 725).

When Sartre speaks of human consciousness haunted by the ideal of perfect Being, or speaks of God as the ultimate project of every man, or says that man solves the problem of God only by his entire life, he *sounds* like a religious man. Christian philosophers and theologians have long spoken in these terms. Where Sartre differs from them is that, for him, God is impossible, and the sad result follows that man's project is always a failure; man endlessly tries to realize a contradiction.

>...the passion of man is the reverse of that of Christ, for man loses himself as man in order that God may be born. But the idea of God is contradictory and we lose ourselves in vain. Man is a useless passion (BN,754).

The divine aspiration that haunts every consciousness cannot be realized, so man is left with no possibility of happiness (BN,110). "For a thoughtful person every enterprise is absurd" (B,31). The world presented by Sartre is the world of God-haunted man for whom God does not exist. It is not a pleasant world and Sartre does not present it as such. He does not regard atheism with the optimism of the nineteenth-century liberals; for Sartre it is very constricting that God does not exist. It is the nonexistence of God that leaves man a failure. "...atheism is a cruel and long-range affair: I think I've carried it through" (W,158).

God is contradictory because he is both consciousness and substance, the two regions of being that are absolutely separated. It is this contradictory ideal that rests at the heart of man. Haunted by the impossible synthesis, man is always aware of his own imperfection. But this imperfection can be said to be of the nature of consciousness. The doubt and the hesitation that Descartes had perceived as an imperfection in his *cogito* is, according to Sartre, nothing other than consciousness itself.

The Sacred, the Magical, and the Fantastic

Some men have frequent experiences that seem to indicate a divine presence; an object suddenly appears to them as hallowed or sacred. The sacred appears through the thing. "The sacred object is an object which is in the world and which points to a transcendence [a consciousness] beyond the world" (BN,457). An object appears with consciousness! It appears to be the divine synthesis. The for-itself, which is always cause of its own nothingness, now seems to be *producing itself as thing* (CRD,457). Sartre quotes Mircea Eliade: "An object becomes sacred insofar as it incorporates (that is, reveals) something other than itself. A sacral stone is a thing and yet in its depths a thing is revealed." Sartre develops the idea:

Appearing through an object, the power preserves a specter of objectivity, but it is itself a subject: the sacred is the subjective manifesting itself in and through the objective by the destruction of objectivity; it is a gaze-object that appears within our universe and in the aspect of a thing, but which robs us of the world and of our own subjectivity by conferring upon us the status of *thing gazed at* (*G*,552).

In the presence of the sacred we experience a loss of our own subjectivity. The sacred thing seems to contain man's subjectivity but it alienates that subjectivity from him in an object. The sacred is "freedom coming back to man as a superhuman and petrified power" (*CRD*,457). The sacred object petrifies me in return, it seems to judge me. The free flow of my consciousness is arrested ("it hardens and thickens like a mayonaise"). I feel myself becoming defined as an object. It is God who ultimately defines my being, but usually the experience is not quite so extreme or ultimate. I am in the presence of the sacred whenever my amorphous consciousness takes on any objective definition. This moment always involves a reciprocal change: the object which affects me appears endowed with consciousness while my consciousness seems to become an object. In the experience I seem to be gazed at and judged. An example of such a reciprocal change can be seen in a verse of Victor Hugo:

> Pendant que je deviens une chose, je sens
> Les choses près de moi qui deviennent des êtres.
> Mon mur est une face et voit; mes deux fenêtres,
> Blêmes sur le ciel gris, me regardent dormir.

> *Demi-sommeil*

As the walls and windows appear endowed with consciousness, the author feels himself becoming a thing.

Sartre often treats this phenomenon and often uses other words than the sacred to describe it. At times he speaks of "the sacred," "the magical," and "the fantastic" as though they were the same. Sartre would not really want to identify the terms, but he does not indicate how they would differ. Several times he contrasts the terms without explaining their difference (*G*,103; *BN*,457). Like the sacred, the magical is said to be the inanimate thing that produces human effects without ceasing to be a thing (*G*,103). The reign of magic is "blinded ideas, plugged by matter, matter possessed by mind and in revolt against mind" (*LPE*,161). The magical is the degradation of the for-itself into an in-itself (*BN*,206). Or, since consciousness is spontaneity and the for-itself is inert, magic is "an irrational synthesis of spontaneity and passivity. It is an inert activity, a consciousness rendered passive" (*E*,84). In trying to differentiate between the sacred and the magical one is tempted to say that the sacred is an object that is endowed with consciousness while the magical is the consciousness that is rendered objective. Such a distinction is not always observed; in the texts of Sartre the meanings overlap. When Sartre elaborates on the fantastic, he again makes allusion to the confusion between subject and object:

It is an entire world in which things manifest a captive, tormented thought....In this world, matter is never entirely matter, since it offers only a constantly frustrated attempt at determinism, and mind is never completely mind, because it has fallen into slavery and has been impregnated and dulled by matter ....The fantastic presents a reverse image of the union of body and soul. In it, the soul takes the place of the body, and the body that of the soul, and we cannot use clear, distinct ideas in pondering this image (*LPE*,62).

The contemporary art that gives us a sense of the fantastic does not show us fairies or goblins. A fairy considered objectively is nothing other than a pretty girl and as such is no longer perceived as fantastic. The fantastic occurs when Nature appears as a human being. It is found in the paintings of Dali and Chirico: stones are pictured as suffering and metals are shown as contaminated with life. Once again the separation between object and consciousness is not properly observed.

The sacred, the magical, and the fantastic each has a religious aspect, but this does not mean that they occur only in what is regarded as a religious setting. The sacred can come into one's life in many unexpected moments; this is what makes atheism such a "long-range" affair. The sacred one or sacred thing is that which imposes a foreign spell on my consciousness. Consciousness is the source of value and it should impose its value on things, but in the presence of the sacred the reverse happens: consciousness feels bound by values imposed on it. Consciousness feels obliged by sacred duties and restricted by sacred taboos. There are pointless acts that must be repeated, there are words that must not be said and thoughts that one must not think. Consciousness is under the spell of an alien determination and this changes its character. Normally, material objects are determined and consciousness is free, but under a spell of the sacred, matter is free and consciousness is spellbound.

When consciousness loses some of its freedom it also loses some of its anguish. In observing its sacred obligations consciousness feels supported by "something warm and living," by a "friendly presence." But in giving up its freedom to the object, consciousness sacrifices some of its own lucidity: so it is that the sacred always involves a mystery, something that consciousness is unable to, or refuses to, analyze. The sacred is an object with consciousness; analysis would reduce it to the complete lucidity of the for-itself and to the complete opacity (absurdity) of the in-itself. But there is no analysis made, there is mystery. Since the sacred object is endowed with subjectivity, it continually suggests an intelligibility, but the intelligibility cannot be brought to light; if it is, the sacred will vanish.

And is it not precisely the sacred which thus manifests itself through the profane without ever letting itself be touched? The world is sacred because it gives an inkling of a meaning that escapes us (G,255).

It was an experience of the sacred when Sartre's grandfather imposed on him the obligation to be a writer, or when stern adults made a thief of the young Genet, or when the fictional Lucien took on the being of an anti-Semite. In each case the spontaneous flow of consciousness was arrested and crystallized into opaque being by accepting a value that it did not create. Consciousness is freedom, but in these sacred moments freedom accepted a fatality, it assumed a determination. Sartre became defined as an author. It was a religious moment, and Sartre recounts the experience in religious terms. In this moment he became defined as an author, and it is God "who identifies and defines him [man] in his ultimate and fundamental project" (BN,694). This definition came to him through his grandfather, so he speaks of his grandfather as Moses dictating the New Law. Flaubert has a definition given him by his father; now he will undergo life "like a sacred ceremony—because it is manipulated by the all-powerful

Relaxation of the Bonds of Being

will of the Other" (*IF*,448-49), "the sacred is the mark of his alienation" (*IF*,392).

In these examples it is adults who impose their determinations on a child, but Sartre sees the imposition of value in all human relations; "man is always a sorcerer to man and the social world is primarily magical" (*E*,84; my translation). But the sacred is also found when other people are not present: it appears in idols or pictures which seem to look at me and judge me; it appears in rooms that seem to be filled with the presence of someone who is no longer there; it appears in rows of solemn books which seem to embody values between their unopened pages. Sartre speaks of a cult of unread books; meaning is frozen, it is not transmitted, the books are "things vaguely bewitched" (*IF*,285-88). Books, rooms, statues, idols, all are objects, and yet they seem to be more than objects for they appear to be endowed with a subjectivity. In the presence of these hallowed objects consciousness feels it has entered into a world where values are objectified, and when values are objectified *everything* is sacred.

Sartre sees the sacred (magical, fantastic) as forming a complete world. One feels a radical transition as one leaves a church and steps into the secular activity of the street. Consider the reactions of a man who seems to be confronted with a talking horse—for an instant the horse appears to be bewitched. But if the horse continues to talk in the middle of quiet trees and a serene landscape, the impression of magic disappears. The man begins to see the horse as a man in disguise, or he seeks some other rational explanation (*LPE*,61). This is because the fantastic is a complete world and dissolves in a rational setting; it either captures and transforms all of our world or it dissolves into nothing.

For Sartre, consciousness always exists in the presence of a world (consciousness always has an object), but this world can be either the world of tools or the world of magic (terminology and contrasts found in *E*,63-94). In the world of tools, objects appear as part of an ordered complex; if one wants a determined effect he must act upon a definite element to bring about a limited change in the complex. This is the world of science, the ordinary human world, the world of men at work using tools to modify their environment for human ends. Here man imposes his purpose on things. It is the human purpose seen in an object that transforms the brute object into a tool. Opposed to the world of tools is the world of magic. Here objects seem to be endowed with a purpose all their own, apart from man. Man is the tool of things. Consciousness may still try to modify this world, but not through the systematic use of tools. Consciousness reacts in kind and tries to act across space and time by spells and incantations. This is the world where the distinction between the in-itself and the for-itself is not observed. "Magic action through influence at a distance is the necessary result of this relaxation of the bonds of being" (*BN*,206).

The world of the fantastic can also be contrasted with the world of tools. The novels of Kafka and Blanchot present a fantastic world, but they do not produce this effect through the use of bizarre objects or extravagant imagery. Sartre sees the effect arising through the presentation of ordinary man-made things that have no human use (*LPE*,64ff.). There is a labyrinth of corridors, doors, and stairways, all of which lead nowhere. Innumerable signposts are along the road, but they indicate nothing humanly intelligible. Messages keep arriving, but no one knows where they come from and they have no meaning. In the world of tools a message presupposes a sender and an intelligible content, but in the novels of Kafka there is the "upset of an entire system of communication" (*IF*,578). In this world the means have isolated themselves and present themselves as ultimate ends. One finds the reverse of the Kantian ethic, which had proposed that man should treat himself and other men as ends, never as means. In the world of the fantastic, man is the means and things are the end. In *The Castle* Kafka presents an anonymous bureaucracy within which everyone seems to be a functionary; men appear as means who scrupulously follow detailed directives that have no human purpose. It is the intelligible world turned inside out: man is the tool of the equipment that he uses. This fantastic world is not limited to novels. It is present whenever man has a sense of Fate that seems to be directing his life. Fate implies a goal that is not human; it lies behind events, and through events it manipulates men for its own incomprehensible purpose. Men feel they are the instruments or the tools of a transcendent project which they do not understand. This is the fantastic: a meaning proceeds from things and events other than the meaning that man has put there.

The world of magic and the fantastic appears whenever there is emotion. Consider the emotion of terror. At night I am alone in a room when suddenly a menacing face appears at the window ten meters in front of me. It is ten meters away, but I experience the influence immediately on my consciousness. In this experience the whole room is transformed, it no longer serves me. There are no tools. I do not see the window as something that has to be broken and the ten meters as a distance that has to be traversed for the menace to reach me. The man need not enter the room, I am possessed already, it is action at a distance. In the experience of terror the window no longer appears as a practical object which protects me, it appears only as a frame for a terrifying face. I am paralyzed into an object, I am a victim of magic. In panic I make useless gestures, but it all takes place as in a dream where I keep pulling the trigger but the gun does not fire. The menace lies beyond the world of tools. My legs become numb and I cannot run. When tools work and distance separates, I find that the horror is gone. The real danger might remain, but in dealing with it rationally I am delivered from terror and the world of magic that terror sustains (*E*,85–90).

My emotion of terror and the terrifying world are reciprocal. Whenever there is emotion, a world of magic appears that denies the world of tools. Consider some other examples. I am walking along a country path when I see a wild beast before me; my heart beats more feebly, I turn pale and faint. My conduct is magical (*E,*62). Not being able to avoid the danger, I have denied it; I swoon and the world is transformed by magic. My emotional conduct does not effect anything, except this global transformation of my entire world. Sartre tells of his own experience in the army in World War II: the Germans were firing on him from in front, and suddenly the French opened fire from behind. There was nothing he could do, so the whole situation suddenly became "unreal." "It is a general fact that when we are in the impossibility of responding to the demands of the world by action, the world thereby loses its reality" (*IF,*666). The world of magic always involves a turning away from the practical world. There is this flight into magic even if the emotion itself is positive, such as the emotion of joy. The man who is overjoyed cannot stand still, he begins and abandons a thousand projects. A woman has just said that she loves him. In his joy he is aware that he cannot realize the pleasure of possessing her all at once; this will come only over the extended period of time that they are together. Now he dances and sings, and by these acts he seems to possess her symbolically all at once; it is a magic conduct that tries to overcome the duration of time. Sartre defines joy as "magical behavior which tends by incantation to realize the possession of the desired object as instantaneous totality" (*E*,69). The man turns from the difficult task of meriting her love; beyond time in the ineffective world of magic, he mimics total possession. In a series of similar examples, Sartre develops his phenomenology of the emotions and concludes:

We shall call emotion an abrupt drop of consciousness into the magical. Or, if one prefers, there is emotion when the world of instruments abruptly vanishes and the magical world appears in its place (*E*,90).

Having presented various magical worlds and the emotional behavior to which they correspond, Sartre adds that consciousness must choose for itself whether "the world is revealed as magical or rational." But he qualifies what he means by "rational." The term does not refer to an objectively rational world which man can contemplate. Rather, it refers to the "technical aspect of the world," it is seeing the world made of "instrumental complexes" (*BN*,544).

For Sartre, a purely rational and logical world is also judged to be magical. If the world were already constituted by a given order, it would not be directed by man; things would be directed by their own individual essences. Spirit would again be involved in matter, but now it would be matter directed by the rational concept. Matter would again appear as directed by "mind," that is, objects would be governed by the "nature" that possesses them. In such a world,

Man, surrounded by ready-made thoughts, the reason of trees and stones, of the moon and water, has only to enumerate and contemplate (*LPE*,54).

Sartre sees such a world in the writings of Aristotle and in mediaeval science. It is the classified world of Linnaeus where everything acts according to its essence; it is not the evolving world of Lamarck. It is a world that is said to be ruled by the white magic of the concept. Since it was Aristotle who founded this world, he is termed the "magician of logic."

Is it not in Aristotle that we find this tidy, finite, classified world, a world rational to the core? Was it not he who regarded knowledge as a contemplation and classification? (*LPE*,57).

For Sartre, knowing is not a contemplation but a practice; knowing is possible only when one is engaged in action: "the Truth is always an enterprise" (*IF*,159). Sartre objects that the world of Aristotle is made for the quietist who contemplates Being, or Nature, with a distant religious awe. Contemplation presumes that Nature has a given meaning apart from the functional meaning man gives it. The desire to see Nature as it is in itself is a "purely theological temptation" (*CRD*,248). It is a theological temptation because one desires to look at the world as a god would look at it, that is, as if he had no relation to it. Such a view assumes that objects are "totalities," that is, that the fullness of their meaning has been already determined. But the meaning of nothing is complete, because man is free and therefore everything in the world is open to an uncertain future. Both the knower and the known are inevitably part of one incomplete process:

The only theory of knowledge which can be valid today is one which is founded on that truth of microphysics: the experimenter is part of the experimental system. This is the only position which allows us to get rid of all idealist illusion (*SM*,32).

If anyone would claim to have discovered a "timeless truth," whether a truth of "pure science" or a truth of theology, he would be caught in this idealist illusion.[1] For Sartre, any such claim would be a vain attempt to transcend the historical perspective and would result only in mystification and illusion. He does not allow the possibility of a pure, scientific knowledge, even in mathematics. It could be said that the mystic is anyone, scientist or saint, who will not resign himself to the temporal and unfinished character of whatever truth he knows.

1. A careful critique of this point is presented in Wilfrid Desan, *The Marxism of Jean-Paul Sartre*, p.254.

The desire to see the world as a constituted totality could be described as a theological temptation because it assumes that objects have an objective and absolute meaning. Because Sartre denies the existence of God, he cannot accept the possibility of an objective intelligibility or the objectivity of Nature. Sometimes Nature appears to be objective, but Sartre tries to explain this phenomenon otherwise. To the farmer, nature appears as a utensil and the animals are simply "cattle." The cherry trees came from afar and were planted there for commercial reasons. But when the city-dweller takes a holiday, it is a different world that appears. It is the world of "Nature." Objects are simply there to be contemplated. But what is the "Nature" that the city dweller sees? It is "nothing other than the external world when we cease to have technical relations with things" (G,266). Then reality changes into a setting. A plain country road between two potato patches presents Nature to the city-dweller. But is it really natural? The road has been laid out by engineers and the potato patches were planted and tended by farmers. The city-dweller does not see the tilling. It is a kind of work that is foreign to him. To the man who does not work there, even the quiet growth of the forest reflects the image of a human finality (G,266). The city-dweller has this vision of nature only because he does not work the fields and does not tend the cattle and does not share the hopes of the farmer; he is a stranger on the farm. But it is possible to extend this vision of strangeness even further. One can withdraw not only from the activity of farm, but from all human activity, from all human hopes and needs. This is the theological temptation: to want to stand apart from man and look at him from afar. This is what the quietist, the ascetic, and the mystic systematically try to effect. They assume a divine point of view beyond the human species and look down on the human enterprise from above, much as one might watch the labors of bees or of ants. The quietist, the contemplative, the ascetic then begins to see the world charged with a miraculous power. He has withdrawn from the world of tools in its entirety so that he now looks at the whole world as the city-dweller looks at Nature. He does not share the goals of men so he does not see that objects have only the purposes that men give them. For the quietist,

Human ends are dead, they float with their bellies up. Petrified ends, ends corroded from below, invaded by materiality, seen from without by an angel or a beast, ends *for others*, for a zoological species to which the quietist does not belong (*G*,259).

When one observes the human enterprise from a distance, it all appears strange and fantastic; it is the attitude of the viewer that has made the difference, "contemplative quietism renders imaginary what is contemplated" (*IF*,666). For example: a school bus becomes "a huge, absurd hornet whose idiotic task is to pour out an uninterrupted stream of travelers." If a bus is not seen as a human tool, it too reverts to being a part of "Nature" like the utensils of the farmer; it becomes "a voluminous assemblage of metal and dead wood." Yet it does not remain as pure Nature. Matter that has been ordered by man retains the traces of human purpose. It is this trace of consciousness that makes it appear awe-inspiring or fantastic. The school bus is first regarded as a purely natural object, an assemblage of metal and wood, an object that should observe the law of gravity. Then, as the bus descends a hill, it surprisingly draws to a halt beside a child who beckons to it; to the man who has withdrawn from the human enterprise the "assemblage of metal and dead wood" has escaped the laws of gravity "because a young, hairless animal has lifted a finger." The bus seems endowed with a "magical power" only because the viewer has withdrawn from human activity; when he looks down upon tools from a distance, the tools seem to be functioning on their own (*G*,259; see *CRD*,362). Such a vision suggests that there is a strange intelligence at work behind objects and events. Sartre quotes the astronomer Eddington:

…we have discovered a strange footprint on the shore of the Unknown and…after having constructed one theory after another to explain its origin we have finally managed to reconstruct the creature who left the footprint…this creature happens to be ourselves (*LPE*,63).

This is how Sartre understands the fantastic (and seemingly the magic and the sacred as well): it is the human world seen from without; it is matter acting spontaneously; it is the in-itself acting under the influence of the for-itself. After all of the theories have been considered by which man tries to understand Nature, its origin turns out to be man himself. Man alienated from his own work contemplates it from a distance and sees in matter the traces he has left there. The person who sees human traces from afar seems to be witnessing a miracle. The in-itself appears to have a mind of its own. The miracle is an ontological one; the very bonds of being appear to have relaxed: a substance is endowed with consciousness! This is the experience of the sacred.

Being and Action

There is a unifying theme behind all of the experiences considered; it is that man either cannot or does not effectively act. Consider the examples that have been presented. Before the wonders of Nature the quietist has adopted a purely contemplative gaze; before the menacing face that has appeared at the window I am paralyzed with fright; before the wild beast I faint; when man is directed by fate, the end result has been determined in advance and his acts will not affect the outcome; in the novels of Kafka and Blanchot men busy themselves with endless details but nothing is ever accomplished. In each case, man is no longer using the world as his tool, and it is then that the world takes on its magic luster.

> When the instruments are broken and unusable, when plans are blasted and effort is useless, the world appears with a childlike and terrible freshness, without supports, without paths (*WL*,30).

This is the world of magic. Man does not act in this world, because significant action appears to be impossible. This does not mean that man is totally passive. He can still make gestures. A gesture differs from an act in that it is not made to accomplish a result, it is made to present a state of being. A man can walk to get somewhere or he can walk to make a gesture. As a gesture, the walking manifests an archetype, it is the walk of *the* wise man, or the walk of *the* carefree sailor. It is not invented as it goes along, it seems to exist per se, it is a unit already constituted, like a dance step (*G*,322). This is the essential characteristic of a gesture: it has already been made and can thus pass indifferently from one person to another.

For the gesture is *sacred*: it is the gesture of an emperor or of a hero; I borrow it from those terrifying beings; it settles on me, tightens my consciousness, which is always a bit slack, imposes an unaccustomed rhythm upon it: it is a sacrament (*G*,322).

A gesture is a fixed movement and therefore somewhat foreign to consciousness. In making a gesture I feel its foreign power within me. This power is measured by the might of the one who first established the gesture. The gesture then serves as a ritual and sacralizing communion with the ancester of the clan or the eponymous hero.

In slipping into my muscles it retains the stamp of its origin: in fact it instills within me the person of its first executant (*G*,323).

It is as though the being of an object descended on me and ruled me by its determinism. Action is the prerogative and special character of consciousness, while the in-itself is unchanging in its plenitude. In the gesture, action is subordinated to the fixed stability of being, consciousness assumes a determinism. The gesture is the act of the human being in the world of magic; it can also be called "an inert activity, a consciousness rendered passive." It is one more attempt to realize the impossible synthesis of in-itself and for-itself. When one feels that he is in the presence of the sacred, gestures are called for, not actions. When one lives in the world of the sacred, life becomes a grand liturgy, all is ceremony; objects are no longer tools but only "appurtenances of the cult."

This opposition between action and being gives rise to what Sartre terms "two incompatible world systems," and the two systems form a constant theme in his writings. At times he will speak of living with two dialectics or playing in two tableaux, but it is the same opposition between action and being that he is referring to. The two systems are incompatible, but a man does not necessarily live only according to one or the other. Sartre speaks of leaping from one system to the other at one's convenience, or of one's mind becoming a "whirligig of two ideologies at war with one another" (*IF*,839). He sees Flaubert as claiming infinite guilt (as responsible for his actions) and infinite innocence (doomed to commit his acts by his fate) (*IF*,266,442). Sartre sees the two tableaux in his own childhood: he wanted to be established in being as a gift of heaven (a self independent of what he might do), and at the same time he wanted to be the result of his own activity (a self-made man). He sees this opposition as basic to the faith, so he writes of his boyhood desires in religious terms: "I was of the Church. As a militant, I wanted to save myself by works; as a mystic, I attempted to reveal the silence of being by a thwarted rustling of words" (W,157). To compare the two categories, Sartre sets up a list of opposing ideals. In the category of *action* he includes: freedom, will, the subject, consciousness, life, and the will to live. In contrast to these, the category of *being* includes: magic, substance, the object, soul, death, and fatality (G,61-62).

If one lives according to the category of *being*, he is dominated by a contemplative ideal and stands in awe before that which is: "one must be open to Being as the mystic is open to his God" (G,63). The contemplative soon becomes a quietist, but quietism is not total inaction, rather all actions are directed toward rendering oneself passive, pure, and vacant. It is at this moment of infinite stillness "protected against the least vibration," when one is at the point of annihilation, that the creature will receive his infinite justification: "The reflection of the infinite in the finite — with the inverse and complementary ecstasy of the finite out of itself in the infinite — constitutes the entire dignity of the creature" (IF,511). The will need only wait in blessed passivity in order to receive being like a divine manna, a manna not like the bread that one must work to gain. In the view of the quietist everything has been arranged in eternity. What a man might *accomplish* is of no importance; it is what he *is* that counts. All has been determined beforehand, he can only watch it unfold. He is only a means, so he tries to behave like an object, and consequently his acts become gestures. Life is a ritual which can accomplish nothing. One need only make the gestures of living, for it is gestures that suggest the archetypes of eternal being. It is as though one were already dead.

In contrast with the category of being is the category of *doing*. Here consciousness does not render itself passive before being, rather consciousness acts and determines being through what it does. Now a man is not judged by what he is, rather he is judged by his deeds.

The two sets of categories are opposed, but that does not mean that a man lives in either one set or the other; in fact, Sartre sees the syncretism of these two conflicting sets as the characteristic of the "religious nature" (G,249). He often presents this conflict in religious terms, as when he speaks of the conflict in his own life between being a mystic and a member of the Church militant. It is this opposition that Sartre sees as underlying the conflicting theologies of salvation by faith and salvation by works (G,248-49). He elaborates on the two opposing attitudes. Salvation by faith corresponds to passivity before Being.

For faith is not simple belief in the Supreme Being. It becomes a humble and passive awaiting of His coming. Moreover, would it seek Him if it had not already found Him? Could it await Him if He were not already there? It is God who awaits himself through the believer. It is God who will attain himself in the mystical ecstasy, which is a fusion of the Subject and the Object. There is thus nothing to do but to await the sudden fulguration that will fill us with *being*, that will make our fleeting consciousness the sheath of God (G,247).

Opposed to this, is the belief that salvation comes through one's own activity:

But all religions aim at governing our conduct. It is by action that we acquire merit, provided our intentions are pure and spring from the heart. It would be vain to seek God, to await Him; we are not in the world to enjoy Him but to serve Him (G, 248).

Sartre finds both of these attitudes in "the religious nature." He finds both present in the one-sentence prayer: "Lord I will *do* Thy bidding, I will *be* Thy servant." Each attitude is said to have its disadvantages. The one leads to quietism, the other to formal dryness and pharisaism. "In any case," Sartre sums up his objection, "militant action, which is prescribed by sacred books, cannot be reconciled with passive waiting for God" (G,248). The two attitudes conflict, but it is just this conflict that characterizes the religious nature. The attitudes correspond to the categories of being and action. Each attitude involves a complete system, and they cannot be resolved. So the religious man does a whirligig and leaps from one system to the other. His mind seeks only the Absolute — but he has found *two of them!* All and Nothing. The mind makes total leaps but it does not compromise. Pure being characterizes the in-itself and pure action characterizes the for-itself. These are the two areas that are irrevocably separate but whose synthesis would be God. Unable to find God, the religious nature assumes both of the divine components. Still Sartre would insist there is no synthesis, it only appears that way. There is only the rapid and unresolved whirligigs of the religious mind.[2]

Sartre is notably unsympathetic to whatever presents itself as the sacred. His criticism is often extreme, but one cannot overlook the fact that what he is saying has many roots in the religious tradition. When he defines man as the being whose "project is to be God" or says that man is fundamentally "the desire to be God," he is not trying to be blasphemous. To most Christians today it would sound more acceptable to say that man desires to be *with* God, or that man desires to *know* God. But that man should *become* God is not unknown in the Christian tradition. In the Eastern church the Fathers commonly spoke of man's divinization and of deifying grace. In the West this terminology was not widely used, but the German mystic Meister Eckhart went so far as to write, "God and I are One....I am the unmoved Mover that moves all things." Eckhart adds that between God and the soul "there is really no distinction" (*M.Eck.*,232,214). In the Mass, Christians daily have asked to share in Christ's divinity (*ejus divinitatis esse consortes*). Such expressions have a scriptural basis: the Second Epistle of St. Peter speaks of men becoming "partakers of the divine nature," and Christ quoted the Old Testament to the effect that "You are gods."

When consciousness is in the presence of the sacred, Sartre speaks of it thickening and becoming an object. Such a phenomenon would also be part of the Christian tradition. St. Augustine addresses the Lord, "I will become solid in You" (*Solidabor in Te* [*Conf.*11.30]). Teilhard de Chardin speaks of himself in a way that could recall the insubstantiality of Sartrean consciousness: he tells of feeling "totally without consistence." Later, through the experience of faith, Teilhard came to refer to God as "my consistence" or "sovereign Consistence." (See the note in Teilhard's *Writings in Time of War*,p.123.) Alfred North Whitehead wrote in a different tradition; still, he would seem to have experienced God in a similar way for he speaks of God as the

2. It is pure action that is characteristic of the for-itself. This absolute action is not the same as the creative, finite action referred to in most of this chapter. In the opposition between being and action Sartre has come to endorse action—but not as an absolute. The question is treated again in the final chapter.

Relaxation of the Bonds of Being

Principle of *Concretion* (that which makes concrete). These would seem to be examples of the phenomenon that Sartre opposes in his criticism of the sacred.

The basis upon which Sartre rests his critique is fundamentally ontological: the for-itself cannot take on a true consistency as this would be a violation of the laws of being. It is this desire of consciousness for consistency that Sartre is referring to in saying that man is the desire to be God. Man is essentially frustrated, because God is not possible; and God is not possible for ontological reasons. The ontological reasons would be sort of a reverse form of St. Anselm's ontological argument. St. Anselm, by a logical analysis of the definition of God, wanted to show that God must exist by the very definition of what was meant by God. In *Being and Nothingness* the atheism of Sartre does the reverse: by a logical analysis of the definition of God — that is, by a consideration of the opposing properties presented in chapter 2 above — Sartre maintains that God is contradictory and therefore cannot exist. Sartre develops the meaning of the in-itself and the for-itself until the opposition between them includes such oppositions as being and action, object and subject, being and nothingness, and so on.

Sartre would argue that God is impossible because such differences are irreconcilable. One might try to dismiss his objection by claiming that these oppositions have arisen because of Sartre's peculiar ontology. But Sartre would not be alone in seeing that the existence of God involves the union of contrary properties — particularly the contraries of being and action that were presented at length in this chapter. St. Thomas spoke of the *Being* of God as *Pure Act*. St. Augustine spoke of God as "always *acting* yet always *at rest.*" Nicholas of Cusa wrote, "Thou, Lord, dost *stand* and *move* at the same time, at the same time Thou dost *proceed* and *rest*" (Happold,*Mysticism*,pp.335–36). Sartre has argued that the religious nature is one that tries to duplicate this set of divine contraries. The best-known recent scholar of mysticism, Evelyn Underhill, would seem to agree: "This double activity, this swinging between rest and work...is truly the life of man...because this alone represents on human levels something of that "ever active, yet ever at rest" which they [the mystics] find in God" (*Practical Mysticism*,p.157). The alternation between being and action is present in the Benedictine monastic ideal: *Orare et Laborare*. The monk would alternate between the passivity of ritual and practical activity. The absolute character of both action and passivity is brought out by Ruysbroeck, a late mediaeval mystic who explains that the spiritual man lives in "two ways; namely, in work and in rest. And in each he is whole and undivided." All those "who do not possess both rest and work in one and the same exercise" have not reached the ideal (Happold, *Mysticism*, pp. 288-89). Teilhard de Chardin also sees great significance in the unity of activity and passivity; for the Christian they unite to form "an astounding equilibrium" (*Divine Milieu*, p. 95, 119). It is this ultimate unity of being and action that Sartre will not allow; rather he speaks of an alternating whirligig and thus expresses both his atheism and his understanding of human failure. But it is obvious that he is dealing with a theme that is integral to the religious tradition.

Aside from the opposition between being and action, Sartre speaks of a whole series of oppositions that were likewise involved in the meaning of God. This is also acknowledged by authors in the religious tradition. Nicholas of Cusa was famous for his way of speaking of God in terms of oppositions: "Thou hast shown to me that Thou canst not be seen elsewhere than where impossibility meeteth and faceth me" (*Hap.*, 336). Arthur Lovejoy points out that this way of speaking was widespread:

The notion of the *coincidentia oppositorum*, of the meeting of extremes in the Absolute, was an essential part of nearly all mediaeval theology, as it had been of Neoplatonism...in plainer language, the permissibility and even the necessity of contradicting oneself when one spoke of God (*Great Chain of Being*, p. 83).

Lovejoy goes on to say that the difficulty was alleviated by what theologians called the *sensus eminentior* of words. That is, when a word was applied to God it had to be understood in a somewhat different but analogous sense. The contradiction was thus in the speaker and not in God. Sartre does not accept this analogous use of words and thus sees God simply as an impossible contradiction.

In the Middle Ages the reconciliation of opposites was not only a theological problem but was also the goal and the experience claimed by a long tradition of mystics. The same goal and

Relaxation of the Bonds of Being

experience are even more evident in the mysticism of the East. William James used drugs to induce artificial mystical states. Again, the same conclusion was suggested:

Looking back on my own experiences, they all converge towards a kind of insight to which I cannot help ascribing some metaphysical significance. The keynote of it is invariably a reconciliation. It is as if the opposites of the world, whose contradictoriness and conflict make all our difficulties and troubles, were melted into unity (*Varieties of Religious Experience*, p. 298).

For Sartre this reconciliation is the goal of every man, and it is in terms of this understanding that he has defined man as the desire to be God. Many mystics have testified to the reality of this synthesis, but it is the rejection of this experience that is the fundamental point in Sartre's critique of the sacred. However, Sartre writes that the integration of the in-itself and the for-itself "is always indicated." He explains that "everything happens as if the world, man, and man-in-the-world succeeded in realizing only a missing God" (*BN*, 762). Though everything *seems* to indicate such a synthesis, Sartre does not accept the possibility and clearly states his reason: it is ontologically impossible for the for-itself to unite with the in-itself, it only appears that way. The synthesis "is always indicated and always impossible" (*BN*, 762).

In terms of "always indicated and always impossible" it is worth considering the Sartrean method. His early writings were done under the influence of Husserl, and he considered himself a phenomenologist. Sartre modified the phenomenology of Husserl and came to criticize him because Husserl never passed beyond the pure description of the phenomena as such. Sartre felt that Husserl should be called a "phenomenalist" rather than a "phenomenologist" (*BN*, 89). The subtitle of *Being and Nothingness* might be the best way of characterizing the Sartrean method: *An Essay on Phenomenological Ontology*. As a phenomenologist, Sartre clearly subordinates the phenomena to the ontological analysis. It is ontology that is in control and that determines which experiences are valid. The phenomena of the sacred are rejected for the ontological reason that it is impossible to have a relaxation of the laws of being.

Sartre also presents himself as an existentialist. He insists that existence is prior to essence. But in the last analysis it is an *essential* reason (the essential impossibility of synthesis) that has the final say concerning the *existence* of a God that is always indicated in experience.

But Sartre's critique of the sacred is not totally opposed to what is found in the religious tradition; there are many points of agreement. To begin with, he has referred to consciousness as nothingness. This is the way that mystics have always spoken, but Sartre would seem to be the first Western philosopher to defend the literal accuracy of the term. For Sartre consciousness is nothingness because it is purely intentional, and intentionality is lost if consciousness becomes clouded with the opacity of the in-itself. A famous Buddhist text would also unite the themes of emptiness and intentionality:

> The mind is like a clear mirror standing.
> Take care to wipe it at all times.
> Allow no grain of dust to cling to it.

St. John of the Cross makes the same comparison; he speaks of the soul as a mirror which becomes clouded so that it cannot receive a clear image (*Ascent of Mount Carmel*, p. 47). It is only the pure of heart who will see God, therefore some experiences must be rejected lest they render the spirit dense and opaque. The mystics have never been sympathetic with magic visions which disturb the soul; these have been rejected as temptations. Much of Sartre's critique is thus directed against the same experiences that the mystics have always rejected. In *The Childhood of a Leader* Sartre told of Lucien and of his sacred experience of anger (see chap. 1 above). Lucien found that the emotion of anger gave a solidity to his otherwise insubstantial being. In this instance and throughout his treatment of the emotions Sartre would be in agreement with the many spiritual writers who have warned about the harmful effects of the passions. The passions were said to mislead the spirit and render it heavy and dense. The practice of asceticism was aimed at disciplining the passions in order to purify the eye of the soul. But Sartre will reject this purity as futile and meaningless.

Spititual writers would agree with a large part of Sartre's analysis, but they would maintain that ultimately there is a valid experience of the sacred. The phenomenology by which this valid experience could be distinguished from its imitations would be the subject of the many treatises on the discernment of spirits. Perhaps the terminology of Sartre could be used to formulate a criterion of discernment: in the false experience of the sacred, consciousness becomes heavy and dense, it loses its transparency. In the true mystic experience, consciousness would take on fullness and consistence but lose nothing of its transparency. To ask whether such an experience is possible is to ask whether transparency and consistence are mutually exclusive, and this is to reintroduce the fundamental question of the in-itself-for-itself, or the possibility of the *coincidentia oppositorum*. Many mystics would say that it is possible and appeal to their experience; Sartre would say that it is not and appeal to his ontology.

4

I Am Not Alone

The Interior Life

If consciousness could see itself as an object, it would then be the in-itself-for-itself. But the for-itself escapes itself, and objective self-knowledge is impossible. Nevertheless consciousness is involved in an endless effort at finding itself. The effort is the act of reflection; the effort is Narcissus fascinated by his image; the effort is the adolescent trying to find his uncertain identity; the effort is the sinner ashamed of his being before God; in short, the effort is the interior life. Consciousness does not have a within, so in one sense there is no interior life. But the efforts that consciousness makes to find an interior give rise to something new: the psyche.

I Watch Myself

The elements of the psyche were elaborated by Sartre in what can be considered his first philosophical work, *The Trans-*

cendence of the Ego, an article written in 1934 and published two years later. At the time Sartre was strongly under the influence of Husserl and the phenomenologists, but he felt that phenomenology was hampered by a faulty understanding of the Ego. Husserl had accepted an Ego that was in some way behind each consciousness and would form part of the necessary structure of consciousness (*TE*,37). Sartre objected that such an Ego was harmful to one of the basic insights of phenomenology: the intentionality of consciousness. Consciousness should be all lightness (*légèreté*) and translucency, but Sartre argued that if such an Ego were introduced into consciousness it would be like an opaque blade (*TE*,40). Possessing an Ego, consciousness would become heavy and lose the total transparency that intentionality requires. Husserl, in developing the idea of intentionality, had purified consciousness of the object known. Sartre demanded that consciousness be further purified, purified of the knowing subject. He does not deny an Ego altogether, but he does not accept an Ego that is part of consciousness or an Ego that is behind consciousness as a subject. Rather, the Ego is an object known by consciousness, it is in front of consciousness somewhat like an object in the world.

When a man engages in many of his daily activities, there is no Ego involved. If he is running for a bus, he is conscious of the bus that must be reached. If he is reading a novel, he is conscious of the plot and of the heroes of the novel, but no "I" can be said to inhabit this consciousness (*TE*,47,48). The "I" only comes into the situation when the man reflects on his activity and sees it as his. In reflecting on the act of reading or on the act of running, he assumes the act as his own. He adds the act to the series of his acts; this series of his acts together with his psychological states could be said to be his Ego. The Ego is not something given to start with, from which our acts proceed; it only appears in an act of reflection that is subsequent to the act. To understand the Ego, one must first consider the structure of reflection.

Reflection can be of two types: pure and impure. In pure reflection the consciousness that reflects is identified with the consciousness that is reflected on. Reflection is a type of knowing, but pure reflection differs from other types of knowing in that here one does not adopt a point of view in regard to what is known. There is no point of view, as what is known is fully known and what is known is identified with the knowing. The knowing is total (*BN*,189), it is a lightning intuition without relief (*BN*,195), it does not teach us anything since it was all known already before the reflection began. It could be better considered as a recognition than as a knowledge (*BN*,189). Because in pure reflection the knowing is identified with the known, this type of reflection is a privileged intuition where error is impossible. The phenomenologists, therefore, require that this reflection serve as the starting point for any philosophy (see *BN*,182).

But all reflection is not pure. As soon as reflection gets out of that lightning intuition without relief in which the reflected-on is given without a point of view, as soon as it posits itself as not being the reflected-on and determines *what* the reflected-on *is*, then its character is changed. Then the reflection effects the appearance of an object distinct from itself. The object is an in-itself. This in-itself is capable of being determined and qualified and studied over a period of time. An example would show the difference between the two types of reflection: if in seeing Peter I experience repugnance, I can say that I now have a violent repugnance for Peter. Repugnance is a consciousness. I can reflect on this consciousness and recognize its content. I know its content with full certainty and cannot be deceived (*TE*,62). This recognition has no point of view and reveals nothing new. It is a pure reflection. But the situation is different if I say that I hate Peter. Hatred is not a consciousness. Hatred is a state and extends beyond my present consciousness; it expresses a permanence. I have not the same certitude when I say that I hate Peter. I might be wrong. Tomorrow I might say that I did not mean it. But a repugnance is different; tomorrow I will not be able to take it back, today I am repelled by Peter. This is known in pure reflection, and in pure reflection to *be* and to *appear* are one and the same. This is why it cannot be mistaken. The being of the repugnance, or of any other consciousness, is its appearance. But a hatred is different, it is never wholly present to my consciousness; its being extends beyond its appearing; it seems to include a whole series of past experiences and it engages me for the future. The past and the future, however, are not part of my present consciousness. Now I am repelled by Peter, but beyond this repugnance my hatred appears. The hatred presents itself in and through each movement of repugnance but it is not limited to the present experience (*TE*,63). Hatred implies that it will continue even when I am not actually thinking of Peter. In this the hatred shows again that it is not a consciousness. Hatred has a being that extends beyond its appearance, while the being of consciousness is only to appear. There can be error in impure reflection for the same reason that there can be error in perceiving any object in the world: the being of that which is perceived is other than its appearing.

The hatred that I have seems to involve my consciousness, yet it is seen as an object. It is not fully objective being; it is consciousness degraded and hypostatized as an in-itself. Sartre calls it a mere shadow of being; it cannot simply be said to be, it is made to be (*est-été*) (*BN*,196). It is made by impure reflection. Impure reflection is an attempt at playing a double game: consciousness tries to step aside and regard itself as an object from a point of view. But when consciousness does this, the reflection is no longer the reflected-on. After having stepped aside to regard itself, consciousness wants to return and affirm its identity with what has been seen as an object. The effort cannot succeed. Impure reflection can thus be defined as "an abortive attempt on the part of the for-itself *to be another while remaining itself*" (*BN*,196). It is impure reflection that underlies the phenomenon of bad faith.

In impure reflection one can come to see his acts, his states, his qualities, and his Ego. These, taken together, Sartre calls the psyche. The psyche is the inner world that can be known objectively, and in this it differs from consciousness. The psyche is what is studied in the objective science of psychology. The spontaneity of consciousness would render a similar study of it impossible.

The states and the actions that make up the psyche are seen to have a certain unity; this unity is the Ego. The Ego is not some kind of a subject X, a center which supports all of the psychic phenomenon. Sartre compares it to a melody (*TE*,73). A melody is not a given X which supports all of the notes which make it up. A melody is the concrete sum of the notes which make it up and nothing more. So the Ego is the concrete totality of my states and actions and nothing further. A melody is nuanced differently by each succeeding note, and so my Ego is nuanced differently by each succeeding action or state. Before the melody has finished, it is capable of diverse resolutions. So while I am still alive, my Ego is open to the uncertain acts of my future. My Ego will only be full and determined when I have died; while I live, the character of my Ego is always in doubt. This doubtful character does not mean that I have a true me, which I have not found. A true me would imply something formed and complete, while my Ego will be formed only by the still undetermined acts of my future.

In reflection the Ego presents itself, deceptively, for the Ego is seen as producing its states. Each new state or action seems to be reattached to the Ego as though the Ego were its *source*. At the same time as the Ego is seen as a source, it is seen as an object; but all objects are wholly passive (see chap. 2 above). A passive object seems to be spontaneously productive. Such an idea is termed irrational. But however irrational it may be, this is what impure reflection sees when it intuits the Ego as source of states and actions (*TE*, 80). In rejecting the validity of this intuition Sartre opposes the common-sense view that would see my *being* as source of my *activities* (a view in which an ultimate subject or Ego would produce a hatred and the hatred would then determine my present consciousness of repulsion). According to Sartre, what is really first is the consciousness; across the consciousness the states are established, and across these the Ego (*TE*, 81). My acts do not arise from my being, rather the opposite — my subjectless acts are the source of my being. In scholastic terms one could say: *Esse sequitur agere*; my being does not determine my act, it follows after the act and is determined by the act. The Ego is not the source of my activity, it comes into being only upon subsequent reflection. A person might exclaim, "Me — could I have done that!" There is surprise because the Ego was envisioned as source of the action. It is not. The source is really the wholly spontaneous consciousness.

In reflection, consciousness projects its proper spontaneity onto the Ego to give it creative power. But spontaneity belongs only to consciousness. If spontaneity is degraded into an object, the object appears magical. To explain, Sartre compares the magic of the Ego to the effect produced by a good mimic (*TE*, 81). The mimic presents us with the *Erlebnis* of another person, but it is degraded.

The play between the two, the *Erlebnis* of the one imitated and the reality of the mimic, fascinates us. In a similar way our own Ego seems to be possessed by a consciousness that is not its own. It is a conscious-thing! We are sorcerers for ourself each time that we contemplate our Ego (*TE*,82). This inner magic is not limited to our experience of the Ego, it extends through all of the elements of the psyche. This is because the psyche is made to be; it is a synthesis of the for-itself and the in-itself and so appears as a world filled with magic.

It is necessary to give up trying to reduce the irrational element in psychic causality. This causality is a degradation of the ek-static for-itself, which is its own being at a distance from itself, its degradation into magic, into an in-itself which is what it is at its own place. Magic action through influence at a distance is the necessary result of this relaxation of the bonds of being (*BN*, 206).

Others Watch Me

In reflecting upon our Ego, we have the impression that that which is interior to consciousness is posed as an object before consciousness. Therefore Sartre terms the Ego a contradictory complex (*TE*,84). It is interiority seen from without. But at the same time it cannot really be seen from without in the way that an external object can. It always seems to be just beyond my gaze, it is too present to consciousness to be seen from a real point of view. For example, I ask myself if I am lazy or industrious. But I am too close to myself to determine the answer. I can ask those who know me, or I can collect facts about myself and interpret them; but to interpret them means to judge myself *as if it were a matter of judging another* (*TE*,86).

But it would be useless to address myself directly to the *me,* and to try to benefit from its intimacy in order to know it. For to the contrary it is the intimacy that bars the way. Thus "really to know oneself" is inevitably to take toward oneself the point of view of others, that is to say, a point of view which is necessarily false (*TE*,87; I have amended the English translation, which presents the "me" instead of the "intimacy" as barring the way. The French uses the feminine *elle*).

It is only by getting rid of all intimacy that I can come to know my own self. It is only when I adopt another's point of view that I am able to see myself and judge myself. If I am able to become conscious of even one of my properties objectively, then other people are already implied (*BN*,331). But is what I find through the judgments of others really myself or is it only an image that others have made?

Sartre has made a long and perceptive study of interpersonal relations. The presence of other people effects a radical change in me. In their presence my subjectivity seems to slip away; before their gaze I feel myself becoming an object. Others judge me, their look tells me what they are thinking; the swift flow of my consciousness seems to harden and become a thing, the thing that I am for them. They continue the process that was suggested in impure reflection. By impure reflection I can never quite determine what I am, I am always too close to see. But with the help of other people I can come to see myself with their eyes: I am the object that others know.

Sartre often refers to the objective being that we have as our Being-for-others. This being is fundamentally the same as the Ego, and sometimes Sartre will use the terms interchangeably (*BN*,320). Sartre has not always been rigid in his terminology; a whole series of terms is used to indicate man's objective being: Being-for-others, Being-as-object, self, Ego, character, nature, essence, person, soul, and so on. The terms are not identical, but it is often difficult to see how Sartre would distinguish them. The term Being-for-others emphasizes the nature of our being, that we have being only through the presence of other people. Sartre explains by an example: I am watching through a keyhole when suddenly I hear someone behind me. Someone is looking at *me*. In shame and confusion a radical change takes place for me. Consciousness is not now in a relation of knowing but of being. Beyond any knowledge which I can have, I am this self which another knows (*BN*,320). I am an object which another is looking at and judging. The shame I feel reveals to me another's look and myself at the end of that look. The world that I was living in seems to be alienated from me.

Pure shame is not a feeling of being this or that guilty object but in general of being *an* object; that is, of *recognizing myself* in this degraded, fixed, and dependent being which I am for the Other. Shame is the feeling of an *original fall,* not because of the fact that I have committed this or that particular fault but simply that I have "fallen" into the world in the midst of things and that I need the mediation of the Other in order to be what I am (*BN*,354).

The experience of myself as an object is not limited to the times when I am in the actual presence of others. Consider again the situation where I am looking through the keyhole. I think I hear someone behind me. I turn, but there is no one there; it was a false alarm. I return to looking through the keyhole, but

far from disappearing with my first alarm, the Other is present everywhere, below me, above me, in the neighboring rooms, and I continue to feel profoundly my being-for-others....Better yet, if I tremble at the slightest noise, if each creak announces to me a look, this is because I am already in the state of being-looked-at (*BN*,340).

My being-for-others originates with other people, but it does not require their actual presence. Perhaps even when there is no one there I may see how ridiculous I appear and I may stop looking through the keyhole. In seeing myself as "ridiculous" I am seeing myself as an object, but I am doing this only by seeing myself as I would appear *to someone else*. It is my objective being that I seem to experience, but in order to have the experience I find that a foreign element is required: the subjectivity of another. In order to think of myself, I have to implicitly think of the other for whom I am that self. The experience can be said to have three dimensions: "*I* (consciousness) am ashamed of *myself* (my objective being) before *another*." If any of the three dimensions is missing, I cannot experience my own being (*BN*,355). If I do not experience the presence of another's subjectivity, then I cannot "find myself." This is the scandal of my dependence. My being comes to me only through others. My "truth" is in their hands.

When I experience shame in the presence of another I can try to overcome my distress by reaffirming my own subjectivity. This can be done by demeaning the Other; I can regard him with scorn until he is finally reduced to the level of being only an object for me. But when the Other is finally seen as an object, I can no longer perceive what I am, for I must be affected by the subjectivity of another in order to find my own self.

The attempt to reduce other people to pure objects can finally lead to the acts of the sadist. The sadist cannot bear that another should look at him and judge him. He tries to overcome his shame at being an object, he abuses others in order to destroy their subjectivity and thus regain his freedom. The masochist makes an opposite attempt. In the presence of others he too feels shame; but in the experience he perceives very vividly his Being-as-object. This is what he has been seeking, so he does not try to overcome the experience; he tries to intensify it. He desires that others treat him as a thing, for this eases the anxieties of his subjectivity. Yet the attempt of the masochist is vain for he knows all the while that he submits voluntarily. His being is only a phantom being, he knows that at any time he can call off the whole project and again his being will vanish.

It could be said that Sartre builds his analysis of the inner life around two elements: consciousness and the psyche, that is, consciousness and consciousness degraded as an object. To know ourselves we have two very different sources of information: consciousness which knows itself with absolute certainty, and the judgments of others. When we are told about our qualities or our character we can feel we are misjudged. We feel this way not because what we are told is necessarily false, rather because the two sources of data are not of the same nature. What others tell me about myself is what I am in respect to them; it is usually a practical truth to be used in dealing with me. But this type of information is not soluble in consciousness (G,32). Others may say that I am intelligent. My consciousness can know that I am thinking, but to know that I am intelligent is a very different matter. Intelligence indicates an intellectual swiftness considered from the outside and indicates that the person judging me trusts my decisions in a certain area. If I am *thinking* I know it with absolute certainty; it is a consciousness. But knowing I am *intelligent* is radically different; it is always more or less doubtful, as it depends on the estimations of other people (G,32). A person does not have an intelligent being or an intelligent nature which produces his intelligent acts. "Intelligent" refers to myself as an object that is seen by others; again, it is a practical truth that they use in dealing with me. But sometimes a person can ascribe more reality to what others tell him about himself than to the certainties of his own consciousness; then the judgments of others become metaphysical principles. Sartre presents an example: a young woman is having marital difficulties and fears that her husband is slipping from her. She flounders about in a state of anxiety and finally gives way to frequent ourbursts of anger. She employs magical conduct, that is, she becomes emotional. The situation requires tact, but she reacts with fits of temper. Her husband tells her that she is irascible. In a sense this is true, but it is only a practical norm for him and for others to use in dealing with her. The difficulty arises when the woman accepts this social data as an absolute truth; it then becomes her "irascible nature."

...if she accuses herself of having an *irascible nature*, if she projects behind her, into the darkness of the unconscious, a permanent predisposition to anger of which each particular outburst is an emanation, then she subordinates her reality as a conscious subject to the Other that she is for Others, and she grants to the Other a superiority to herself and confers upon what is probable a superiority to what is certain. She endows that which had no meaning other than social with a metaphysical meaning, a meaning prior to any relationship with society (*G*,33–34).

A person's nature — his being or Ego — comes to him from society. This being is not in consciousness, nor behind consciousness as a subject, it is before consciousness as an object. "I is an other," wrote Rimbaud, and Sartre quotes him many times (*TE*,97; *B*,158; *G*,138–149; *IF*,771). It could be said that Sartre builds his analysis of the interior life around these two elements: consciousness and one's objective being. This objective being is secondary to consciousness, having been formed by impure reflection and the judgments of others; it is consciousness objectified.

Because our objective being is consciousness seen as an object, or the for-itself degraded as in-itself, it seems endowed with sacred power. Finding our being is a religious experience:

Is not the religious moment par excellence that in which a subjectivity, ceasing to disperse itself indefinitely in everyday reality, regains its eternal being, becomes a calm totality in full possession of itself? Eternity invades the state of flux, the absolute manifests itself, something new happens beneath the sun (*G*,63).

It is a moment of time that seems to contain all time; The extended duration of living is concentrated into a totality. Since one's whole life was contained in that moment, future experience will not add anything to what he already is. The moment itself can be endlessly repeated (this is "the eternal return") but the moment can return eternally only because novelty has been ruled out by the totality of the experience. Insofar as one remains faithful to it, "the succession of his *'Erlebnissen'* can only refer back to an archetypal event" (*IF*,482).

Such a moment gives peace; consciousness feels calmed and sanctified, for beyond its restless striving its eternal self is bestowed. The being that is bestowed is consciousness tranquilly resting as an object. Sartre sees the perception of one's ego as part of the experience of many mystics; he too uses the language of the mystics to describe it.

The garrulous and amorous consciousness will passively receive its visitation; it will enter the consciousness as a lover enters his mistress; consciousness will love this being as the woman loves the male, as the faithful love their God....It *will be his being* by virtue of a mystic marriage (*G*,64).

Consciousness awaits the arrival of its being as the mystic awaits the visitation of God. But, like the divine visitation, one's being cannot be found at will. It appears suddenly in the eyes of someone who is looking at me. From him or from them I receive my own self—but it always has a dimension about it that is not quite mine; it has been made by others. I grasp for my being, for being gives peace—but it gives peace only in limiting my freedom.

I can change my life into the effort to fulfill the nature, the vocation, the being, I have been given. If I do, then I am under the spell of someone else. "Hell is other people," writes Sartre. But it is a hell I cannot avoid even if I live alone. Perhaps those who gave me my nature are now long dead, but still I am bound. I feel their gaze judging whatever I do, the hell comes with me. I try to be alone, but being-for-others is part of me. My depths have been transmuted by a gaze and before the gaze I stand endlessly accused. In the depths of my mind I busily explain over and over again my innocence, but no one seems to hear. I am possessed by another, I am divided against myself, my own interior life is no longer my own. A dialogue takes place within me; it is consciousness and another who speak. Consciousness rambles on in its own defense, it assumes attitudes and postures as though it were taking part in a dramatic performance. But it is all of no use, I cannot

I Am Not Alone

get away. Hell is other people, and other people have been fixed within my own psyche.[1]

God Watches Me

Descartes began with the *cogito* and then proceeded to present thought, that is, consciousness, as a substance. Sartre also begins with the *cogito*, but for Sartre consciousness is not a substance. It is wholly insubstantial — this is the cause of its anguish. There is a radical difference between the substantial *cogito* of Descartes and the vacant *cogito* of Sartre. Sartre sees the difference in the gaze of God.

If Descartes has substantified thought, it is because he believes that God sees him: as an object for an absolute being who knows what is true and what is false, his truth is to be an absolute object (*G*,241; see also *TE*,50).

The gaze of God renders everything objective, even subjectivity. The gaze of God is "Medusa's petrifying glance" (*R*,152), or it is "a crystal whose perpetual touch produces a perpetual crystallization" (*G*,241). Before the gaze of other men I can take measures to end my shame. I can regard them in return, see them as objects in my world and thus regain my subjectivity. Before God I am seen, but I cannot see in return. God is the eternal Subject who cannot become an object. My shame is eternalized. My phantom being becomes eternally fixed. "*I* am ashamed of my eternal *self* before the eternal *subject*." My being-as-object has been hypostasized and rendered absolute.

The position of God is accompanied by a reification of my object-ness. Or better yet, I posit my being-an-object-for-God as more real than my For-itself; I exist alienated and I cause myself to learn from outside what I must be. This is the origin of fear before God (*BN*,355).

1. Desan (*The Tragic Finale*) argues from the texts of Marcel to show that the Other is not the Enemy, but the Savior (p.188). This would seem to be the direction in which Sartre's own thought has been moving. Raymond Aron points out this development in Sartre's thought and in this sees him allowing a way out from the helpless world of *Being and Nothingness* and *No Exit*. He sees Sartre's *Critique* tracing man's inhumanity to man to *scarcity*; this is only an *accidental* cause, and therefore one that is not integral to being human (*Marxism and the Existentialists*,p.170; see also p.175).

In his novel *The Reprieve*, Sartre portrays an experience of religious conversion. One of the characters, Daniel, has long felt his lack of being. He was always disturbed by the Cartesian *cogito*: "I think, therefore I am." The more he thought, the less he seemed to be. Every view that he could get of himself seemed absorbed in an inner insubstantiality (*R*,313). Whatever he had done was done for the benefit of onlookers. One September afternoon as he sits alone and almost dozing in a garden chair, he awakens with a start. His consciousness seems to be brought to a focus; he is amazed, awed, and delighted.

At long last the husk bursts and opens. I am myself for all eternity, homosexual, mean, coward. *They* see me — no, not even that: *it* sees me. He was *the object* of looking. A look that searched him to the depth, pierced him like a knife-thrust, and was not his own look; an impenetrable look, the embodiment of night, awaiting him in his deepest self and condemning him to be himself, coward, hypocrite, pederast, for all eternity. Himself quivering beneath that look, and defying it. That look! The night! As if night was the look. I am *seen*. Transparent, transparent, transfixed. But by whom? *"I am not alone,"* said Daniel aloud (*R*,103).

He finds his being; it is a shameful being, but still it gives him peace and a pleasure that is greater than any pleasure of the flesh (*R*,103). In the days that follow he is staggered by similar experiences. He reflects on what the look was like:

I can easily describe that look: it is nothing; it is a purely negative entity: imagine a pitch-dark night. It's the night that looks at you, but it's a dazzling night, in fullest splendor; the night behind the day. I am flooded with black light; it is all over my hands and eyes and heart, and I can't see it....What anguish to discover that look as a universal medium from which I can't escape! But what a relief as well! I know at last that I am (*R*,315).

Daniel changes the wording of the Cartesian *cogito* to make it conform to his own experience: "I *am seen*, therefore I am." In excitement and joy he writes to Mathieu, his friend.

I need no longer bear the responsibility of my turbid and disintegrating self: he who sees me causes me to be; I am as he sees me. I turn my eternal, shadowed face towards the night, I stand up like a challenge, and I say to God: Here am I. Here am I as you see me, as I am. What can I do now? — you know me, and I do not know myself. What can I do except put up with myself? And you, whose look eternally follows me — please put up with me. Mathieu, what joy, what torment! At last I am transmuted into myself. Hated, despised, sustained, a presence supports me to continue thus forever. I am infinite and infinitely guilty. But I *am*, Mathieu, I am. Before God and before men, I *am*. *Ecce homo* (*R*,315).[2]

When I come to discover "my true being," or to "find my real self," God seems to be present as part of the experience. The "real self" that is discovered is my being-for-others absolutized. Being-for-others has always implied another subjectivity *for whom* I am that being. If I should find my "absolute being," it can only be through the presence of the Absolute Subject by whose gaze my being has been absolutized. If I discover who I "really" am and what I "really" must do, the discovery has taken place in a divine presence. "God is first 'sensible to the heart' of man as the one who identifies and defines him in his ultimate and fundamental project" (*BN*,694). Sartre, though, does not believe that there is a God and does not believe that man has a true being. His rejection of the one coincides with his rejection of the other. For Sartre, the gaze of God is the gaze of human society internalized; and it is with this understanding that Sartre interprets various literary references to God as references to human society. The God of Mauriac is "society as a concrete totality of the Others" (*G*,143), the God of Parain is "that quintessence of the Other" (*LPE*,173), and the God of Kafka is "only the concept of the Other pushed to the limit" (*BN*,326). For Sartre it is only human society that looks at man, that chooses the elect and that gives out vocations. It was human society that saw Daniel as coward and homosexual, it was human society that told Genet he was a thief: "his election comes from the society of decent [self-righteous] people. The error is to attribute it to a metaphysical being" (*G*,142).

The error of attributing one's being to God is one made in bad faith. In pure reflection one finds that he is free and realizes that any value his life might have must come from himself. But in fear he refuses to be his own God and chooses a God outside of himself who will give him his being. Thus Sartre becomes an author and

2. The translation has been modified. I do not see how, in the context, "supporter" can mean "support." I have translated it as "put up with."

Genet becomes a thief. Consider again the experience of Emily (*A High Wind in Jamaica*), presented in the first chapter. Her consciousness idly reflects on itself and suddenly regards "Emily" as an object apart. She wonders *if she is God* and finds the idea terrifying. Suddenly, consciousness can stand apart from the Ego and realize its own total freedom. It can see itself as escaping the Ego on all sides, free of the Ego and sustaining it by a continuous creation. This is pure reflection and it is anguish, "it is this dread, absolute and without remedy, this fear of itself, which seems to us constitutive of pure consciousness" (*TE*,102).

Sartre comments on the clinical case of a woman mentioned in the writings of Pierre Janet. The woman was filled with terror lest she go to the window of her home and start summoning in the passers-by like a prostitute. She was a respectable woman, that is, her Ego, her being-for-others, was that of a respectable woman, but she was terrified by her own freedom. Sartre proposes that the essential role of the Ego might then be to mask from consciousness its own spontaneity (*TE*,100).

Everything happens, therefore, as if consciousness constituted the ego as a false representation of itself, as if consciousness hypnotized itself before this ego which it has constituted, absorbing itself in the ego as if to make the ego its guardian and its law (*TE*,101).

But pure reflection can break away from this guardian and law; then consciousness sees itself in full transparency, and this is anguish.

It was Kierkegaard who first introduced anguish into modern philosophy. But Sartre maintains that even Kierkegaard invented opacities for himself in dread of transparency. In *Fear and Trembling* Kierkegaard tells of Abraham undertaking an act beyond human comprehension: he went out to sacrifice his son. Abraham suffered anguish — this Sartre acknowledges. He suffered anguish in that he went beyond the norm given to human nature. But Sartre objects that Abraham is still not pure, for there is an element of alienation in his ascesis: "whatever his uncertainty, for God he either is Abraham or is not. God's gaze has constituted him from without: *Abraham is an object*" (*G*,186).[3]

3. In *CRD*, Sartre reconsiders Kierkegaard's Abraham and would seem to

Abraham was not completely pure, for he would not accept that man was the only God; therefore, he was constituted by God from without. For Sartre that age is over. God is dead.

As long as God was alive, man was at peace: he knew himself looked at. Today when man is the only God and man's look makes everything hatch forth, man turns his neck to try to see himself (*S1*,289; see also *S1*,153).

It was the gaze of God that once gave creation its meaning; now it is man's gaze alone that can give the world whatever meaning it has. But what can give meaning to man? Nothing, that is man's anguish, that is the price one must pay now that man is God and man himself must establish all values. Instead of paying the price, man turns his neck to see himself, he tries to catch his own meaning, a meaning *given* to him. This is impure reflection. It is Narcissus fascinated with his own being as object. It is man under the spell of his Ego.

In his recent study of Gustave Flaubert, Sartre has offered an understanding of the regard of God that is difficult to reconcile with his earlier writings. He presents this by envisioning the acts of paternal adoration that Gustave experienced as a child: "When the child perceives himself so pure, so vast, and so calm that he believes he is on the point of abolishing himself, the All-Powerful does not disdain to mirror himself in his vacuity" (*IF*,510). Such moments are the highpoints in the life of the child and they give him his dignity as a creature. Sartre elaborates:

the created being, limited but undivided, makes itself by its total nothingness the host of an infinite power, which, at the same time, deigns to content itself within this narrow lacuna, sanctifies it, valorizes it, overflows it, suppresses its limits and reabsorbs it into itself (*IF*,511).

Gustave had been baptized as an infant, he was catechized, and he made his First Holy Communion. In the context of the faith, his mystical experiences make obvious sense: he has been created to worship his Creator. But Gustave's parents are not believing

---

understand Kierkegaard differently: "For Kierkegaard, man is the Signifying: he himself produces the significations, and no signification points to him from the outside (Abraham does not know whether he is Abraham); man is never the *signified* (not even by God)" (*SM*,10; *CRD*,18).

Christians: his father is an atheist and his mother is a deist. Gustave's baptism and religious education were just conventional ceremonies practiced by the rising bourgeoisie. When Gustave first senses his father's disbelief he is amazed: he hears sarcasm directed against the God he was taught to love and to which he had responded so well. Now his adoration makes no sense; his soul still wants to pass out of itself in adoration, but the highest authority (his father) indicates there is nothing adorable. Gustave gives way before authority and accepts atheism as his way of speaking, but beyond language God remains the great unspoken he has known.

Sartre explains that Dr. Flaubert espoused the utilitarian philosophy of the day with its atomistic psychology. This psychology saw each man composed of a particular set of elemental drives (psychic "atoms" such as fear, ambition, and the like), and the ego was the ultimate atom — in short, the psychology that Sartre has always rejected (BN,683). This psychology included an ethic of egoism and hedonism with which Gustave is not able to identify: he is too uncertain of who he is to be an egoist and is confused about what he desires. While he accepts the utilitarian philosóphy on the principle of authority, Christianity continues to offer a very tempting alternative, for it would permit his yearnings to result in worship (worship is nonutilitarian and nonegoistic). Sartre explains that the believing Christian does not really attribute the act of worship to his nature as man. Rather it is the action of the All-Powerful who breaks apart man's essence (nature) by his vertiginous and fascinating existence: facing God, how could one not feel inessential (without essence)? Sartre explains that a dialectic is involved: it is by man's determination (his ego-essence) that the believer stands before God; but the moment *before* God is only the abstract moment of the dialectic which first presents this negation (ego-essence) only to deny it. In more conventionally Christian terms, what Sartre is saying is that the Christian comes to know himself as man (his human nature before God) only to know that his human nature is denied (that is, "elevated"). Thus, the supposed nature of the Christian is not really his nature at all; it is just an abstraction that is affirmed in order to be denied by the *super* natural vocation he has been given. Thus Christian worship involves man in super natural actions, actions that do not proceed from his essence (ego, nature). Sartre is sympathetic with such an arrangement, for thereby actions are not subordinated to being. The psychological atomism of Dr. Flaubert is seen to have an opposite effect: its array of precise desires can arise only among those

who take their determination [essence] as the positive source of their reality, that is to say, that egoism is only the consequence of atheism, of a blindness to God and of a malign aberration which would palm off non-being as being and the infinite being as nothingness (*IF*,513).

The infinite being mentioned here is obviously God and the nonbeing would be the interior life of man reified into an ego-essence ("non-being as being") by the atheism of atomistic psychology. Thus Sartre presents the analytic regard of Dr. Flaubert (analytic because it would reduce Gustave's psyche into a set of basic desires) as in direct opposition to the absolute regard of God, which would free Gustave of his ego-essence in the act of adoration. Gustave is tempted by the Christian faith; what he wants from it is that it

transform his soul, or, better, that it efface the rakings and the crosshatchings of analysis to finally reveal it to him in its natal transcendence (*IF*,513).

Elsewhere in his study of Flaubert, Sartre writes a prayer to portray Gustave's attitude in a time of crisis:

Hidden God...I am defeated in all that men have given me, look at me naked and alone, virgin wax as on the day of my birth (*IF*, 2,077).

Perhaps in these passages Sartre is only trying to interpret the mind of Flaubert, but this is not altogether evident. In any case, the act of worship is hierarchic (nonegalitarian) and therefore Sartre is not sympathetic. However, it should be noted that here the absolute regard of God does not solidify Gustave into an absolute essence; it would free him from the essence his father has given him (*fait éclater notre essence*) by the presence of a vertiginous and fascinating existence. The divine regard is not the look of society absolutized, as this was presented earlier in this chapter. Rather it involves a liberation that opposes the look of the father and any other human look; it would efface the human "crosshatchings" and free Gustave of "all that men have given" him. He would be born again, he would again become "virgin wax," restored to his "natal transcendence."

The experience of Gustave closely resembles the experience described earlier in this section where consciousness could stand apart from its ego and realize its total freedom — the vertiginous and fascinating moment when the ego-mask is removed and consciousness finds itself apart from any law. In Gustave's experience the moment is presented as worship. But the study of Flaubert was written years after the earlier passages from *The Transcendence of the Ego* and *The Reprieve,* and in the intervening years Sartre came to have many reservations about the experience, as will later become evident.

Mental Prayer and Mortification as Found in the Writings of Genet

Sartre has written book-length studies of four French authors: Baudelaire, Genet, Flaubert, and himself. Each study presents Sartre's analysis of what might be termed the inner life of the respective authors. In the 625-page treatment of Jean Genet the religious experience is often considered. As for Genet himself, he has led a bizarre and openly immoral life; in no sense can he be considered a believer. Still Genet has had experiences which could be termed religious, and religious themes abound in his writings. As explained in Chapter 1 above, the young Genet was caught stealing and was branded as a thief. According to Sartre, this naming provided Genet with a monstrous and guilty Ego. His later life was to revolve around this incident.

Until the "crisis," he lived in the "sweet confusion" of the immediate, he was unaware that he was a person. He has learned that he is and, by the same token, that this person is a monster (*G*, 22).

Everyone seems to see the monster that Genet is; only he cannot. He seems to feel it breathing down his back, and turns to see nothing. "Thief" is only a social truth, a word others use in dealing with him, but Genet comes to accept it as his substance, his metaphysical being. Sartre interprets the life of Genet as his attempts to perceive the being that defines him. Genet cannot find his being; in seeking it within himself, he has interiorized a social truth with the result that he progressively becomes a stranger to himself.

He sacrifices his inner certainty to the principle of authority. He refuses to hear the voice of the *cogito*. He decides against himself in the very depths of his consciousness....He is a wrong-way Descartes who applies his methodical doubt to the content of the "I think," and it is hearsay knowledge that will provide him with his certainties. Out of a reverse idealism it is to himself that he applies the famous *esse est percipi*, and he recognizes himself as being only insofar as he is perceived (*G*,36).

Wherever he went and whatever he did, Genet was regarded as an object of contempt. His nature seemed to weigh on him like a curse. Finally he began to rebel aainst the curse. He decided to *will* the contempt that he had long received and went out of his way to provoke it. He decided to correspond to the image that others had of him. He writes: "I decided to be what crime made of me." But Sartre objects that "to be" is here a transitive verb, it seems to mean "to throw oneself into one's being in order to coincide with it" (*G*,59). At the same time there is a second meaning: "to be" suggests that Genet has, as a being, a preexistent substance that produces his acts by necessity. If he has a nature as source of his acts, everything is determined by that nature, including the movement he makes to lay claim to it. On the other hand, if he has the power to assume his nature, he also has power to reject it; if he is free, his nature is only a decoy. Genet wants both. He wants to *make* himself a criminal by committing crimes, and at the same time wants to commit crimes because he *is* a criminal. He shifts continually between the two positions, between being and acting. In his desire for action he tries to provoke contempt. He wants to be freely responsible for the events of his life. Then he reverses his stand and assumes that men do not act, their "acts" are simply the attributes of the substance that they embody. He waits for his substance, for an inner principle that will come and take over his inner life, rule and determine his acts by a strict necessity. He wants to be carried along by overwhelming passions. Awaiting this principle, he adopts a quietism; he still acts, but only if the act will have a happy effect on his inner life. Acts are subordinated to being, they become gestures. While breaking into a house, he makes all the right gestures; then he tries to catch a glimpse of himself as "thief." "With a bit of luck, being will shimmer in his gestures, will alight in his open hand, and Genet will catch it" (*G*,71). He watches himself. He awaits the least beginning of a feeling, he tries to force it and then quickly withdraw and examine it with borrowed eyes. Sartre describes the process with religious terminology: "The miracle must be solicited, one must become a prey in order to tempt the angelic Visitor." But in the end the effort is a failure: "The soul is prepared for the visitation, but the angel does not come" (*G*,65).

Genet has spied on his inner life, but nothing comes of it, for the spy and the spied-on are the same. He watches himself in the mirror. Mirrors present us with what others see. He tries to catch about the eyes and the lips the secret that others have found. (Looking at oneself in the mirror is a frequent motif in Sartre's fiction: [*N*,16; *NE*,19,etc.; also *B*,155-57]). Genet begins having homosexual relations, which Sartre interprets in metaphysical terms as a search for objective being. His relations are with criminals or with those who look like criminals: big, senseless brutes who push Genet around. Sartre regards these partners as the being Genet is seeking. They are criminals, they are indifferent to him the way a substance is indifferent to its accidents, and like a substance they are solidly built. They must overpower him, for that is the way his being should be. Genet is physically weak but very intelligent; his partners are the opposite. Sartre interprets the relationship as that of reflexive consciousness (Genet's) illuminating the immediate consciousness (the criminal's). In the relationship Genet sacrifices himself and tries to be nothing but the pure manifestation of the criminals who serve as his being. He wants to be nothing but "a phosphorescence that radiates from this handsome body," or "the indispensable brilliance which draws that great and terrible figure from the shadow." But his partner must reciprocate "in recompense, it [the criminal] will alienate itself within him, it will be his essence, his goal and his Ego" (*G*,85). There is the godlike figure of the stupid criminal united with him, and he is nothing but its brilliant revelation. The couple is formed; they are two and yet they are one. The couple is the divine unity of reflective consciousness gazing at immediate consciousness, consciousness objectified.

But in practice the whole arrangement does not work. Genet realizes only too well that he is not overpowered by the brutes; he submits voluntarily. He has been driving himself on without rest, all the while knowing that he is getting nowhere. He finally decides that he is not able to find his nature, so he reverses the whole situation: he resigns himself to never seeing his nature, provided he is seen by it. Sartre calls this change an "imperceptible displacement" (G,143). By it Genet makes himself an object before an invisible gaze that touches him like a magic wand and endows his wretchedness with a sacred dimension (G,143). Now Sartre finds that the situation has changed:

He feels himself to be a reflected consciousness with respect to a reflective consciousness, with one difference, to wit, that the reflective consciousness is in heaven, out of reach. But it sees him, it guides and approves him....Thus, by a sudden reversal, consciousness becomes an object, and the imperceptible object of consciousness assumes the rank of an absolute subject which watches him (G,144–45).

Sartre terms the result "*sacred* Genet haunting the everyday soul of profane Genet" (G,145,296). Genet constantly talks to this sacred friend within and calls it to witness the events of his life. Sartre regards this as a dissociation of the personality that is common among solitaries (G,146).

If this "imperceptible displacement" is taken literally, it reverses the basic psychological structure outlined by Sartre. In this shift, the Ego, which first arose as object in impure reflection, is now the *subject* of a reflection. The triad consciousness, Ego, and Other (*I* am ashamed of *self* before *another*), is now reduced to a dyad: profane Genet and sacred Genet. Profane Genet is consciousness, while sacred Genet seems to be a composite of Ego and Other! The really radical change introduced by the shift lies in the way that the gaze of others has been internalized. The gaze had always been internal in the sense that it seemed to watch our being even when we were alone. But now the gaze of others seems to be identified with our being and sees not our objective being but *consciousness itself.* By this "imperceptible displacement," the Sartrean structure seems to be altered. Consciousness is left with something behind it (*G*,297). This would seem fundamentally unacceptable in terms of Sartre's understanding of intentionality (*S1*,32–35) and of the Ego (*TE*,37ff.). This transformation would allow that a person's acts proceed from his being.

The decisions he makes from day to day are only the coin of the great fixed and eternal choice which constitutes him to the depths of his being (*G*,144).

The gaze has also changed its character. It no longer condemns Genet, it lovingly approves of whatever he does.

Sartre offers little explanation for this displacement. He describes it with a certain rhetorical playfulness and he is probably not altogether serious; still, he does use this reformed structure to interpret Genet. It is within this context of what may be called reversed, impure reflection (Ego as reflecting consciousness, while consciousness is the reflected-on) that Sartre analyzes Genet's religious experiences.

After the change an omnipotent gaze seems to thicken Genet's consciousness with a secret objectivity. "To think, to speak, to feel, are henceforth to worship this Demon, which is oneself, or to offer words as sacrifice in propitiatory ceremonies; all is religious gift, all is worship" (*G*,149). Genet continually speaks to this inner divinity, but not as one would speak to a person of flesh and blood. A divinity understands all that is said even before one speaks. Genet finds that a single word or a short phrase can have a magical effect in his mind. Words seem to contain a secret meaning that escapes him. It is this meaning that Genet offers up to his divinity when he mentally pronounces words. In ordinary discourse words indicate what is understood by the person speaking. But in pronouncing words to his divinity, Genet uses words to bear the meaning that he does *not* understand, the meaning that seems to escape him. Now words do not designate things, they do not convey meaning, they are only part of a ritual. Genet repeats the words, and beyond his consciousness the sacred One sees and understands.

It [a word or phrase] suddenly allowed a glimpse of something unrealizable over and above its prose signification, something which, beyond the place and the moment, above Genet's head, required a supreme consciousness that alone was capable, intuitively, of bringing this signification into being...it gives proof of God by the necessity of a consciousness that deciphers its esoteric meaning (*G*,298).

Words pass freely through Genet's mind. Then they begin to assemble on their own, they form groups as if they possessed an objective finality apart from the finality he might give to them. It is as if Another was speaking through language, Another speaking through him and giving him sudden illuminations. Genet does not so much feel that he is speaking as that he is spoken (*G*,298). This impression seems to resemble what is often experienced in the writing of verse. The poet feels inspired by words that come together of themselves. But Sartre has little sympathy with such poetry or with mental prayer; this poetic process implies that language has a truth of its own apart from its pragmatic ability to tell another what one is thinking. If one uses language as if it had a truth of its own, he is acting like the woman who believed she had an irascible nature: beyond the practical use of a word she was looking for a metaphysical reality that escaped her. This is what Genet is doing. For Sartre language is an interhuman phenomenon and should be kept that way. If there were a non interhuman aspect to language there would be an order of truth transcending the human and therefore a God maintaining this truth. This Sartre does not allow. "Language is being-for-another. What need have we for God? The Other is sufficient, any other" (*LPE*,173). Since language is bound to our being-for-others, Sartre traces Genet's poetic sensitivity to the moment when he was branded as a thief (*G*,297–98). A word had absolutized his being, which can now be addressed only by the absolute sense that seems to underlie language. In being called a thief, he was exiled from human society and human values. Afterwards he will borrow human language, but he does not share the values that language expresses. He will use it like an outsider, the meanings escaping him. Language suggests to him an absolute world that transcends his comprehension. But for Genet that is all right. A heavenly consciousness gathers comprehendingly the absolute meanings that escape.

Sartre considers emotions as magical attempts to transform the world and to confer on an object a quality that is not present (see chap. 3 above). Genet experiences poetic emotion. He gives lofty names to the objects and experiences of his wretched condition. By these names the objects are transformed and his life takes on a nonhuman value. His miseries become the splendid signs of his election, they are his Stations of the Cross; the prison he is in is his palace, and he is a prince (G,296). Giving new names seems to transform Genet's life. "In this ceremonious naming, each object that loses its contingency assumes the rank of appurtenance of the cult" (G,398). In giving new names he appeals to a higher Judge who alone can see the deeper meanings that lie hidden in words and events. This is his prayer.

In addition to this poetic form of prayer, Genet adopts the practice of mortification, that is, he goes against his immediate desires and causes himself distress or pain. Underlying this practice is the human experience that it is the frustration of immediate desire through failure, pain, hunger, and the like that gives rise to reflective consciousness. Referring to a time when he was mad with fear, Genet writes: "I had never been so aware of myself as in such moments." Sartre concludes: "Thus, the moment in which Genet's immediate consciousness borders on annihilation is precisely that in which his reflective consciousness *exists* most" (G,240). Sartre sees Genet torturing himself in order to bring about the supreme lucidity of reflective consciousness. But Sartre makes a further distinction: Genet's reflective consciousness in its full lucidity *exists* most, but it *is* not. In pain or anguish reflective consciousness attains to pure transparency (existence). It frees itself from the opacity of being, it grasps itself as a purified nothingness. This is anguish, but as pure nothingness it is at least one part of the desired in-itself-for-itself. Now pure nothingness must be transmuted into being. This is the function of the sacred Genet. The sacred Ego regards his consciousness in its moment of supreme lucidity and by this very regard renders lucidity objective. The for-itself is objectified. The self-torture was only a purification of consciousness; at the moment of total lucidity it is transfigured into the plenitude of being. The miracle is worked by sacred Genet, his divinity, or that which Sartre terms "the pure medium in which existence is refracted into essence" (G,242). In a blinding instant a sinner is transformed into a saint. All is reversed. Genet speaks often of achieving sanctity and Sartre explains what he means:

[Sanctity represents] the instant in which the destructive changes back into the constructive, in which zero is identified with plenitude, in which the mystery of the impossible nothingness reveals that of the ineluctable substance (G,508; see also 242).

For Sartre this transformation means that the purity of consciousness emerges as the solidity of being. He illustrates by a quotation from the writings of Genet:

In the midst of this suffering, it seemed to me that there remained — shame having burned me all over — in the midst of flames or rather the vapors of shame, an unattackable matter, of a shape formed by sharp, severe lines, a kind of diamond rightly called solitaire (G,242).

Genet sacrifices his miserable self in order to have access to the sacred. To accomplish this sacrifice he tried to live reality in all its sharpest conflicts. He does not seek peace or unity for himself, only laceration and division. These are the openings to the sacred. When Genet's miserable subjectivity seems to be in ultimate pain, it is all redeemed elsewhere, it appears as absolute object. Genet is thus petrified at the moment when his existence is most intense. Beyond the anxieties of existence his "true being" is formed out of unattackable diamond.

And since this reflection which goes over to being is precisely the sparkling lucidity whose maximum intensity coincides with the radical dissolution of the human, since the extreme limit of annihilation marks the supreme intensity of the reflexive consciousness, the maximum of *existence* becomes, for the gaze which *fixes* consciousness at this crucial moment, the inverse: the maximum of being (G,241-42).[4]

Sartre finds that Genet's method of transformation strongly resembles the method of Descartes. Adopting a position of universal doubt, Descartes found his ego; he emerged as total plenitude, that is, as a thinking *substance*. What Descartes achieved by the *cogito* Genet achieves in *praxis*. The principle that underlies both transformations might be stated as follows: when consciousness attains absolute purity as for-itself, it is divinely transformed into absolute in-itself. Sartre has no sympathy with the principle, but it is one that he finds in many authors, stated in

4. For purposes of clarity I have retranslated the final phrase.

many forms: Extreme poverty is wealth; refusal is acceptance; total loss is total gain; he who loses his life will save it. Sartre is unimpressed: "Twenty-five centuries of philosophies have rendered us familiar with these unexpected returns where all is saved when all appeared to be lost" (*S1*,173). He considers the transformation as it is found in the writings of a contemporary mystic (Bataille) who claims that he knows nothing. This Sartre will allow, but he wants Bataille to stop there.

But if I make my ignorance a substance? If I transform it into a "night of not knowing"? Behold it has become positive. I can touch it. I can dissolve in it (*S1*,182).

Sartre brings a similar objection against Meister Eckhart ("When you are neither this nor that, you are all things") and St. John of the Cross ("To succeed in being all, strive to be nothing in anything"). For Sartre this is only "inefficacious rhetoric," a few operations performed on language (*G*,202), a "fundamental hypocrisy" that one cannot help but suspect (*IF*,533). In his autobiography Sartre reflects on his own life and asks himself if he has not been playing the same game: offering the pretense of despair but ultimately only playing a game of loser in order to win. But whether or not loser-wins has played a part in Sartre's own life, he still has no sympathy with the principle: there is no gaze that can transmute loss into gain and no medium in which existence is refracted into being. Man's actions, man's language, and man himself have only a human meaning, and mystical transformations are only a misuse of language. For Sartre, he who loses his life has lost it; not knowing is ignorance; and the wretched, suffering life of Jean Genet or of anyone else is just a wretched, suffering life. In each case the reason is the same: there is no God and therefore there is no magic to give things more than their human value.

In his analysis of reflection Sartre is developing his basic understanding of man as the desire to be God. The for-itself is presented as continually escaping itself, then in reflection reversing and trying to coincide with itself as object. If the for-itself could succeed in this reflection, it would be God. Sartre's identification of God with the ideal act of reflection has many roots in the

I Am Not Alone

philosophic and religious tradition. Aristotle had identified God as "self-thinking thought." Plotinus wrote at length of that reflection in which "knower and known are one"; he saw this act of knowing as the source and goal of all creation (*The Enneads*, 3.8.30). In mediaeval theology Nicholas of Cusa would locate God in the reflection "where seeing is one with being seen." *The Bhagavad Gita* would see God as "the one to be known and the knower." Shankara, a Hindu philosopher, objects to such a type of reflection: even Brahma cannot know himself; Brahma "is the Knower, and the Knower can know other things, but cannot make itself the object of its own knowledge, in the same way that fire can burn other things but cannot burn itself." Sartre would seem to agree with Shankara that there can be no "self-thinking thought," but still he would see this as the impossible ideal that the mystic is seeking. The effort of the mystic gives rise to the "interior life." Sartre quoted the passage from *A High Wind in Jamaica* where a young girl is disturbed by her own act of reflection. She seems to be self-thinking thought and wonders if "perhaps she herself is God."

It might be said that the mystic is one who tries to pursue this intuition. The mystic tries to eliminate every distraction from his mind, his method requires intense concentration. Some mystics value the concentration itself, but the goal of the mystical ascesis is said to involve a direct and immediate knowledge: "gone is the distance between the thought and the object of thought," the knower is one with the known. Sartre will allow this type of awareness if by it the mystic means pure reflection. "Pure reflection" is an immediate knowledge, it is a lightning intuition without relief, and the knowing is identified with the known — but there is no object. This type of knowing can bring liberation, and Sartre saw it as fundamental to phenomenology. The mystics are also aiming at liberation, but it could not be said that most of them are aiming at pure reflection. The final mystical stage involves an element of *otherness* that pure reflection will not allow. That is, the object known must be the *same* as consciousness and at the same time it must be *other*. The double character of this goal is frequently expressed in paradoxical form. For Plotinus the goal was to achieve a knowing that would be "no longer a duality, but a *two* in *one*" (*The Enneads*, 6.7.34). Perhaps this double character is nowhere stated with greater precision than when Teilhard de Chardin writes that the essential aspiration of all mysticism is *"to be united* (that is, to become the other) *while remaining oneself"* (*Divine Milieu*,p.116; italics and parenthesis are Teilhard's). For Sartre this double element means only that one is playing a double game; the double element renders the reflection impure. Sartre's definition of impure reflection ("the attempt on the part of the for-itself to be another *while remaining itself"* [*BN*,196]) is strikingly similar to Teilhard's statement of the goal of all mysticism. Sartre's objection to this type of reflection is obvious: it is a confusion of subjectivity and the object. It violates the fundamental principle of phenomenology: the intentionality of consciousness; it tries to unite the in-itself and the for-itself. In impure reflection a foreign element has been introduced into consciousness in its own act of reflection; the mystic is in bad faith! Faith involves an element of otherness in the act of reflection.

There is a passage in Kierkegaard where faith is presented as introducing otherness into reflection, but for Kierkegaard faith is the highest possible ideal. He explains: "he who loves God without faith reflects upon himself, he who loves God believingly reflects on God" (*Fear and Trembling*,p.47). Again it is faith (belief) that introduces the divine Other into reflection.

Sartre is obviously dealing with the same phenomenon that has been treated in the mystical tradition. Perhaps his systematic analysis might offer a framework within which one could consider the diversities found in the teaching of the mystics. All religious traditions have agreed that man has a possessive, individualistic, striving self, an Ego, the "old Adam," which is regarded as an artificial construct and something to be renounced. Many traditions would then add that, by the surrender of the Ego, man discovers his true Self, his soul, the "new Adam." But this second part of the teaching is not universal: the Buddhists would seem to resemble Sartre in their doctrine of *anatta*, according to which there is no ultimate self, no individual spiritual substance. One Buddhist scholar has written, "no acting subject besides action exists, and nothing that perceives besides perception." For the Buddhist, whatever self or character that one might have is simply the accretion of his previous thoughts and deeds (perhaps even a residue from his deeds in a previous incarnation), and apart from this residue there is no ultimate self. This accumulation of selfhood constitutes a man's karma; it is something that must be undone in order to experience the truth of anatta — the liberation from all forms of selfhood. Sartre would seem to agree with the Buddhists in that the Ego is simply the residue of past deeds, and that the liberation from the Ego would free one from all forms of selfhood.

In order for there to be a truth or in order that man have a true self, Sartre argues that God would be necessary. Thus in his writings there is an essential connection between objective self-knowledge and the knowledge of God: Daniel finds his true self and God in a single illumination, Lucien sees his own back (self as object); Sartre and Genet find their vocations (self objectified as "author" or "thief"), and in each case the experience is religious. This link between objective self-knowledge and God is frequently exemplified in the religious tradition. The quest of St. Augustine had a double object: *Deum et animam cupio scire*. And when Augustine recounts the central experience of his Christian conversion, he tells of seeing himself as object:

But you, Lord, while he [Pontitianus, a friend of Augustine] was speaking, were turning me around so that I could see myself; you took me from behind my own back, which was where I had put myself during the time when I did not want to be observed by myself, and you set me in front of my own face (*Confessions,* 7.7).

The same double quest presented by Augustine (*Deum et animam*) is found in Julian of Norwich: "Whether our urge is to know God or to know our own soul matters little" for in either case "we come to know them both together" (*Revelations of Divine Love,* pp.160-61). Eckhart would put it that "To be conscious of knowing God is to know about God and self" (*Meister Eckhart,* p.80). In the Hindu tradition Coomaraswami also refers to the double quest: "What is God?" and "What are we?"; he concludes that theology and autology are the same science (*Hinduism and Buddhism,*p.15). Sartre would agree that the two quests are one and that theology and autology are the same science; his rejection of one coincides with his rejection of the other.

Sartre argues that consciousness is objectified into a self only through the regard of another, the regard giving the new reality. In a similar way Thomas Merton tells of the divine regard conferring a new reality:

Our discovery of God is, in a way, God's discovery of us....His seeing us gives us a new being and a new mind in which we also discover Him. We only know Him in so far as we are known by Him (*New Seeds of Contemplation*,p.39).

In *The Reprieve* it was through the experience of *being known* that Daniel came to know God. Merton puts it in much the same way:

We know Him because He knows us. We know Him when we discover that He knows us. Our knowledge of Him is the effect of His knowledge of us (*No Man Is an Island*,p.173).

The same significance of the divine regard is found in Kierkegaard:

God looked upon me in my conscience, and now it is impossible for me to forget that he sees me. And because God looked upon me I had and have to look towards God (*Journals*,p.125).

It is even implied in St. Paul's Epistle to the Galatians:

now that you have come to know God, or rather *to be known* by God, how can you turn back again to the weak and beggarly elemental spirits, whose slaves you want to be once more? (*Gal.*4:9).

St. Paul reproves the Galatians for falling back into the slavery of superstition. For St. Paul the Galatians have been liberated from the spell of elemental spirits because they have *been known* by God. For St. Paul, and for a long series of mystics, to be known by God is a liberating experience. For Sartre being-known is not liberating: being-known destroys one's own subjectivity and renders the one known the slave of the one who knows. Sartre developed his theory of interpersonal relationships out of a passage in Hegel concerning the look the master has for the slave. This type of knowing is presented in *No Exit* and *Being and Nothingness* and is undoubtedly one type of knowing and beingknown. But there would seem to be a very different way that a man can know and be known, and that is in the experience of love. In love a man feels that he is fully known; at the same time, he has a sense of liberation, his subjectivity seems to gain a new intensity. This is what many have found in the human experience of love, and this is what the mystic has experienced in being known by God; but this is what Sartre does not allow. For Sartre, a man can know himself as known only at the expense of his own subjectivity. Otherwise man would realize the impossible synthesis of the in-itself and the for-itself.

Once again Sartre's ontology is seen to dominate the phenomena. He acknowledges that many authors tell of self-knowledge and he acknowledges that many mystics have spoken of the experience wherein their nothingness was transformed into plenitude, their infinite poverty into infinite wealth, and so on. But he dismisses what they have written as "inefficacious rhetoric." Once again twenty-five centuries of phenomena are dismissed for ontological reasons. This should not be surprising, Sartre considered the in-itself-for-itself "always indicated" even though it is always impossible.

Still it would seem that in one very significant case Sartre's ontology does not totally dominate the phenomena. Consider his whole treatment of Being-for-others. According to Sartre a man becomes aware of the existence of other men through a transformation that takes place in the man's own *cogito*. In this experience a man knows himself as the object that he is for others; his knowledge is immediate and therefore absolutely certain. This can only occur in pure reflection. But what is the ontology of this experience wherein the for-itself is objectified? How in any sense can the Sartrean subjectivity (as presented in chapter 2 above) be objectified? This, after all, is what is said to happen. To justify what he is saying, Sartre appeals to the experience itself yet never gives an ontological explanation of how the transformation effected in this experience would be possible.

Another ontological question that is fundamental to Sartre's whole treatment of the other concerns *who* this other is. Sartre sees it simply as other men, leaving God to be only the "quintessence of the Other," that is, as a generalized notion of otherness. Martin Buber has written a critique of Sartre in which he asks: "But what if God is not the quintessence of the Other, but its absoluteness?" In this context, there is an interesting passage in *Being and Nothingness* where Sartre considers the fact that, at times, a person may sense that he is the object of a look, although actually he is mistaken. There is no one there. Such a mistake causes a problem for Sartre because for him the existence of the other is known in the *cogito* with the absolute certitude of the *cogito*. Yet here the *cogito* seems to be mistaken! Sartre answers the objection by saying that the actual convergence of someone's eyes upon me is the "pure *occasion* of realizing my being looked at" (*BN*,339). Thus the being-watched that effects the transformation of the *cogito* transcends any actual situation; it is this transcending sense of being watched that makes the actual situation possible.

> . . . the appearance of a man as an object in the field of my ex-perience is not what informs me that *there are* men. My certainty of the Other's existence is independent of these experiences and is, on the contrary, that which makes them possible (*BN*,343).

Sartre insists that the Other he has come to experience through the transformation of his *cogito* is identical with the men he knows objectively; but to justify this important identification he appeals to no more than an occasionalism. He compares the appeal to the act of the Platonist who turns to philosophy on the *occasion* of finding contradictions in the world of sense. This occasionalism shows how tenuous is Sartre's identification of *who* this other *is*. The Other who seems to gaze at me is one who follows me wherever I go and from whom I cannot escape: an ability in the Other that seems to transcend the human. A very different identification of the Other is possible: Plato saw objects in the physical world as reminders of heavenly truths. Perhaps the gaze of other men is only the reminder of a radically different Other who makes his demands on me. The gaze of other men would then be the occasion (even though sometimes it distorts) when I experience the transcendent Gaze that pierces my human transcendence.

It is obvious that Sartre would not allow any such identifica-tion; he insists on restricting the meaning of experience to its interhuman value. The Absolute is an illusion that one turns to in bad faith, there is no appeal beyond the judgments of men: "If God doesn't exist, there is no way of escaping men" (*DGL*,142). Truth itself is only a human fabrication, and "man is immanent to the human" (*S1*,185).

In evaluating Sartre's objection, one could ask if man's imma-nence to the human is to be taken as a tautological truth or as a norm. It seems to hesitate between the two. One accepts it as a tautology, but then it becomes a norm used to reject that large part of experience wherein man seems to be aware of what transcends the human. In denying the reality of any transcendent truth, one seems to be affirming at least one transcendent truth by the act of denial. A set of similar objections could apply to the following paragraph of Sartre:

And if there is a "torture" for man, it is his inability to leave the human in order to judge himself, the inability to look at the underside of the cards. Not because someone hides them from him, but because it is by his own light that he sees them. From this point of view, the mystic experience should be considered as a human experience among others, it is not privileged. Those for whom immanence is intolerable invent ruses in order to see themselves with inhuman eyes (*S1*,185).

In saying "it is by his own light that he sees them," Sartre has stepped outside the human condition to render this absolute verdict upon it. To deny that the mystic's experience is privileged requires an overview that compares and evaluates human experi-ences. To speak of "ruses" is to imply that there is a transcendent norm that could distinguish the ruse from the genuine. Sartre gets into these difficulties because he presents man as wholly confined to the human, but in order to see that man is so confined, Sartre himself has had "to look at the underside of the cards" in order to render his absolute verdict on what the human is not.

Return to Nature, Unnatural Son

The Religious Life

"Freedom is one," Sartre observes, but under the appearance of unity he finds that Descartes has presented two rather diverse theories of freedom. In 1945 Sartre published an article explaining the two theories, and in the course of the article he used the texts of Descartes to present his own theory of freedom. Sartre finds that when Descartes considers his own power of judgment in the *cogito* he uses one theory, but when he simply wants to save some human autonomy before a rigorous system of ideas, he uses another.

Two Freedoms

Sartre first considers the theory of freedom that Descartes developed out of a reflection on his own power of judgment. To understand this freedom consider first a student of mathematics: no matter how good his professor may be, there comes a moment when the student finds himself alone with the problem. He is in control: if he does not decide to seek the relationships involved, if he does not provoke an illumination, the words remain as empty signs. When I reflect on my own experience I likewise see there is something in intellection that is not mechanical. It has been said that no man can die for me, but Descartes would press it further to include every act of the judgment: no man can understand for me. Every man has a total autonomy, and all of the force in the universe cannot take it from him. It is because of this total independence of the will that Descartes saw the human will as the image of God in man. Man's liberty is so total that Descartes saw no difference between the free affirmation made by man and the free affirmation made by God. (Descartes regarded affirmations [judgments] to be acts of the will.)

He allowed that the affirmation made by God's will is more effective, but nevertheless, when man's will is considered only in itself, it is no way less than God's. Each man has total autonomy, with the result that God himself cannot have more. Freedom must be entire, or not at all. But there is a distinction between freedom and power. Man's freedom is infinite, but his power is finite. The magic mentality (treated in chap. 3 above) does not make this distinction; it tries to proceed from unlimited freedom to unlimited power. It tries to transform the world in its entirety by emotions or ritual gestures. When consciousness extends absolute freedom to absolute power, the world of magic appears, the imaginary world where wishing makes something be so. Sartre rejects the world of magic and likewise rejects an opposite understanding that would speak of freedom even where there is no power whatsoever. Descartes recognized the absolute character of freedom; and Sartre notes that at least sometimes Descartes recognized that his freedom did possess some power. His freedom could create. "I have *formed* a method," he wrote; he was able to make something.

Now consider the student of mathematics after he has correctly made an addition. He was free to make the addition or not, but after he has made it he has not added a new truth to the universe. Thousands have performed the same addition before him. His free act has not created anything new. Sartre asks how it is that Descartes thought he could reconcile the fixity and the necessity found in mathematical essences with the absolute freedom found in the judgment. This incongruity brings up the second understanding of freedom that Sartre finds in Descartes: now Descartes is not considering the absolute freedom of the judgment, rather he is trying to save some human autonomy before a rigorous system of ideas. According to this second understanding man cannot create truth or form truth, he can only discover the truth already established by God. The man of action can look at his enterprise and say "This is mine," but not the man of science. As soon as the scientist discovers truth, it is no longer his. It belongs to everyone —and to no one. Descartes even says that if the scientist clearly sees a relationship, he is not even free to doubt it. But what has happened now to the absolute freedom of the judgment? Now Descartes writes:

I could not help but judge that a thing which I conceived clearly was true, not that I found myself forced to do so by any external cause, but only because the great light that was in my understanding was followed by a great inclination in my will (*LPE*,186).

Descartes still persists in using the word "free" to qualify this irresistible adherence to the evidence; but it is only because he has introduced a second understanding of freedom. This adherence is free only in the sense that it is not made under the influence of an *external* constraint. The first presentation of freedom saw the will with absolute power to determine itself before the ideas formed by the understanding. But a very different understanding is involved when Descartes writes:

the more I incline toward one [of two contraries], whether because I know from evidence that the true and the good meet there or because God thus disposes the inner working of my thinking, the more freely do I choose and embrace it (*LPE*,187 [from 4th Meditation]).

Here Descartes says he is the more free the more he is determined. In saying "God thus disposes the inner working of my thought," he is referring to his Christian faith, which a man has by God's grace acting directly within him. Sartre protests that it is something of a scandal that this autonomous and infinite liberty is suddenly affected and disposed by grace to affirm and accept something that it does not really understand. But Sartre makes even a more fundamental objection when he asks: "But, at bottom, is there a great difference between natural light and this supernatural light which is grace?" (*LPE*,188). In the act of faith it is God who is said to act through the mediation of my will. But Sartre sees the very same type of interference whenever the clarity of an idea compels the will to make an assent. If my will is irresistibly inclined to affirm an idea, it is because the idea weighs upon me with all of its being and all of its absolute positivity. It is this pure and dense being, without fault or emptiness, which affirms itself in me by its own weight. God is the source of all being and positivity so that this wholly positive affirmation, this plenum of existence that is a true judgment, does not have its source in me but in God. In this case it can be asked, "Who does the affirming?" If the assent is irresistible, can I still call it *my* act? Here Descartes seems to adopt the same position as Spinoza: it is transcendent truth that *affirms itself* within the individual consciousness in which it is present. But if this is the case, what is left of the human subject? When man's thought is unclear, confused, or erroneous there is subjectivity; but when the truth clarifies itself, the man disappears and truth affirms itself within his consciousness. Here, only error and confusion are personal to the subject: insofar as man is right, objective truth affirms itself. But if man is subjective, then he is in error. This is what Sartre sees implicit in Descartes' second understanding of freedom.

Descartes extended this second understanding of freedom into morality: if one judges well then one acts well. Sartre concludes:

The thesis is now complete. The clear vision of the Good entails the act as the distinct vision of the True entails assent. For the Good and the True are one and the same thing, namely: Being (*LPE*,189).

If the human act necessarily proceeds to what is Good, is there still any human autonomy? It seems that an irresistible force inclines men to the Good, just as the quiet power of the evident obliges men to affirm clear and distinct ideas. Before the transcendent Truth affirming itself, man is nothing; he retains his own subjectivity only by his confusion, ignorance, and error. Here, before the full positivity of the Good, man is able to remain himself only by Evil. But the Good and the True are full Being, so they can be said to be God or at least are from God. God is an infinite plenitude of being; as such he is not able to rule nothingness or even conceive of it. The result, Sartre concludes, is that it is only by man's dealings with Evil and error that he can escape from God.

Cartesian man and Christian man are free for Evil, but not for Good; for Error, but not Truth. God takes them by the hand and, through the conjunction of natural and supernatural lights which He dispenses to them, leads them to the Knowledge and Virtue He has chosen for them. They need only let themselves be guided. The entire merit in this ascension reverts to Him. But insofar as they are nothingness, they escape Him. They are free to let go of His hand on the way and to plunge into the world of sin and non-being (*LPE*,193).

Man now has a one-sided freedom: he is free only for ignorance and error. Since the order of truths exists apart from man, the only way that he can define himself as autonomous is by the refusal. It is by refusing until he cannot refuse further that man finds his autonomy. Sartre objects that now it is not in an affirmation that one finds the prototype of the free act, but in the nonbeing of the methodic doubt. The wholly negative character of freedom is evident when Descartes writes:

we experience our freedom in that we are always able to abstain from believing those things which are not clearly investigated and certain (*LPE*,189,190).

Doubt is the rupture of contact with being; by doubting, man has the permanent possibility of disengaging himself from the existing universe. Man, as this pure negation, this pure suspension of judgment, resting immobile as someone holding his breath, is able to withdraw from all that is, from the world, his memory, and his body (*LPE*,190). In this moment he is a pure No, nothing else, but it is in this moment of total refusal that man experiences his liberty. Man is not man insofar as he is a plenum of existence in a world without lacunae, but only insofar as he refuses and disengages himself by the disengagement of systematic doubt. This is the consequence of the second type of freedom that Sartre finds in Descartes.

It could be said that this type of Cartesian freedom can appear in two forms. In the positive form, the will is still called free but it has lost its autonomy because the great clarity of what is understood determines the assent; in the negative form there is a true autonomy but it is limited to a refusal of what is unclear and confused. In either form, if the *act* itself is considered, it is found to be defective, for it is not free. For Sartre a free act must be a creative invention. A free act is one that was not determined by and was not contained, in germ, in a former state of the universe; it introduces something wholly new and as such must be a creation. But the second type of liberty does not allow for creation: in the positive form man does not create but discovers; in the negative form man is motionless in his refusal, he cannot even produce an idea, for an idea has a certain being which cannot derive from a refusal.

Sartre does find a true understanding of human freedom in Descartes, and this understanding is in the texts where Descartes is speaking of the freedom of God. According to Sartre, the God of Descartes is the freest of all of the Gods forged by human thought (*LPE*,194). The God of Descartes is the only God not bound by eternal principles or bound by a sovereign Good before which he could do only the construction work. The God of Descartes created not only the world, but also the laws which govern the world. This God could have made the radii of a circle either equal or unequal. The God of Descartes was not forced to decide which was the better thing to do, rather it was by his act that the Good was invented. This is the absolute liberty that Descartes placed in God. Sartre sees Descartes finally presenting *in his theology* the true character that he found in his own human liberty. Descartes had presented man's absolute freedom of the will as the image of God's absolute freedom. But when Descartes considered the system of eternal verities and their effect on consciousness, he allowed man only the negative autonomy of ignorance and error. Sartre calls for the positive autonomy wherein an affirmation creates the truth that it affirms and determines for itself what is its good and evil. To have a positive form of autonomy, the affirmation cannot be necessitated by a transcendent truth that determines the assent; the assent must determine the truth. This is the radical liberty that Descartes saw in God, and it is also the total autonomy that he saw in himself as image of God. But when Descartes considered his faith and the order of eternal truths, he denied this creative liberty in man and spoke of the will being irresistibly moved to make the assent. Sartre argues that the world has changed since the time of Descartes: now it allows no faith, and in its science it allows no eternal truths. He adds that it took centuries of crises in faith and science finally to restore to man the full creative liberty that Descartes had placed in God.

The Search for Positive Being

In his second theory of liberty Descartes had presented himself as being the more free the more his assent was determined by the evident truth. For Sartre this is not liberty, but determinism. It leaves man really free only insofar as he is in ignorance or error. But such a theory of liberty was not first proposed by Descartes. Sartre sees this as Christian liberty as well as Cartesian liberty, and in some ways he is justified. Augustine had spoken of the will being free only when man submits to God's law (*Conf.*9.1; *Civ.Dei.*12.6), while what man can accomplish on his own is wholly negative. The decrees of the Council of Orange present the same limit to human autonomy: they state that if there is any truth or justice in man it comes from God, while all that man has of his own is lies and sin (*Nemo habet de suo nisi mendacium et peccatum*) (Denzinger,*Enchiridion,*#195). This understanding of man that allows him autonomy in his evil but sees his goodness wholly dependent on God entered into the Christian tradition. It can be seen again in the ninth-century controversy over predestination: Gottschalk had taught that man was divinely determined for either heaven or hell, a theory that would deny man's autonomy for either good or evil. He was condemned by the official Church, which agreed that indeed some men *were predestined* by God to eternal life. The remainder perished, but they were *not predestined* to perish; for this they were themselves responsible (Denzinger,#316,#322). (However, it might be said that lacking God's predestination to life they could not have done otherwise.) Dag Hammarskjold offers a similar theology: "The responsibility for our mistakes is ours, but not the credit for our achievements" (*Markings,*p.91). In a Hindu context Coomaraswamy explains that "'we' are the authors of whatever is done amiss, and therefore not really 'done' at all; while of whatever is actually done, God is the author" (*Hinduism and Buddhism,* p.37). For Sartre this is part of the general system wherein the objective truth determines man's assent, and man is free only in ignorance and refusal. Sartre explains the mentality:

It is as a nothingness and insofar as he is involved in Nothingness, Evil, and Error, that man escapes God. For God, Who is infinite fullness of being, can neither conceive nor govern nothingness (*LPE*,189).

Sartre would see this one-sided freedom implicit in the ideal of Christian sanctity. The asceticism of the saint is only a systematic attempt to remove the nothingness for which he alone feels responsible. He wants to be determined wholly by objective Being.

Christian saintliness is a negation of negation. It rejects only that part of ourselves which comes from us, that is, from our nothingness: error and passions....At the end of the renunciation there remains only being, absolute positivity without any negative counterpart, that is, the creature insofar as he relates to God alone (*G*,207).[1]

The saint sees his own autonomy capable of only evil and error. Progress in sanctity consists in surrendering one's autonomy, that is, in losing one's nothingness and accumulating a little more being with each denial (*G*,243).

Sartre's objection is not simply against a pessimistic picture of man that has formed a part of the Christian tradition. His objection is equally against the mentality of the scientist, for the scientist sees himself as a pure nothing, a simple gaze before the infinite weight of the truth that he contemplates (*LPE*,188). The scientist strives to have his consciousness determined only by the objective evidence. If his science is faulty, it is because he has been subjective; if his science is true, it is because the subjective factor has disappeared and the objective truth has been able to manifest itself. Subjectivity is seen as introducing only confusion and error into his calculation. When the confusion is cleared and truth affirms itself, the scientist has disappeared before the

1. St. Thomas explains that "insofar as men are sinners they do not exist at all" (*Sum.Th.*I.20.2ad 4).

impersonal truth he has discovered. The scientist who wants to eliminate his own subjectivity and the Christian who wants to conform to objective norms are both working with the same vision of man. Both want to get rid of their subjectivity and attach themselves to objective being. The scientist could also be said to maintain that *Nemo habet de suo nisi peccatum et mendacium*.

This effort to attach oneself to objective being and avoid subjectivity takes many forms. Sartre calls it the attitude of serious man. Since it is an effort to divest oneself of subjectivity before objective being, Sartre sees it as a religious effort. The serious man hides from himself the consciousness that he has of his own freedom (*BN*,711). This is the fundamental doctrine of the materialist. The doctrine of serious man was proposed by Karl Marx when he asserted the priority of the object over the subject (*BN*,711). Since materialism is an attempt to gain objective being, a man is said to enter into this philosophy as a man enters into a religion (*LPE*,215). Materialism is also a flight from oneself, and once again, like the scientist and the Christian, the materialist is said to be ashamed of his own subjectivity.

If this mentality characterizes the materialist, it also characterizes the self-righteous man. In a long analysis of the self-righteous man, Sartre develops the meaning of Good and Evil, which turn out to be human constructions that have been invented by self-righteous men. The self-righteous man mistrusts his own subjectivity and autonomy. To rid himself of the anxiety that goes with subjectivity,

he cuts the negative moment away from his freedom and casts out the bloody mess. Freedom is thus cut in two; each of its halves wilts away separately. One of them remains within us. It identifies forever Good with Being, hence with what already is (*G*,24).

Man denies the negative moment that is part of his freedom for it causes him anxiety, it is the refusal that isolates him, that is, makes him autonomous. He attaches himself to the group, for the group is positive: to be alone and to be wrong are one and the same thing. He puts negativity outside what he will recognize as himself. He comes to define himself narrowly by traditions, by obedience to the values of the group and what amounts to the determinism of the Good. He seeks to empty himself of his own individuality and submits mechanically *perinde ac cadaver* (the Latin phrase quoted by Sartre [*CRD*,601; *IF*,49], that St. Ignatius uses to describe Jesuit obedience). The "decent man" makes himself like a corpse, blind to what he does not want to see; he is the one who has eyes and does not see, ears and does not hear (*G*,25). But this blindness ultimately causes problems for him. The rejected half of his freedom does not leave him undisturbed: "Poor right-thinking man; he wanted, in the beginning, to concern himself only with the positive and with Being, to obey unerringly" (*G*,25). He wanted to become entirely positive, but he finds that he cannot affirm without denying what is opposed to what he affirms, he cannot love without hating the enemy of what he loves. The man who pretends to conform to good principles, "who is chock-full of Being and turns everything to the glory of the Good" is really the man who is rotted deep underneath (*G*,168). He accepts a norm of conduct, but in the same impulse his freedom suggests that he violate it. The self-righteous man "shuts himself up in a voluntary prison and locks the doors, but his stubborn freedom makes him leave by the window" (*G*,35). It is by limiting his freedom to what is positive that he causes the negative to rise up as a temptation. The negative becomes that vague, swarming self that is wild and free outside the limits he has set for himself. How is it that one first becomes aware of Evil? It is by accepting an *objective* norm of what is good, and this is what Sartre opposes. Sartre quotes St. Paul to explain the origin of evil: "By the Law is the knowledge of sin" (*G*,25).[2]

When man sets the negative half of his freedom outside of what he considers himself, the negative freedom comes back to haunt him; it becomes a rage to destroy that contradicts what he wants to do and contradicts itself; it is Evil. Evil is the unity of all of man's negative impulses to doubt, to reject, and to criticize, but only insofar as he refuses to *recognize* these impulses as the normal exercise of his freedom and only insofar as he relates them to an external cause (*G*,25). When man limits his self-understanding to what is positive and good, he sees the negative part of himself coming to him as a threat from without. Then the negative is what

2. In the French, Sartre misquotes St. Paul; cf. Romans 3:20.

he wants, although he does not want to want it. It is the object of a constantly rejected will which he considers as other than his "true will." Evil appears as his anxiety, his disbelief, or the individuality that still keeps him from a perfect identification with the group. Evil comes to him from without, like another himself that is wild and free and tempting. Evil is always other, yet it is himself, it is the part of himself that he has rejected and made other. Evil is the other than Being, the other than the Good, and the other than Self (G, 35).

Since the self-righteous man will not see evil as part of himself, it seems to withdraw from him and goes to lead an independent existence elsewhere. It is projected on others, thus giving the self-righteous man the catharsis that he needs: now evil is no longer a temptation, it is an object of horror that is apart from him. Who is the evildoer? Sartre answers that we each have our own. The evildoer is the man who in some way presents to us objectively and in broad daylight the obscure temptations of our own freedom. He presents that which we will not accept in ourselves. The man who hates the homosexual is the man for whom homosexuality is his constantly rejected temptation. He rejects homosexuality, but suddenly there is a shifty something that appears about persons and things: he becomes alarmed, it is as if the world is about to open up and become dizzying. What frightens the "good" man when he sees the "evildoer" is only his own freedom. Evil is the negative half of freedom when freedom is not accepted and is projected without. Evil is that part of freedom that we deny and throw on others like the robe of Nessus (G, 151). Evil is a manufactured concept, made by the society of self-righteous folk for the express purpose of getting rid of temptation in themselves.

Evil is never more perceptible than in time of war. In war, the enemy is the evildoer par excellence; the enemy is clearly identified, everyone agrees on who he is. Therefore, it is during a war that the "good" man has the clearest conscience. All of society has had a catharsis, it is in time of war that there are the fewest lunatics (G, 30). Apart from the time of war, Sartre sees society forming its own "professional evildoers": it develops its quota of criminals, the poor, racial minorities, and others. We project on them our own secret fears, we see them as objects with evil in their expressions or in the color of their skins or in the different way that they dress. But evil is a concept for external use only; the man whom we call evil does not see himself that way. Evil is a myth that was created by the self-righteous man; it does not exist, it cannot exist, it contains a maze of antinomies. To show this, Sartre considers what is meant by evil: As a pure negation it reduces itself to *pure nonbeing*; but since it exists before us as a temptation it must also *be*. The Christian may reply that the being of evil has been borrowed from being. Sartre answers that, in order to borrow, it must itself be. He applies the concept of evil to consciousness. The evil of consciousness is hebetude, darkness, and opacity. But, on the contrary, it can be said that consciousness is evil only when it wills itself evil in *full clarity*. Again a contradiction! That which is evil must be an object of loathing to the one who commits it, otherwise the evildoer would be in harmony with the evil, and harmony is a good. On principle, evil is disorder since all of its effects are aimed at destroying order. Yet for it to be effective in destroying order, it too must have a certain technique and order. Evil then has to be the disorder of all order and the order of all disorder (*G*,26–27). Evil can contain all these antinomies because it is only a catchall concept. It is only a construction that was invented by the self-righteous man to rid himself of his unwanted freedom.

Liberty as Creation

In the article that Sartre wrote on Cartesian freedom, he identified freedom with creation. A free act was

an absolutely new production, the germ of which could not be contained in an earlier state of the world and that consequently, freedom and creation were one and the same (*LPE*,195).

The man who refuses to accept his full liberty will also refuse to be creative; he is struck with awe in the presence of being. The pure scientist does not want to create, he does not want to interfere with the real, he only wants to discover and comprehend the world as it is. The materialist also does not want to create: for him everything that happens is part of a determined and inevitable process; there can be no creation.

The self-righteous man is another who refuses to create. For the most part he is a conservative. He has reverence for being and wants to conserve it as it is. He is afraid of "knocking down the edifice." "Everything is full, everything hangs together, everything is in order, everything has always existed, the world is a museum of which we are the curators" (G,24). Creative action would break up the old order, any construction implies an equal amount of destruction. But destruction is negative, it is what the self-righteous man refuses to allow. He has identified the Good with Being. But in order to create, a man must see the good in what is presently missing. He must see a goal that does not now exist. This lack in Being is what the conservative man refuses to see: having identified Being with the Good, he cannot see goodness in that which as yet *is not*. He refuses the vision of nonbeing that must precede the creation of the new. Upkeep, maintenance, restoration, and renewal, these are the only activities he can understand and permit. They are wholly positive, they can be performed by the man who has no vision of what is not.

Like the materialist and the conservative, the saint also has a fundamental attachment to Being. For the saint, however, Being is identified differently; it lies apart from this world of nothingness. Like the conservative man, the saint also does not try to create, he merely tries to realize a bit more of eternal Being. Sartre has come to adopt a Marxian understanding of history and interprets sanctity as a phenomenon of a consumer society. In such a society men work but they do not understand their work as creative; consumption is the ideal.

The work is merely a *preparation:* servants dress the bride; consumption is a nuptial union; as a ritual destruction of the "commodity" — instantaneous in the case of food products, slow and progressive in that of clothing and tools — it eternalizes the destroyed object, joins it in its essence and changes it into itself, and, at the same time, incorporates it symbolically into its owner in the form of a *quality*...in the case of food, fullness of being emerges in the moment it melts in a mouth and releases its flavor (G,196).

As the product has value and fullness of being only in the moment of its destruction, so it is with the saint, "who is sucked by God like a piece of candy and feels himself deliciously melting into an infinite mouth" (G,196). The sense of "fullness of being" is only at the moment of destruction. This gives rise to what Thorstein Veblin called "conspicuous consumption" and also to the conspicuous waste that is central to any religious sacrifice. A consumer society will glorify the military hero. Before his death, the hero is lavishly feted. Then he must die in battle — no other death is fitting. His slaughter is a ceremony in which he is immortalized, and his spiced soul "will delight the palate of the great Taster" (G,197). The martyr is like the military hero: he attains eternal being not by the work he has done but through the act which consumes him. So it is in the offering of a sacred sacrifice: a people stands blissfully by and watches their goods eternalized as they go up in smoke. This is consumer society. Its guiding myth is the destruction of the world, not its creation (G,199).

Sartre sees "generosity of consumption" as the aristocratic ideal of the late Roman Empire, an ideal that was then adopted by the Christian church. Knights outdid one another in shows of extravagant waste, just as churches outdid one another in elaborate ornamentation. But it is the saint that Sartre sees as the truly fine flower of consumer society. The saint presents the whole community with its own image of self-destructive generosity. He internalizes the military drama and plays it in slow motion. He begins by offering his own wealth to God only to find that that is not enough. "It is the entire world that he wants to offer; to offer, that is, to destroy in a magnificent potlatch" (G,201). The aristocrat made gold useless by applying it to the walls of a church. The saint makes the world useless by refusing to use it. He dies in hunger among riches. The poverty of the saint is not the same as the poverty of the poor man (G,199). For the saint, it is necessary that the riches exist, they must exist in order to be scorned. The saint will come to define himself by what he has renounced. Therefore, slaves, artists, and cooks must labor

so that the Saint, rejecting royal dignity, ivory, precious stones and the beauty of women, may lie at death's door, barren and disdainful, heaped with *everything* because he accepts *nothing*. Then the world, abandoned, empty, rises up like a useless cathedral. Man has withdrawn from it and offered it to God (G,201).

Once again the theme of Sartre: useful objects become sacred by being removed from human use. The saint tries to put everything out of use; by total renunciation he will sanctify the world.

The conservative, self-righteous man did not create because he identified the Good with what is, with Being—he could not accept the negative act of destruction. The saint has a similar attachment to Being. He does not consider his systematic rejection of the world to be a rejection of Being. His rejection always takes place in the direction of the metaphysical hierarchy. Sartre compares the renunciation practiced by the saint with the renunciation practiced by the Platonic philosopher. The Platonist rejects the shadows of the cave to arrive at the Platonic ideas, which are said to contain all Being. In this movement the physical world is rejected, but nothing positive is lost, as anything of positive value in the physical world is contained in its perfection in the intelligible world. So Sartre describes the mentality that he sees behind the saint's asceticism:

To renounce human love for the love of God is to find all the being of the former in the latter. One does not cease to love the creature: one loves him in God. Cured of its deviation, purged of its nothingness, firmly applied to its sole real object, love is an opening on the All, it is all loves in a single love, the infinitude of my finiteness and the plenitude of my emptiness (*G*,209).

When Kierkegaard takes leave of Regina, he takes pleasure in thinking that she is restored to him in her entirety (*G*,211). The goods that are renounced in the saint's refusal, or the goods that are destroyed in sacrifice are not lost, they are retained in their quintessential form by the consciousness that has made the renunciation. Everything is restored inwardly to the consciousness until the consciousness comes to know itself as the unity of these rejections. Sartre sees Hegel as the one who stated the principle behind the saint's asceticism, for Hegel wrote that transcendence preserves what it rejects (*G*,209). Kierkegaard rejects Regina in time, and it is thereby that he possesses her forever. Plato rejects physical beauty and through the very rejection gains eternal Beauty. So it is in the mind of the saint: he does not see himself as losing what he rejects. Whatever is renounced by consciousness is restored to it inwardly, eternally preserved. All that the saint has really renounced is nothingness, and with each renunciation he has gained a litttle more Being.

The saint tries to acquire the perfect Good that exists from all eternity. His ideal is not to create, for the Good already exists. It could be said that the saint resembles the self-righteous man in that he too is trying to preserve. But it is a preservation set in the context of a Platonic or Hegelian metaphysics where it is the act of rejection that preserves in inwardness the world that was rejected. Sartre refuses with disgust the whole system of sanctity. Transcendence does not preserve what it rejects. The saint is using guile to gain the world, and sanctity is a gangrene (G,201;S4,18).

The materialist, the pure scientist, the self-righteous man, and the saint, all have made the same fundamental error: they have identified Being with the Good. They each feel religious awe in the presence of what is established; before the majesty of Being, they deny their subjectivity. They have implicitly accepted Descartes' second understanding of freedom and will not allow themselves to create.

Orestes and His Crime

In several works of fiction Sartre presents man breaking with the world of Being and thereby achieving consciousness of freedom. In *The Age of Reason* a young boy arbitrarily breaks a valuable and ancient vase. By this negative act he feels liberated from the fullness of the world. The act was arbitrary; if it were done for a reason, that reason would be a good and would leave him in the full world of Being.

In *The Flies*, the negative act is a double killing. After the killing occurs in the story, Sartre pleads with great eloquence his case against God, the Good, and the world of positive Being. *The Flies* recounts the Greek legend of Orestes, who returns to Argos and there kills his mother and his step-father. Zeus appears to Orestes and urges that he repent of his crime. Zeus speaks:

Orestes, I created you, and I created all things....the world is good; I made it according to my will and I am Goodness. But you, Orestes, you have done evil, the very rocks and stones cry out against you....Good is everywhere, in you and about you, sweeping through you like a scythe, crushing you like a mountain. Like an ocean it buoys you up and rocks you to and fro, and it enabled the success of your evil plan, for it was in the brightness of the torches, the temper of your blade, the strength of your right arm....No, Orestes, return to your saner self; the universe refutes you, you are a mite in the scheme of things. Return to Nature, unnatural son.[3]

Orestes does not quarrel with Zeus's picture of the goodness of the universe, but answers that he is different:

Your whole universe is not enough to prove me wrong. You are the king of gods, king of stones and stars, king of the waves of the sea. But you are not the king of man.

Orestes explains the change that has come over him: Yesterday he felt at one with Nature. This was the Nature that was Good and was made by God and sang to Orestes the praises of the divine Goodness. But,

suddenly, out of the blue, freedom crashed down on me and swept me off my feet. Nature sprang back, my youth went with the wind, and I knew myself alone, utterly alone in the midst of this well-meaning little universe of yours. I was like a man who's lost his shadow. And there was nothing left in heaven, no right or wrong, nor anyone to give me orders.

In losing his shadow Orestes has come to accept the negative half of his freedom that he had projected outside himself. Good and evil are no longer objectively given. Zeus tells Orestes that he is isolated by this new-found freedom and offers Orestes forgiveness, but Orestes answers with a description of Sartrean freedom:

Outside nature, against nature, without excuse, beyond remedy, except what remedy I find within myself. But I shall not return under your law; I am doomed to have no other law but mine. Nor shall I come back to nature, the nature you found good; in it are a thousand beaten paths all leading up to you — but I must blaze my trail. For I, Zeus, am a man and every man must find out his own way.

Descartes had compared his absolute freedom to the absolute freedom of God. Orestes does the same.

What have I to do with you or you with me? We shall glide past each other, like ships in a river, without touching. You are God and I am free; each of us is alone, and our anguish is akin.

3. I have changed the translation of the final words. The French reads: *Fils dénaturé*. This and the following passages are in *NE*,119-22.

Before the freedom of Orestes the might of Zeus is of no avail. As the play ends, Orestes strides forth triumphant, free and alone.

Being and Nothingness, published in 1943, was dominated by its treatment of the in-itself and the for-itself. They were presented as the two ultimate and irreducible regions of being. In the latter works of Sartre these irreducible regions of being hardly occur and the in-itself and for-itself terminology seems to have been dropped. Some of the old division remains, but not between regions of being. In 1952 the contents that were once termed the in-itself and the for-itself are presented again but under different names. They are now *Good* and *Evil*. Consider the meaning of the in-itself as it was presented in 1943: the in-itself was Being; it was wholly positive, absolute plenitude and Parmenidean Being (*BN*, 752). Nine years later the Good is presented with the same characteristics: the Good is Being, absolute plenitude (*G*,155); the Good exists by itself, it is absolute positivity (*G*,158); it is also Parmenidean Being (*G*,186). There is likewise a close parallel between what was called the for-itself in 1943 and what is called Evil in 1952: the for-itself was nonbeing, other than self and other than Being (*BN*,726); it took its own marginal existence only if one fixed his gaze on Being (*BN*,756), and by its negativity man was free in the otherwise full world of the in-itself. In 1952 it is Evil that has these properties: Evil is pure nonbeing (*G*,186), it is other than self, "other than Being, [it] is always *elsewhere*, always elusive" (*G*,163); it also can be seen only out of the corner of one's eye (*G*,30,163). By its negativity man is free in the otherwise full world of the Good. Earlier the for-itself was seen as an explosion and the cause of itself (*S1*,32; *TE*,82); now it is Evil that is described as the explosion and cause of itself (*G*,28,19). Between 1943 and 1952 the terminology has changed, but the contents remain the same—with one major difference: *now the contents are no longer two regions of being, they are only two artificial constructions.*

In 1952 Sartre often treats of Good and Evil, repeatedly using the terms, but he by no means defends their validity. Rather, he rejects the "abstract separation" by which Good and Evil are separated from each other. In 1943 the in-itself and the for-itself were "two regions of being" irreconcilably opposed; but in 1952 when the same *contents* are considered again, they are presented as abstract constructions that divide a true unity! The unity that Sartre proposes unites the old oppositions: Being and Nonbeing, full positivity and lack, and so on. It is the separation of these terms that is rejected. (It could be objected that the terms were never more radically separated than they were in *Being and Nothingness*.) Now the whole labyrinth of Good and Evil, Being and Nonbeing does not involve two regions of being; it is only an artificial construction invented by the self-righteous man on the day that he cut his freedom in two (*G*,186). Sartre asks that Sovereign Good and Sovereign Evil, Being and Nonbeing be rewelded together so that freedom may be reestablished in its prime dignity (*G*,186). He expects their synthesis at some future date in the form of a Hegelian *Aufhebung* (*G*,186). But what is this *Aufhebung* other than the *reconciliatio oppositorum* that Sartre would not allow?

In 1943 it was this very synthesis that was said to be impossible, and this impossible synthesis was said to be what men mean by God. Now Sartre calls for the synthesis—but he has not come to accept God. God is not accepted because what Sartre means by God has also undergone a change. God is no longer the synthesis of the opposites; He is now one of the opposing terms that *prevents* the synthesis: the Good "exists by itself, it is God" (*G*,158). God is Being and infinite plenitude of Being (*LPE*,189); God is all positivity (*G*,214). The God envisioned in *Being and Nothingness* was composed of the positivity of the in-itself and the negativity of the for-itself. Now the God rejected by Sartre is said to be so identified with the positive that he cannot govern or even conceive of the negative. It is a different God. It is simply full positivity, or what was presented in *Being and Nothingness* as the in-itself.[4]

Man is said to have alienated from himself the positive half of his freedom. The half that has been removed is called God or the Good, or some such term that is wholly positive, and the freedom that is left for man is the freedom of pure negation. The positive half of man's freedom is given to God and this is what constitutes man's alienation: God is Good, or Being is Good; this much having been said, all that is left for man to do on his own is to

4. This wholly positive God was also suggested in *BN*, 120.

Return to Nature, Unnatural Son

disrupt, deny, or damage the Good that has already been established. *Nemo habet de suo nisi peccatum et mendacium.* In *Being and Nothingness* man was also presented as alienated, and "God" expressed the ideal but impossible harmony of man. Now "God" has changed; he is no longer the ideal harmony of man, he is only one of the opposing terms by which the present state of man's alienation is continued.

6

Strange Hell of Beauty

The Spiritual Life

The saint, the self-righteous
man, and the materialist all
have something in common:
they seek to hand over their
freedom to an external law —
the saint to the laws of God, the
self-righteous man to the laws
of society, and the materialist
to the laws of matter. Each of
them tries to divest himself of
his freedom and assume the solidity of objective being. A totally different choice is possible, however, a negative choice
that denies the whole of being
and chooses only the freedom.
A man can feel glutted with
goodness and his own blind
submission to the law; he can
rebel against it all, perversely
affirm his freedom, and go
forth into nothingness and the
pure transparency of spirit.
Spirit always surpasses the "given." With Stoic determination
and metaphysical pride, spirit
can assert itself to be radically
independent of society, God,
and the universe.

When consciousness had tried to subordinate itself to objective being, Sartre had called it religion. Now when consciousness renounces objective being and asserts its freedom, Sartre calls it spirituality. Religion and spirituality are, then, opposite movements: one is the attempt to be pure being, or in-itself, and fuse pantheistically with all that is; the other is an effort to be pure existence, or for-itself, and purify oneself of all that is. The spiritual life is the rejection of positive being; since positive being is also the Good, the spiritual life is interpreted as a quest for Evil. This might seem like a wholly arbitrary way of defining the spiritual life, but it is not. Sartre's presentation of this life is based on his study of such French literary figures as the Marquis de Sade, Flaubert, Baudelaire, Genet, and Jouhandeau. All of these authors wrote of spirituality and practiced some form of it; at the same time, each made a more or less explicit commitment to evil. In presenting spirituality as wholly negative, it is this mentality that Sartre is trying to explain. He acknowledges that the spirituality of the Middle Ages was different (*WL*,124). Still, both spiritualities have common elements, as will be seen.

The Purification

The saint regrets the nothingness that limits his being, but the sinner regrets the taint of being that sullies his nothingness. Sartre studied the sin-mysticism found in the works of Jouhandeau and explains the mentality involved:

Since the Positive is God within him, since only the *limit* comes from him, he will become a limit: "It is my own limits, those which God imposes upon me, which deliver me [Jouhandeau]." He delivers himself little by little from God; he systematically rids himself of "whatever was exigent and sublime in his desire," unlike St. Theresa who retains the quintessence of hers (*G*,214).

To escape divine omnipotence, Jouhandeau asserts his pure finitude, which is "the infernal kiss that Nothingness gives to Nothingness." Whenever one has knowledge of that which is, there is something positive involved; therefore, it concerns God. But in the relations the soul has with itself there is nothing positive; Jouhandeau writes that this relation is "not quite God's concern." Sartre explains the mentality:

. . . as a being I am encircled and hemmed in by being, God's eye sees me. But since God, the infinite Being, cannot even conceive nothingness, in nothingness I escape him and derive only from myself (*G*,159).

Jouhandeau sought to disappear into the darkness beyond the gaze of God; he will escape into the negative, since God is all positivity and is blinded by his omnipotence.

In order for the divine understanding to conceive the negative, it would, to a certain degree, have to be affected with negativity. Thus, the nothingness which is secreted by the creature is a veil that hides it from the sight of the Almighty, like the ink in which the cuttlefish envelops itself (*G*,214).

Jouhandeau sets out with the explicit desire to be Evil, and Sartre considers the complex mentality involved in this desire. Evil is a secondary quality in that it first presumes the existence of the Good, for Evil can be Evil only in corrupting what is already Good. The man who perceives Evil must therefore perceive a double reality. "In short, since Evil is a negation, one cannot discover it unless one first, or at least at the same time, perceives what it denies" (*G*,152). The will that is good simply desires the Good, but the evil will is more complex: it must first pose the Good and will it and then at the same time not will it. If something evil is desired, then it must in some way be a good. In order for an act to be truly evil it cannot be desired; it must repel even the one who commits it. "I shall know unmistakably that an action is evil when the very idea that I might commit it horrifies me" (*G*,152). There can be only one motive for evil, and that is the very lack of motives. Any other motive would have a positive content and would therefore taint the act with goodness: if a prisoner kills a guard only to escape, the aim of the prisoner is not murder but only to escape. Insofar as the prisoner's intention is concerned, the aim is good and only the means are evil. The evil the prisoner does is subordinated to what he sees as a greater good. The ideal evil act is one not subordinated to a good. Sartre presents an example that he bases on an incident in the writings of Genet. A man is alone in the country when he suddenly notices a child at play. The child is charming and happy, and the sight of the child awakens in the man feelings of sympathy and love. But love immediately awakens in him the idea of murder.

The idea first manifests itself in the form of anguish: it would be *awful* to kill the child. Or, if one prefers, if only I'm not seized with a desire to kill him! That is all. No hatred, no sadism, no resentment....With all his heart he wants the child to live, he would like to talk to it, caress it, make it happy...beads of sweat stand out on his forehead; he rebels completely against this abominable possibility, which is nevertheless *his* possibility. *Precisely because of that,* he will kill (*G*,153).

It is the sight of the Good that arouses the will to harm. Goodness is awakened in the evildoer, but it serves only as the first indispensable moment in evildoing; it is awakened only to be thwarted and trampled on (*G*,154). This is how Sartre interprets the act of the fallen-away priest who says a Black Mass. The priest hates God for only one reason: because God is lovable. He sets his will to refuse the established order of Good, but in refusing it he affirms it more that ever (*B*,69). It is this tearing apart (*déchirement*) that defines "consciousness in evil." But in this moment of anguish and division, consciousness is faced with itself. This is "the infernal kiss that Nothingness gives to Nothingness."

The Good is all-perfect, it exists by itself and has no need of me. In doing Good I surrender myself, I lose myself in Being, I abandon my particularity in the universal good that exists as the norm for all men. But Evil is different: it is all weakness, I am its cause and conserver, its wavering being needs me in order to exist. Good comes from God, while Evil is what I do on my own. Hence there is in the Good which attracts me a motive for turning away: the Good is already there and has no need of me. I lose myself in the good act, I forget myself and swoon in a kind of pantheistic ecstasy as my good becomes part of the universal Good (*G*,159). In the Evil that horrifies me there is almost a motive: it is of Evil alone that I can say it is wholly mine.

...if being is everywhere, if error is *nothing*, if evil is *nothing*, if everything one may want or conceive or love is also being and, hence, an aspect of Good, then the temptation of Evil begins, that is, freedom tempts itself. The universal subject looks down into the well and sees at the bottom his own image as a negativity, a particularity, a freedom. And furthermore, nonbeing attracts me, or, if one prefers, I attract myself from the depths of nonbeing (*G*,159).

This is the dark temptation of Evil: in Evil I do not merge into the

Good, I assert my own individual difference. "Indeed, I find myself in it, I am never more present to myself than in that grating consciousness of wanting what I do not want" (*G*,159). This dazzling presence to oneself is spirit. As a being thinking about being, I am a creature of God, I depend on him. Spirit is different; as a nothingness thinking about nothing, I am my own cause (*G*,160).

Usually the spiritual man does not oppose the Good quite so explicitly. More often, he directs his purification against the material world, or what is simply the brute, unintelligible given. The religious man had offered a certain homage to God in accepting creation; creation was good, it was a *gift* from God. The spiritual man will not accept the given; he practices a form of Catharism in which he tries to purify himself of matter, of the world, and of his body. He does not praise creation, he scorns it. He performs an ascesis to liberate himself from whatever is natural. "Nature was the first movement, spontaneity, immediacy, pure uncalculating goodness. It was first and foremost the whole of creation, the hymn which rises up to its Creator" (*B*,116). It is of all creation that the Catharist tries to purify himself, for if he accepts creation as a given he is no longer *Causa sui*. To do this he must fly in the face of all the evidence:

this will, which is bent on denying the evidence and on rejecting being, burns alone in defiance of all, infinitely alone, and feeds on itself....Emerging from nothingness for the purpose of supporting nothingness, this freedom knows that it will return to nothingness and is glad that it will. It can thus set up against history, which rejects it, a kind of negative eternity which is its own lot (*G*,68-69).

This is metaphysical pride and the purity of evil.

Sartre develops this mentality in his study of Baudelaire. Baudelaire made a fundamental choice of himself in opposition to the universe. After that, he could not afford to be natural. If he were natural he would lose himself in the crowd and be at ease in the world, and this is exactly what he did not want. He chose to be the perpetual jarring refusal, to hold his head above the water and watch the universe with a mixture of disdain and terror. He felt obliged to sustain a perpetual inner tension and dissatisfaction with the world and thereby maintain his difference. He constructed for himself an antinature; he adopted artificial mannerisms, disguised his foods with heavy sauces, and dyed his hair green. He had relations with women but these relations were never natural and earthy. Sartre sees in them a pathological Platonism that was directed to women who were pale, frigid, and disinterested in Baudelaire. To avoid the natural, he made love to women who were dressed in theater costumes. With them he was often only a *voyeur*, for a *voyeur* does not compromise himself. He worked out a cult of frigidity, which Sartre analyzes. The cold is Baudelaire himself, sterile, gratuitous, and pure. His verse speaks of polished metals, cold, and pale. The moon is one of his symbols, for it is isolated in a dark sky and sheds a cold and infertile light on the earth; it resembles nonbeing, which *is* only insofar as it is a pale reflection of being. Baudelaire envisions a landscape according to his taste: the vegetation has been removed and the trees torn out, "a landscape composed of light and minerals with water to reflect them" (*B*,108). With his friends he assumes an icy and ceremonious politeness: "many friends, many gloves." In the artificiality of his tastes and behavior Baudelaire was defining himself in opposition to nature; he was living out his basic choice not to contaminate himself with Being.

Baudelaire despised work but praised the act of creation: a creator does not have to demean himelf and accept something from the world to work with. A creator is not affected by what he does, he is not compromised, he remains aloof. A worker must always partially submit to the material he is working with, and this is what Baudelaire refused to do. He had a horror of any direct action of the universe on him. He became a poet who could not accept "inspiration," for inspiration is experienced as given and thus as something for which Baudelaire did not feel responsible. Sartre explains that in a deterministic age Baudelaire had "an intuition that the spiritual life was not something given, but something which created itself" (*B*,135). His efforts at refusing the world and denying whatever was natural were part of his efforts to create himself, and this is spirit. "To hold oneself in, to put a bridle on oneself, was a way of bringing into being beneath one's fingers and the reins the *Self* that one wanted to possess" (*B*,135).

Sartre does not limit this spirituality to Baudelaire; he finds a similar orientation in numerous writers. Flaubert is said not to have married because he felt a horror of procreation (*IF*,214–15). He despised the needs of the body and once rested several days without eating. He wrote in his notebook: "I understand well those people who fast and revel in their hunger and rejoice in privations, it is a sensuality much finer than the other." He practices chastity and explains the reason to a friend: "A normal, regular, nourished and solid love would take me too much out of myself, it would trouble me" (*IF*,2,053). He adopts a reflective disgust with the world and the human condition and announces that he writes to demoralize others (*IF*,444). At the summit of misery he places himself; the proof of his demonic aristocracy is that he suffers infinitely. Sartre speculates on the intent of Flaubert:

I know my limits and this knowledge is a wound of the Pride I am: I hold myself in the air without roots, above men, damned alone....I am the herald of silence, the *mortal* enemy, in every sense of the term, of the All-Powerful, an enemy who always loses, and is proud to lose because his defeats make him endure each time his All-Powerlessness (*IF*,566).

The scorn of one's natural needs is the act of the aesthete, who "must derealize the vulgar requirements of his body, hunger, thirst, fear" (*G*,379). Sartre sees this attitude in the "principle of delicacy" advocated by the Marquis de Sade. He tells of a young girl who could not bear to be invaded by sleep; to sleep is to give way to nature. She took stimulants to fight back this alien intrusion (*B*,109;*R*,18). Sartre finds this Catharist tendency even in his own childhood. Recalling his attitudes when he was about six years old, Sartre writes, "I fled my unjustifiable body." He would feel distressed by his own physical presence and would want to avoid it. He tells of his fascination upon hearing his grandfather announce that someone was absent:

bodily presence is always a surplus. But intact, reduced to the purity of a negative essence, he [the one absent] retained the incompressible transparency of a diamond (*W*,58).

He was repelled by what was simply the "given" and tells of blaming himself for a toothache in his effort to derive only from himself.

Genet, who has "a most Christian horror of the flesh, a most

Platonic horror of all matter" (*G*,414), also practices a type of spirituality. To his intense mind, matter makes no sense, so he invents for himself imaginary pleasures that are devoid of this senseless intrusion. He looks at food that he does not eat; he prefers to feel the empty, nonmaterial process of digestion that takes place within him. Matter is the unintelligible outrage. In the poems of Genet everything is dematerialized. Sartre regards this poetry as a "kind of Platonic ascesic which aims at eliminating the outrage" (*G*,391). Genet's ideal is to make a poem that would be pure form without any content, for in pure form he would escape the given and would make something appear for which he was the sole creator. He tries to eliminate matter because he "wants both to show his rejection of the divine creation and to manifest, in the absolute, human impotence as man's eternal reproval of God and as the testimony of his [man's] grandeur" (*G*,392). The result of these "spiritual exercises" is that the world begins to appear strange and immaterial; it seems to be composed only of signs and abstract symbols. "Reality is worn so thin that one can see the light through it" (*G*,14). If one carries out this systematic deprivation of oneself to the limit

one will still be living in the world, but the world will then be only a flat painting, an optical illusion. One will know that sounds and lights, words, smiles, blows, are only glittering appearances at the surface of a dark emptiness (*G*,182).

Matter has been removed and the world emerges as spirit. But when the world is transformed into spirit that brings a new revelation: Beauty.

Beauty

The religious man was seen to have difficulties in that he was never able to surrender the last of his freedom. The spiritual man also has difficulties, but they are very different. As an evildoer (a spiritual man), all goes well for me as long as I remain in solitary rumination; my princely *cogito* reveals to me my unique particularity beyond all being. In this *cogito*, I have shelved the world, everything human is alien to me. I transcend all law and nothing which *is* can define or limit me. I become whatever I like, and then I rapidly escape whatever I have become by willing the contrary. My whim is my only law, and whim is contradictory, fleeting; it baffles all definition. I exult in a wonderful and dizzying freedom wherein Being is lit up by the dim light of my own nonbeing. The moment is awesome, and Sartre asks, "How could I fail to want to eternalize by an act the wonderful instant in which Nothingness holds being suspended in brightness?" (G,235).

But this is where the difficulty lies. In the princely *cogito* I find that I transcend all law, I am wild and free. Then I desire to express my transcendent glory and eternalize it by an act. The act must be like the *cogito*, it too must exceed all law; therefore I commit a crime. The crime takes place. "All at once this whole phantasmagoria breaks like a bubble: I am again a being in the midst of other beings" (G,235). The crime I had envisioned became a reality, and as a reality it is incorporated into being. The will to evil was transformed into an act, an object; now it is not transcendent at all, it is an object situated among the other objects of the world. The princely *cogito* vanished in becoming a deed. Beyond the universe, I had indulged in reflection like a lordly monster, but when I try to act like a lordly monster it is all over: my *act* is studied and catalogued, it is objective. Psychiatrists and sociologists compare my crime with other similar deeds, it becomes a statistic. The princely subjectivity has vanished; I awaken from a glorious dream of Evil, for Evil has tried to pass into Being. I find I am defeated as God brings the goodness of fact out of my effort at Evil. But if everything that is, is Good, then where is Evil to be found? Orestes has killed Clytemnestra, his mother. It seems to be a crime, yet Zeus explains that goodness is everywhere; it was the good that permitted the success of the killing. The strength of Orestes' arm and the temper of the blade he used in killing, the torch that furnished the light for the deed—these are all good (NE,120). After the killing, a body is there; the dead body is being and all being is good. Where in the whole process is there any Evil to be found? Sartre answers quite simply that Evil is not in the deed; Evil is not done, it is imagined (G,356).

Evil is beyond being and so is that which is imagined. Consider the moment of evil experienced by the man who arbitrarily kills a child. "The moment of absolute Evil is that in which he dreams of killing a child and in which suddenly, without ceasing to be a dream, the imaginary terminates in a decision" (*G*,160). I do not make use of Being when I imagine, I imagine on my own. "Being and the true, which are guaranteed by the Almighty, get on very well without man, but the false and the imaginary constantly require him" (*G*,358). The man who has set out to escape the gaze of God can imagine; in contemplating an illusion, he has found what is entirely his own.

Sartre explains that God does not understand what people are doing when they play the three-card trick. God, who knows all being and all truth, knows the truth of the playing cards. In his omniscience he sees the front and the back of the card that is slipped dexterously from one pack to the other; he knows it is the ace of spades. Then, "One of the players turns it over: well, yes, it was the ace of spades; what about it? God is surprised at the audience's astonishment" (*G*,358-59). The trick requires that one make an error in perception—but God does not make errors. God knows the world of being, and in the world of being there is only the truth. Whatever God produces is being and true, therefore it is only illusion that manifests the kingdom of man. *Nemo habet de suo nisi peccatum et mendacium.* Only man can produce an illusion; God is limited to the truth. The aspirant to evil has found a way out: "since man as a being comes from God, he will choose himself resolutely imaginary so as to derive from himself alone" (*G*,359). Evil draws men away from God, but illusion does the same: the imaginary is evil and evil is the imaginary. Sartre speaks of the great mystics doing the opposite: they tried to pass beyond appearances into the fullness of the real. They tried to tear away all images and thereby attain a dazzling blindness. But the aspirant to evil is repelled by any encroachment of the real. He takes refuge in the only place that is left: empty imaginings that transform his mind into an unsteady kaleidoscope of fakery and delusion. He sets up his own private hell.

But hell is not silence or darkness, it is a swarming of images, of flashes which one *thinks* one sees and which one does not *see*, of sounds one *thinks* one hears and which one *knows* that one does not hear (*G*,359).

The man who lives in the imaginary is tortured in the dream that he has created himself. But in Satanic pride he will not let go, for this flickering hell is the one thing man can really claim as his own. *Nemo habet de suo nisi....*But with it all, what has he accomplished? He is at the same impasse as before: he is confined in the *cogito*. His evil has damned him to utter solitude while the world of Being has not been effected at all. Evil remains as impotent as always, for each time the dream tries to pass over to the real, Evil is overcome by the goodness of Being.

But suppose the process could be reversed: suppose the dream does not change into the real, suppose the real could change into a dream. Such a transformation actually does occur. It occurs at the end of the three-card trick. The trick itself is only an illusion, but when it is performed the gasps and sighs of the spectators are *real*. The false and imaginary have disrupted being; the real activities of the spectators are directed into illusion. The process could be enlarged. By a series of mirrors and a well designed set of illusions, the most serious of men will begin talking to empty space or will thrash at shadows. The talking and thrashing are real activities but they are directed into that which does not exist. In illusions the dream passes into reality but it does not lose its dreamlike character; it is the real that loses itself in the appearance. If tricks and optical illusions could be systematically constructed, the real world would seem lightened and begin to fade away.

The self-righteous man is a serious man. He works industriously in the service of being. But on his day off he allows himself a "break"; he spends an evening at the theater and all is reversed. Before him there are actors with imaginary feelings or there is a white screen where flickering shadows form the illusion of men. The real world seems to fade away and be replaced by another. The serious man senses the difference. He has paid to enter the theater, part of his real work has been directed towards this evening, but now his work empties into shadows and illusion. Here in the theater the evildoer breaks out of his impotence and has a real effect. "Let him become an actor in real life: through him the evil powers of the theater will destroy the seriousness of existence" (*G*,370). By systematically inscribing illusion into the real, the evildoer has his revenge on being. On a block of marble he will inscribe the image of Venus, on a flat page he will inscribe perspective, the illusion of depths. And then the marble and the page are no longer seen for what they are but *for what they are not*. In this, once again, he escapes from God. God knows things for what they are; beyond what things are there is only trickery, and God is not taken in. He sees the flat page with markings upon it. But the very idea of perspective is something that God does not understand. To see perspective requires that objects be placed at varying distances from the viewer, but "God is absolute proximity, the universal envelopment of Love. Can he be shown from afar His universe?" (*S4*,37). Perspective requires distance, removal — in short, negation — but God is universally present and entirely positive.

Only a being which is not entirely can have the sense of non-being; in order to grasp a card trick and to see a Venus in a block of marble, one must suffer in one's very heart from a void which it is impossible to fill; in order to form an image, one must disconnect oneself from being and project oneself towards that which is not yet or that which no longer is. In short one must *make oneself a nothingness* (*G*,359).

Seeing Venus in a block of marble can give an experience of beauty, yet it is illusion, it is not real. Sartre would go even further and say that reality itself is never beautiful. The difficulty is not that reality is poorly made, simply that it is real. "Beauty is a value applicable only to the imaginary and which means the negation of the world in its essential structure" (*PI*,281). One may argue that there is beauty in nature; but Sartre argues that beauty is not *in* nature at all. When one is captivated by the appearance of beauty in a landscape, one is really perceiving in the manner that one imagines (*G*,372). In such an experience, things gleam with an unwonted brilliance, they seem to be floating. Everything remains present — the trees, the spring, the peasants, the wheat — and yet we feel we have entered an image. At such moments we say that we "think we are dreaming." It seems like the landscape has been created to manifest a distant finality, being seems to manifest something beyond being. The whole reality of the objects before us seems to lie in the witness they bear to what lies beyond them. But in that case reality is no longer itself, it is only a sign, a symbol, an image; "one might as well say that being is pure appearance, for it *is* only insofar as it bears witness; thus, the being of being is its appearing" (*G*,372). This is the illumination of beauty: things are not what they are; they are seen as what they are not. The world has been derealized and beauty is the process of derealization. It is the process in which a block of marble, spots of paint on a canvas, or a landscape are no longer themselves but only an appearance. The lover of beauty does not like things for what they are but only for what they are not. "Beauty is neither an appearance nor a being, but a relationship: the transformation of being into appearance" (*G*,377). The lover of beauty does not create works of art because he cannot have the real; it is rather because he does not want the real, he wants the artificial. When he goes to the theater, he does not want to watch a real man in real deliberation, he wants to watch the imitation of Hamlet in fake deliberation. He buys art not because he wants to see a street in Montmartre; he wants to see paint that forms the optical illusion of a street. It is illusion that the aesthete is seeking, for illusion presents him with less of the material. Illusion confronts him with emptiness, less of the given, and less of nature.

As I gaze on the statue of Venus, the block of marble and the room that it is in both become transfigured. I reach out to touch. Venus fades and the room seems more dreary than before as my hand rests on a block of dusty marble. The world regains its thick and commonplace density. I sit in a theater and am gripped by the magic spell. The play ends and I step out into the street. Reality presses in on me and I feel its disturbing presence with a nauseous distaste (*PI*,281). Beauty is the transformation in which the real passes into an empty appearance. But when the transformation is over, only the emptiness remains. Beauty "is a tremendous nightmare in which the world is swallowed up and it is a revelation that gives the key to the world: being is meant for nothingness" (*G*,377). Beauty leaves its aftertaste. After the experience is over, reality appears nauseous and vacant. "Strange hell of Beauty," writes Genet, and Sartre adds: "Strange hell, indeed: Beauty does not fill, it hollows; it is the frightening face of Negativity" (*G*,378). Beauty and Evil, terms that have been coupled so often. Neither has any reality of its own, but each refers to the same parasite that eats away Being and the Good (*G*,390).

The serious, right-thinking man rarely has intuitions of beauty, he is afraid of them. He has chosen the positive way and rejected the negative half of his freedom. But perhaps one night he goes to the theater and unexpectedly is moved to tears. Sometimes tough-minded men cry before what is only illusion; "for the moment they become that which they would have been if they had not spent their lives hiding their freedom from themselves" (*WL*,45). But it is only for a moment. Afterwards they try to dismiss the experience and say, "It is only fiction, what does it prove?" Fiction is only an illusion; what it proves is nothing. But that is why the tough-minded men are afraid: nothingness is the one reality they cannot allow.

In the presence of the beautiful the evildoer does not weep and he is not afraid. In order "to see Venus in a block of marble, one must suffer from a void which it is impossible to fill," "one must disconnect oneself from being," "one must make oneself a nothingness." This is what the good, tough-minded man has found so disturbing; but it is precisely this that the evildoer has been engaged in for so long. "Yet, it is a fact: the evildoer is very often an aesthete; the aesthete is always an evildoer" (*G*,370). The aesthete-evildoer has chosen nothingness; but being overcomes his every act, for every action is good. It is only by an unbearable tension that the evildoer is able to maintain his transcendence. But when beauty appears before the aesthete, suddenly everything changes. The real seems unsure of itself, it flickers and fades into what is not. For an instant the tension can relax. The nothingness that he had tried to maintain with such difficulty is objectified before his gaze. The aesthete swoons momentarily while fully conscious.

The aesthete did not want to contaminate himself with the given so he set out to dematerialize the real. Now beauty comes to his aid: if being is only appearance, if the world is only a stage where a great play takes place, then I am but an actor situated apart from reality. The material world has been left behind and existence is only an optical illusion. Reality is a theater prop, nothing can touch me, it is all part of the act. If being is only appearance, then the role which I play in life does not really count; all that counts is the grace of the performance. This is the world of Baudelaire, Genet, and Oscar Wilde, with their respective cults of "dandyism," "elegance," and "gracefulness."

Baudelaire set out to derealize the world so that "lightened, hollowed out, filled with signs and symbols, this world...was nothing but himself; and it is himself that this Narcissus wants to reach and contemplate" (*B*,179).[1] The universe has been spiritualized; it has been turned into meaning, and meaning is the image of human transcendence. The aesthete can relax for an instant, transcendence meets transcendence, abyss calls out to abyss, and across the universe takes place "the infernal kiss that Nothingness gives to Nothingness."

The Created and the Uncreated World

The young Sartre was fascinated by the early silent films and has recounted his experience. The film might show a helpless victim bound beside a powder keg; the piano would begin to play a selection from *The Damnation of Faust* as the flame raced along the fuse. The hero would arrive unexpectedly and extinguish the flame. But at this moment the villain would return and leap on the hero. A duel with knives would begin:

but the accidents of the duel likewise partook of the rigor of the musical development; they were fake accidents which ill concealed the universal order. What joy when the last knife stroke coincided with the last chord! I was utterly content, I had found the world in which I wanted to live, I touched the absolute. What an uneasy feeling when the lights went on....In the street I found myself superfluous (*W*,78-79).

The silent films and the books in his grandfather's library provided Sartre with a rich, imaginary world, the world in which he wanted to live. When he was still barely able to lift the heavy volumes, he studied the *Grand Larousse*. In the pictures and texts of the encyclopedia he found the "true flowers" and the "true birds"; outside in the garden the flowers and birds were only rough imitations of the archetypes found in the *Grand Larousse*. In books he found a universe that was already "assimilated, labeled, thought"; he adds that, in beginning his life among books and then proceeding to the real, he developed an idealism that took him thirty years to get rid of.

The account of how he was able to get rid of idealism is found in

1. The last phrase is translated differently in the English text. The French reads: "...c'est lui-même que ce Narcisse veut étreindre et contempler."

the semiautobiographical novel *Nausea*. This work recounts a series of experiences through which a man comes to the realization that he is *de trop, an unneeded and excessive existent*. He tells of sitting in a restaurant and feeling such an experience coming on; he gets up and runs awkwardly for the door. Out on the street he hastily boards a passing tram where he sits staring at the seat beside him:

I murmur: "It's a seat," a little like an exorcism. But the word stays on my lips; it refuses to go and put itself on the thing.... Things are divorced from their names. They are there, grotesques, headstrong, gigantic and it seems ridiculous to call them seats or say anything at all about them: I am in the midst of things, nameless things. Alone, without words, defenseless, they surround me, are beneath me, behind me, above me (*N*, 125).

In panic he leaps from the tram and enters a public park; he sits on a bench between the black trunks of some chestnut trees. Words have vanished and so have the "archetypes" found in encyclopedias. He is surrounded by the brute, unexplainable presence of the real. Until this moment all of his life seems to have taken place on the surface, among ideas. Now he is faced with untamed and unclassified existents. He looks at himself and at all of the objects that are around him:

We were a heap of living creatures, irritated, embarrassed at ourselves, we hadn't the slightest reason to be there, none of us, each one, confused, vaguely alarmed, felt in the way in relation to the others (*N*, 128).

He thinks without words and says that he experienced the absolute. But now the absolute is not the universal order that one experiences in the cinema, now the absolute is the absurd. Things are absurd, they are different from whatever one might say about them. The root of the chestnut tree before him is contingent, it is not there by any necessity, its presence cannot be deduced, it is wholly and perfectly gratuitous. It exists as itself in the very measure that it lies beyond any necessity. Everything that exists is gratuitous and, he adds, when one recognizes this, "*Voilà la nausée.*"

Sartre will later explain that this use of the word "nausea" is not metaphorical, not derived from the physiological nausea; it is rather that all concrete and physiological nauseas are derived from this sense of contingency and gratuity (*BN*,415). The experience of nausea can be said to present the total downfall of the spiritual man. Such a man lives with words and images among the airy simulacra of things; he is sometimes bothered by the presence of his body and by the accidents of chance, but he feels that these will be overcome with perseverance. The spiritual world is the world of pure symmetry that the young Sartre encountered at the cinema, when all of the supposed accidents of the duel were assumed into a universal order and the last stroke of the knife coincided with the last chord of the music. In such moments Sartre felt that he was touching the absolute — universal necessity; but in *Nausea* a different absolute is encountered — universal gratuity. This is the experience that ended his thirty-year idealism. The real world is absurd, no reason can be found for its existence and no final harmony can be expected. This is the world that Sartre encountered as he left the theater, stepped out on to the street and with a touch of nausea found himself superfluous.

The imaginary world of the cinema or of a novel is a world that has been created by an author. Each of the small details has been willed and set in place for a certain purpose. The imaginary world is a *creation*, and in this creation "by a special intention there is a place assigned to every creature" (*IF*,1,593). In the imaginary world of the film and the novel the seemingly gratuitous events are only surface appearances; beneath them a final harmony is the absolute. But in the real world it is the reverse: harmony is only a surface appearance and total gratuity is the absolute.

Sartre considers the difference between the real world and the world of art (*WL*,45-46). When he is enchanted by a landscape, he might find that the colors of the blowing leaves harmonize with the distant sky. But he knows that this relation of harmony does not exist apart from himself; this harmony between the distant colors has not been *put* there. He adds that even if he believed in God he could not establish any meaningful relationship between divine providence and the harmony of colors seen from his particular vantage point. Harmony is sometimes seen in nature, but the man who sees this harmony knows well that it is only a coincidence. Nature itself is composed of a random juxtaposition of colors and objects without any interrelated purpose. The amorphousness of nature is nauseating, and sometimes it is also frightening.

If man becomes frightened in the presence of nature, it is because he feels that he has been trapped in an immense, amorphous, gratuitous existence which completely freezes him by its gratuitousness. He no longer has *his* place anywhere; he is planted on the earth without a goal, without a *raison d'être* like heather or a clump of broom (*B*,106).

Nature reflects to man his own gratuitous existence, but art and fiction have an opposite effect. Consider the way that the reader of a novel perceives details and events. A character in a novel is presented in a certain mood, then by the configuration of the city he "happens" to pass through a park. The park develops his mood or perhaps is the place for a chance meeting, and so on. In reading the novel we perceive the configuration of the city as having been made that way *in order to* present the park at the right moment; the park presents itself *in order to* develop or intensify his mood or *in order to* allow the "chance" meeting, and so on. In reading a novel all of the supposed "accidents" are not perceived as accidents, they are perceived as having been *willed*; all of the details are presented *for a purpose*. Ultimately the events and details will fit together and reveal the universal order intended by the intelligence of the author. This is the world of art. It is a created world; everything in it is part of a plan that has been willed by a providence. Every object and every incident in a novel has a place and a value assigned to it, that is to say, they are *creatures*. But the real world offers a radically different experience: objects and incidents do not fit together. Each being is *de trop* with respect to the others. They are there without purpose. Meetings take place which lead nowhere, and that is how they are experienced. I may or may not happen to cross a park while in a particular mood, but in any case I do not perceive the park as having been put there *in order to* affect my state of soul.

There are two different worlds involved and Sartre speaks of them both as absolutes. One is the real world of brute *fact* and the other is the imaginary world where everything has been assigned a *value*. The real world presents truth and the imaginary world presents beauty, but in no way can the two worlds coincide. Truth is never in art (the block of marble is not really Venus) and beauty is never in nature (the landscape is beautiful only when it is seen as an image). The real world presents us with an amorphous mass of unrelated existents, and words cannot even be said to apply to this world. The world of art presents a universal harmony and purpose, but it achieves this transcendent harmony only by purifying itself of all that is contingent, that is to say, of all that is real.

Sartre writes that the last century produced a whole generation of artists who regretted their loss of faith. Cast without reason into an uncreated world, they turned to literature, for there they themselves could form a creation. Sartre considers Flaubert's eagerness to be a creator the result of his awareness that he was not a creature (*IF*,966,1,591). According to Sartre, this generation of artists judged the imagination to be both the grandeur and the weakness of man. It is the grandeur of man as it creates a unified cosmos and thus substitutes for the God who does not exist. But at the same time the imagination is the weakness of man, for the artist knows well that he is only "the ridiculous demiurge of a cosmos that *is not*" (*IF*,1,592).

When we see beauty in the world of nature, we are then looking at nature in the way that the young Sartre looked at the flowers in the garden and saw real flowers as imperfect imitations of the pictures in the *Grand Larousse*. At such moments the flowers seem less real. When an actor plays Hamlet on the stage he does not render Hamlet real, rather he derealizes himself into an imaginary character (*PI*,278;*IF*,662ff.). But such a derealization is not limited to the stage. In real life a woman can come to see herself as "another Madame Bovary"; she will then try to assume that imaginary personality as her own. She becomes less real in the process, she is drawn out of the real situations of her own life under the power of an image. "Madame Bovary" has become a value that interprets her experience, it insinuates itself into her reactions and her decisions. Reading a novel or seeing a painting affects a person's subsequent perception so that he begins to interpret and nuance events as if they fitted into the preestablished order he has seen in art. The events of one's life seem to be ordered to a future. The painting and the novel are serving as archetypes for experience. Oscar Wilde had said that "Nature imitates Art" (*IF*,829). Sartre understands the phrase of Wilde to mean "that the real tends towards appearance and the fact towards value, hence that being aims at being engulfed in nothingness" (*G*,404;see also *IF*,829,1,577,1,589,and *DGL*,184). This is the experience of beauty.

Nature is imitating art whenever we see the world as a creation. At that moment we see reality as if it were an image or a sign, and we see real individuals as if their presence had been given some ultimate purpose. But in seeing individuals directed by a transcendent purpose we are no longer seeing them as themselves. "In the measure that we use the creations of novelists as patterns to decipher real individuals, we derealize these individuals in considering them to be *creatures*" (*IF*,1,589-90).

The characters in fiction are creatures and in this way serve as "traps" for the reader. In recognizing ourselves in a fictional character what we really are doing is installing in ourselves the impossible demand "to be the synthetic product of a divine totalization" (*IF*,1,590). The characters in fiction have been willed as a totality by their author. In taking such a character out of fiction and feeling its influence within, we are trying to make ourselves creatures in reality. All that we actually are doing is derealizing ourselves into the imaginary, for it is only in the imaginary world that creatures exist. In the real world our presence has not been willed and we have been given no purpose; we are unneeded, unjustified, and superfluous.

It is to the person who feels deeply his unjustified and superfluous existence that beauty makes its appeal. Beauty seems to deliver him from the gratuity of life. Beauty offers a purposeful world, it sets up a demand in those who perceive it that seems to say, "Seek always to perceive the world within you and outside of you as if it was the object of a concerted creation" (*IF*,1,589). Beauty awakens the desire to see oneself as a creature directed by a transcendent will, to see the chance events of life as though they were the details in a novel, to see ourselves and all about us as if we had each been given a purpose by the great Author. Again we are in the world of the aesthete: each incident has been planned, the roles have been assigned, and all that counts is the grace of the performance. The world is a stage, that is, the world has become artificial. Reality has been replaced by Creation.

The Image as Negative Theology

A character in the fiction of Genet is called Divine. Sartre interprets the meaning of the name:

Divine is a hole through which the world empties into nothingness; that is why she is called Divine: when she appears she causes a hemorrhage of being....She is divine because of the ease with which she denies the real (*G*,411,414).

Here the divine is not identified with being and the real, but with the denial of them. Sartre considers this position a reversal of the relation that Christians had established between being and nonbeing. For the Christian, God is the being par excellence; we attach ourselves to him insofar as we participate in being. But Sartre observes that in recent times a number of artists have presented a reverse understanding of God and man's relation to him. God is identified with the denial of being. With this radical change the role of the imagination has also been reversed. Now the imagination does not remove man from the presence of God; rather it is the imagination that gives man a presentiment of God, the imagination is "the vain witness of an undefinable Somewhere":

since God is not, it is by the nothingness within that we witness to our vain and inconsolable refusal of his Non-Existence; it is by rendering ourselves imaginary that we render ourselves most like him (*IF*,1,592).

It is by this negative conception of God and the corresponding role of the imagination that Sartre interprets the mind and vocation of Flaubert. Although Flaubert did not express belief in God, Sartre judges that he passed beyond disbelief into a negative theism. His father and older brother were scientists and atheists, but Flaubert began to find that science was limited: it treated only the world of fact and truth. He wanted something else, he would write, "Truth exists; I recognize it, I believe it, and I am opposed to it" (*IF*,532). The scientist is confined to a consideration of what *is* and never treats what *is not*; it is the nonbeing and nothingness in man that required an explanation beyond science — a God. Flaubert felt (according to Sartre) that perhaps God had plunged us into a universe where truth was discovered by science and only illusion gives a presentiment of God.

What if these nothings, these pure appearances, these false like-nesses in their very inexistence and in their lack of reason consti-tute the unique means of communicating with him [God]?[2]

The full world of being is simply there; uncreated and sickening, it needs no God to explain it. But the nothingness and dissatisfac-tion in man seem to indicate something beyond being. Nothing-ness and dissatisfaction then appear as the dignity and glory of man, they lead man beyond being to the negative God.

A God is required to explain why man is the prey to Non-Being. Or, if one prefers, it is by our Non-Being (by our errors, our su-perstitions, our failures and all our repellent phantasmagoria) that we communicate with the absolute Being.

Basically Sartre would see the life of Flaubert as an effort to communicate with the Absolute through the illusion of the image. But the communication is not in the brief moment that one is able to believe in the image, it is in the moment of despair when the image collapses. In this moment an unnamable presence seems to appear beyond the image. Every image is ultimately a failure, for it is only a hollow appearance that disappoints. When failure and disappointment are repeated indefinitely, the reason is persuaded that God does not exist. At the same time, the inexplicability of failure becomes the one mystery that reason cannot explain. Flaubert begins to envision the possibility that he might become the great Artist, that is, he will become a maker of failures.

In his adolescence Flaubert wrote a number of short novels. They were all tragedies showing that failure is the story of the human condition; the higher were a man's aspirations, the deeper would be his degradation. When Gustave was fourteen he wrote *Le voyage en enfer*: "the subject of the novel is nothing other than the world, the child discovers that the world is Hell" (*IF*,959). This basic understanding remains throughout the life of Flaubert.

Through reading the great artists of the past, Homer, Vergil, Shakespeare, and others, Flaubert comes to realize that he lacks the breadth of vision necessary to equal their achievement. He

2. This and the following reference are from an article by Sartre on Flaubert that appeared in *TM*, October, 1966, pp.627-28. The article became part of the book on Flaubert but several paragraphs were dropped. The thought is also expressed in *IF*,2,088.

finds that his images are imperfect and labored, there is always a residue that remains in them; but how could it be otherwise when the world of art is not yet his world? The image is the failure of being, but in the world of being Gustave is still able to succeed. To become a great artist he must be a total failure and show to everyone and to himself that he is an "homme-échec" (*IF*,1,812). Late one night while driving a gig with his brother, he has a nervous collapse and is brought back to the family home for a long period of "recovery." He has entered the world of art, and during the time that he is a semi-invalid he finds that his manner of perceiving the world has undergone a change. He will describe this new awareness as the "aesthetic attitude"; he is helpless, and the world begins to appear fascinating and distant.

The practical man, *homo faber*, sees a very different world than the aesthete; the practical man sees objects in terms of the use that he might make of them. Since he has a project, the objects that he sees are objects that he *might* use, they are not perceived as totalities. That is, their entire meaning and use are not simply given within them; they are still open to the different meanings that the practical man might give them should he decide to use them. This affects the perceptions of the practical man: he *sees* possibilities before him, objects seem to suggest different uses that he might make of them.

But to the extent that one renders oneself a passive spectator, a quietist who uses nothing, objects seem to lose their open-ended character. They are no longer seen as "possibilities" but are fully constituted with a given meaning; they are totalities. This is the world of art. In the world of art each object has an assigned meaning; its future is inevitable because the artist has introduced it for a precise reason and it will serve that purpose alone; it is not open-ended, it is totalized. For a man to "see" totalized objects, he must have no project of his own; to see the world at an "aesthetic distance" he must be totalized himself. If one has a project, all objects can help or hinder this project and thus appear open-ended. Realizing this in an obscure way at the age of twenty-two, Flaubert engineered a nervous breakdown. Gustave lies motionless, and "inert in the hands of his brother he realizes his ancient dream: to become wholly imaginary" (*IF*,1,846). Like the tragic hero of a novel, his life is controlled by a will other than his own;

as for an actor on the stage, the plot of the play is out of his hands; he has entered the world of art. In his swoon Gustave surrenders the *vécu*, he sets life aside with all of its anguish and uncertainty. He no longer has a project or a goal, the world cannot affect him and he cannot affect it; everything seems to change. His life is over, he is totalized and so is his world: "the first artistic step is to consider events and persons as if the totalization were already made" (*IF*,1,965). When human desires are renounced, the world appears at an aesthetic distance.

Objects for him have lost their seriousness. They are pure presences, still glowing and fascinating, but they no longer propose anything to him—ever since he forgot his passions and the ends of the species—and often he no longer understands them (*IF*, 1,942).

Sartre sees Flaubert's nervous collapse as an action aimed at failure—only the man who is defeated can have the vision of art. But in Flaubert's intended failure Sartre sees only a game: *qui perde gagne*, loser wins. Sartre argues that Gustave was only playing the game of losing—losing in order to win—and playing it in two ways. The first way is explained by Flaubert in a novel he was working on during the months after his collapse: *l'Education sentimentale*. The novel tells how to become a great artist; Sartre considers it a theoretical and practical treatise written for Flaubert's own use (*IF*,2,011). As in all of the writings of Flaubert the world is found to be intolerable, and Jules (the would-be artist) realizes that he must have no part of it; to attain this ideal he sets about derealizing his perceptions:

In *l'Education sentimentale* Gustave has revealed to us the technical sense of his project: to disqualify systematically all the impressions received and, placing the *vécu* in parenthesis, to realize himself in depths as a pure serenity, that is, as the absolute equivalence of Being and Non-Being; at the end of the ascesis he will be so empty of self that he can attain self only in the imaginary... thereupon he will become Lord of images (*IF*,2,075).

Flaubert explains that in the interior life of Jules there are "magic illuminations and flamboyant pleasures, the blue sky of the Orient permeated with sun" (*IF*,2,048). As to the exterior life, the world is hell, so Jules has renounced it and left only his body there to be tortured by Satan at will. Satan is Lord of the real, but unknown to Satan an unreal masterpiece begins to take shape within the tortured body; the imaginary vision arises, however, only on the condition that the dreamer remain a dreamer. Therein the would-be artist encounters a problem: he is Lord of images, but Satan is Lord of the real. Jules cannot become an artist after all, for an artist must use *real* means in order to write; but "if one so much as lifts his finger he thereby participates in the Evil with which the world is infected" (*IF*,2,005). He finds he must remain passive, without breath or desire, like an insect helpless on its back. "Jules is king of the irreal on condition that he does not leave" (*IF*,2,009).

The situation of Jules the helpless artist closely resembles that of the helpless evildoer presented earlier in this chapter, except that now all of the values have been reversed. Then the world was good, ruled by God, and the would-be evildoer was unable to realize his imaginary evil. Now the world is evil, ruled by Satan, and the would-be artist is unable to realize his imaginary masterpiece. Jules has sacrificed living in order to produce a masterpiece, but he finds the one thing that he cannot do is produce, that is, he cannot do anything *real*. This is the first form of loser-wins that Sartre finds in Flaubert's nervous collapse, but it contains this basic dilemma that Flaubert himself did not see until he neared the end of *l'Education sentimentale*.

The dilemma is further complicated in that Flaubert had judged that Shakespeare was able to describe every human passion only because Shakespeare had no passion or purpose of his own. Then Flaubert sees that the self-destructive acts of Jules had a purpose all along: he wanted to destroy himself (his passions) *in order that* he might restore himself as artist (*IF*,2,011). Jules had a project after all! Flaubert had even explained that Jules was "enriching himself" through each defeat; how can one speak of the death of all desire if he is "enriching himself" in the process? His failures are a farce: desire has not died, rather all desires have been subordinated to one desire: the desire to write, the desire to be the great artist (*IF*,2,056–57). The losses of Jules were calculated losses, failure was aimed at success, it was the necessary and sufficient condition that a masterpiece might emerge. The artist was expected to rise out of the emptying of man like the butterfly out of the chrysalis (*IF*,2,086). Flaubert had even called the transition "mathematical." He had become a failure as man in order to rise above man as the artist, but it did not work. An artist is not a total failure. Something more radical is required: to become the great artist, he must *fail as artist.* But the artist negated

is not able solely by his defeat to transform himself *into an Artist,* since it is the same concept which the negation ought, at the same time and under the same relationship, to restore in its plenitude; it needs a mediation, which, *from another point of view,* gives to the desperate one that which had been lost (*IF*,2,086).

Formerly the artist was only the nonhuman, now the artist must be the nonartist! Flaubert writes in desperation that art is the quest of the impossible. Something beyond nature is required, something beyond all comprehension. Flaubert fears that he is losing his sanity and writes a letter describing the difference between madness and genius: he tells of some children who are acutely sensitive to music, but finds that their acute sensitivity only causes them shattered nerves and extreme suffering. He explains, "These are not the future Mozarts. The *vocation* was displaced; the idea has passed into the flesh where it rests sterile and the flesh perishes; the outcome is neither genius nor health" (*IF*,1,805). For years Flaubert had been practicing "spiritual exercises" in which he had been trying to dream himself into the world of art, the totalized world, the inert world that is the obverse of the open-ended real world. Then the inert world of which he has dreamed slips from his mind into his body, the idea takes on flesh where it "rests sterile and the flesh perishes." He finds himself a shattered recluse and not another Mozart. His body is passively undergoing the failure of being, the failure of which he had dreamed. His body is the mimic of totality, that is, the mimic of death, for only the dead are totalized. "The vocation was displaced." There are two alternatives: either one can make an objectified failure, that is, a work of art, the beautiful object as failure of being, or one can passively undergo failure in his perishing flesh. But how could Flaubert *make* anything at all? To make something would ruin everything that he values, it would involve him with the evil world of nature that he is straining to deny. But there is almost an alternative: what if he as an individual were summoned by God to be an artist? Then his actions in the world would not be actions with the world at all. They would be miracles; they would not involve him in nature, for as particular exceptions they would violate nature and thus they would not contaminate the great dream. But now becoming an artist would not be "mathematical" at all, it would all depend on an individual vocation; like Mozart before him he must wait for "un appel a l'activité" (*IF*,1,805). Flaubert must wait to see if he has been called to *act* or only left to be *victimized* by the vision he has had. The difference between the great artist and the sickly madman is that the artist has received a divine vocation:

But since it is established that he [the Artist, the genius] contradicts the laws of the universe, it is because an all-powerful will has suspended them in each particular case. A great writer is always something of a Lazurus; he undergoes the common lot, he dies and begins to smell; at that time someone intervenes who snaps his fingers, time is reversed like an hourglass, he rises full of genius (*IF*,2,073).

This is the second form of loser-wins that Flaubert obscurely envisions, it is not automatic at all. First, Flaubert must deny himself as artist. He tries to make himself "indifferent" to art. He explains that writing is only a useless hobby; it is simply an additional body function like smoking or sleeping. He writes, "If you wish to write well, desire nothing, not even what you write or will write." He insists that he could never attain the grandeur of the artist, then he announces that art is a useless vanity without value. When he finished his novel about Jules, he sits helpless at his writing desk for almost three years (1845–47). He must not seek to become the artist, this much he knows. But then as he muses, something else begins to fascinate him — sanctity; particularly the legend of St. Julien, the human outcast who reaches the depths of degradation only to be called by the Lord Jesus. Thirty years later this would become *Saint Julien l'Hospitalier*. Sartre observes that the story of Jules and the legend of St. Julien are the only two happy endings in all the writings of Flaubert; like his other works, they tell of losers, but two of his losers become winners. Loser-wins has two forms, and the radical form is sanctity.

Sartre proposes that Flaubert made a wager something like the wager of Pascal. Pascal bet with his life on the existence of God, arguing that if he were in error he would lose only a temporal pleasure, but if he were right an eternal happiness would be gained. In the second form of loser-wins (losing as artist), Flaubert bets everything he has, not to save his soul, rather to save his last chance on earth — to win as artist! Gustave has all but broken with the world and finds himself on the borders of madness. He throws over his last desire, he no longer tries to be an artist; he is a total failure, now it is up to God (*IF*,2,074).

The second loser-wins (destruction as artist to become artist) requires a God to make sense (that is, one who is beyond contradiction), but throughout his life Flaubert continues to profess disbelief. Sartre argues that he is only following the rules of the game, for if he acknowledged God his loss would not be total: Flaubert must suffer the absence of God throughout his life, for only thus can he live without hope and therefore be pleasing to God. Then "since Heaven is silent and grace is refused him, he will remain at the level of the negative Infinite." It is up to God to decide: if there is no God or if God does not want him, then he is lost in madness and abject folly. Sartre sees Flaubert making the following prayer:

Hidden God, in whom I must not believe and whom, if I had the permission, I would love with all my soul, behold; I am defeated in all that men have given me, look at me naked and alone, virgin wax as on the day of my birth, for I wish to count on none but You (*IF*,2,077).

Then it is that God seems to respond to Flaubert's despair. Something changes; it is as if the All-Powerful gives him a mandate:

You will be born and die in desperation, cursed, you will strive unceasingly to deny my existence, and I will not undeceive you; you will have my invisible assistance only to produce the works which best discourage your species, your merit in my eyes will be double since your misfortune will be extreme and you will infect others with it. Thus wishes the infinite love that I bear you (*IF*, 2,087).

Illusions are the great work of God, therefore it is only the everlasting Father who can call a man to be an artist; then God works through the art to draw men away from being, to fill them with yearning and thus increase their merit by increasing their burdens. From time to time Providence calls forth "sorcerers, artists, and Lords of Optical Illusion" to lead men apart from the kingdom of this world, for reality is Satan's domain. Flaubert wagers on the God beyond reality; he writes, "I believe in the eternity of only one thing, that of Illusion, which is the true truth" (*IF*,2,076). Flaubert the actor has been touched by the one absolute that an actor can allow: illusion. He has been given a mandate; he proceeds to write and announces ten times over that the reason he writes is to demoralize men (*IF*,444). At one time he had compared himself with the Christian hermits: he saw himself another St. Anthony helplessly drawn into the confines of his own imagination where he was tortured by flamboyant visions. This was the first loser-wins. Now he has been selected by Infinite Love to derealize the world by filling it with images; for it is the image that draws man away from the world of being and thereby reveals to man the abyss of dissatisfaction that nature never can fill (*IF*,1,626). The artist systematically turns the real into illusion, the illusion wavers and collapses, and man is wracked with yearning for the great Absence. But that is its purpose. In the real world God can be known only where there is absence: "it is by our failures and all our repellent phantasmagoria that we communicate with the absolute Being."

For Sartre, beauty is the failure of being. Flaubert would agree, but through failure itself he tried to communicate with someone beyond Being. Sartre sees the life of Flaubert bearing witness that God *ought to be*, but he will not accept what he terms Flaubert's "negative theology"; for Sartre failure is nothing but failure and beyond being there is only nothingness. The artist has indeed removed the gratuitousness of life, but for Sartre the gratuitous is also the real: "it is the contingency of the fact which is the best mark of its reality" (*IF*,1,377). Thus for Sartre the artist does not testify to the existence of God, but only that God ought to be. After the illusion of the image (the play or the novel) is over, man is left with a yearning for God; the meaningful world of art has wakened in him the desperate desire to be a creature. But it is all to no avail; art has done nothing but exasperate man's impossible longing. The image is compared to salt water, in that it does not satisfy but only intensifies the thirst. Beauty may fill us with yearning and delight, but for Sartre it is only the vacant face of nothingness; Beauty does not lead to God, but only to images we *think* we see and *know* we do not. We are eviscerated by vacant fantasies that quietly tear us apart. Strange hell of beauty.

Sartre's study of Flaubert is permeated with references to "negative theology"; a brief consideration of the negative tradition in theology could help situate what Sartre is saying. The *via negativa* is often regarded as particularly characteristic of the East: in Buddhism it is associated with zen meditation, in Hinduism with the *neti neti* that leads to nirvana, and in Taoism with the Tao that cannot be known. But there is also a long tradition of negation in the spirituality of the West. In medieval Judaism Moses Maimonides would explain that God "has no positive attribute whatever." The way to God is strictly negative: "every time you establish by proof the negation of a thing in reference to God, you become more perfect." The *via negativa* became strong in fourth-century Christianity after Eunomius had maintained that he knew God by his proper name (the Ungenerated). A series of saints (Basil, the Gregories, Chrysostom) opposed Eunomius and argued that God could be known only in the darkness of incomprehensibility. Pseudo-Denys would speak of God as "the transcendent Dark" and explained the way to find God:

abandon all sensation and all intellection and all objects or
sensed or seen and all being and all nonbeing and in unknowing,
as much as may be, be one with the beyond being and knowing
(*VME*,70).

Pseudo-Denys described God by a series of over fifty negations (not-goodness, not a being, not nonbeing, not affirmable, not deniable, and so on); his writings were of major significance in all medieval theology. Scotus Erigenus would present God as the highest negation; since God is transcendent to all being, he refers to God as *nihil*. St Thomas sees the way to God as a way of negation: "Since we cannot know how God is, but only how he is not; we must therefore consider the ways in which God does not exist, rather than the ways in which he does" (S.Th.Ia.iii.Prol.). Any quality that we can know by our reason must be denied: "And then the mind dwells in the darkness, as it were, of an ignorance. As long as life lasts it is in this ignorance that we are best united with God" (*Scpt*.Ia.St.vii.1). However, this final ignorance is not the same as the original ignorance; the final ignorance can come only subsequent to a process of affirmation and negation. Eckhart writes that "only the hand that erases can write the true thing." This is what has come to be known as apophatic theology: first, something is stated, and then it is denied ("erased"): God is good, but he is not good in any way that we can know. It is only in the ignorance that *follows* the negation that the truth of God can be known. Thus, Eckhart would speak of God as the Negation of negation (*Meister Eckhart*, p.247). God is identified with the denial of negation. This is the tradition of theology in which Sartre would place Flaubert: the image is the negation of being — this Sartre would allow — but for Flaubert the communication with God was in the moment that the image collapsed. The collapse of the image negates the negation of being; this negation of the negation is the God of Eckhart and of the apophatic tradition.

The basic apophatic sequence, presented by mystics and theologians and found by Sartre in Flaubert, recalls the ontological sequence that Sartre presented in *Being and Nothingness* (see the final section of chap. 2). In *Being and Nothingness* the in-itself is first and is entirely positive. The for-itself proceeds out of the in-itself; it is consciousness, the negation of positive being, and therefore secondary to the being which it negates. The third phase is the being beyond the nothingness — God, the in-itself-for-itself. This might be termed the Negation of negation or, again in the language of Eckhart, it is what is written after the erasing. For Sartre the third phase is the ideal for which every man strives, but it is judged to be an impossible ideal that cannot be achieved.

Like Sartre, the holy man would also understand the apophatic sequence as a way of life: it is his own being that must undergo the negation. This is what Sartre sees in the ascetic practices of Flaubert; they are efforts at self-destruction, efforts at rendering himself imaginary, but done with the *implicit* understanding that this destruction itself will be negated. Thus sanctity is presented as the ultimate form of loser-wins. The saint or the martyr is the one who loses totally as man in order that, inexplicably, he might win; this is the third phase, when the human negation is negated and man awakens in God. This is what happens in Flaubert's story of St. Julien: at the moment when he stretches himself in total degradation over the body of a leper, the heavens open and Jesus summons him to enter. The *very moment* his human sensibilities are completely negated, he sees the Lord Jesus welcoming him. St. Augustine writes: "When you become such a man that no earthly thing delights you, believe me, at that very moment, at that point of time, you will behold what you desire." The Christian ideal of self-negation (John of the Cross urging that "the soul strive to work in its own despite") goes back to Christ, who spoke of self-denial with a promise of gain: "whoever loses his life for my sake, he will save it." "Unless a grain of wheat falls into the earth and dies, it remains alone; but if it dies it bears much fruit." Sartre points to the same sequence of loser-wins in the passion of Christ: "the ignominious and accepted death, the frightful defeat of the prophet on earth, is elsewhere, in heaven, a mysterious victory" (*IF*,608). Thus the apophatic sequence involves not only ideas, but one's own self. Man must empty himself, being turns into nothingness, and all one has is the more or less unjustifiable hope that that nothingness itself will be negated. This is the absolute form of loser-wins. It is the inexplicable hope for something-beyond-the-nothingness that has animated the Christian saint, and Sartre sees the same apophatic movement in two men fascinated by the Christian ideal: "St. Genet" and "St. Flaubert."

7

Dirty Hands

The Active Life

It was in 1945 that Sartre wrote his essay on the two forms of Cartesian freedom. In writing this essay he seems to have realized that the same double understanding of freedom for which he criticized Descartes was to be found in his own thought: in *Being and Nothingness* man was said to be free, in that he broke with the full world of being; he discovered his freedom in his questioning, anguish, and uncertainty. Freedom was said to be "really synonymous with lack" (*BN*,692). This freedom resembles the negative freedom that Sartre finds in Descartes; it is free only in uncertainty and revolt. But *Being and Nothingness* spoke of another freedom as well, the freedom that must dispose of some positive power in order to be itself ("choice, being identical with acting, supposes a commencement of realization" [*BN*,592]).

The two forms of freedom are presented throughout the writings of Sartre; as in the writings of Descartes, they are difficult to reconcile with each other. They probably can be best understood if they are situated in a temporal sequence: in the growth of an individual man, in the liberation of an oppressed people, and ultimately in the evolution of mankind. It could be said that the very young child does not really know either form of freedom: "We had our first existence as *absolute objects*" (*S4*,238). Gradually the child becomes aware of his own subjectivity. This is the experience of anguish and emptiness; it is the experience of pure consciousness that Sartre criticizes because it leads nowhere. This freedom is purely negative and must be abandoned in order that the individual might assume the other form of freedom, the freedom that creates. It could be said that Sartre understands three separate stages: first, at the time of his birth, man is an absolute object; then, during childhood, he comes to discover the negative freedom of pure subjectivity; finally, he can assume the active freedom that creates. The three stages occur in sequence, but it would seem that most men do not really pass beyond the first stage.

Sartre does not fully explain the three stages, but they are frequently implied in his writing. They can be found in a consideration of his own development as a writer. Sartre refers to his own bourgeois childhood. The bourgeois could be said to belong to the first stage; throughout their lives they continue to regard themselves as "absolute objects." They have not had or at least have not accepted the experience of their own subjectivity. They continue to speak of themselves in the third person. The slightest doubt or negativity has never crossed their grey eyes (*N*,84). They identify themselves with the solidity of their homes and their city (*N*,158). They feel they are part of the great fixed order of being that must be maintained. They are inert objects alienated from either form of freedom. The child raised in a bourgeois family is systematically persuaded that he has been given an objective destiny to fill; thus he is convinced that he is an object. The family home in which he is born and the possessions he will one day inherit persuade him that he has a predetermined worth that is quite apart from anything that he might *do*. What he accomplishes is of no importance, it is his being that counts. As a member of the bourgeoisie he undertakes some useless study (the "liberal arts") and surrounds himself with the trappings of eternity (great paintings, and so on). The fullness of being has been given to him so he is left with nothing to do. He appears as an ornament at ceremonial occasions of state where he makes official gestures that accomplish nothing. Otherwise he occupies himself with the liturgy of good manners and the pointless rituals of politeness that are expected of members of the higher class (*S3*,185ff.; *N*,44; *IF*,294,613ff.). He does nothing, doing is beneath him; he *does* not, he *is*. In short, he is the self-righteous man, the "religious man" presented above in chapter 5. He preserves established being. He has never accepted the negative freedom of pure refusal. He prefers to be an object. Sartre has endlessly denounced the bourgeoisie, and his denunciations consist in showing that the bourgeois will not acknowledge his own nothingness. These denunciations abound in Sartre's early writings, when he was experiencing the negative freedom so intensely himself.

It was late in Sartre's career as a writer that he became highly critical of "the artist," the writer who claims a transcendent value in his work. The artist (Flaubert, Baudelaire) is presented by Sartre as the man who revels in the empty freedom of subjectivity. The artist abandons the real world in order to construct his own immaterial world out of the thin air of his own nothingness. Unlike the bourgeois, the artist is not spellbound by being, rather he is spellbound by his own nonbeing. But like the bourgeois, he is also estranged from doing. He does not work. He cannot work for he has rejected anything that he might work with; he rejects the "given." He wants to stand apart like a divinity and make pure creations out of nothing. In writing *What is Literature?* (1947) Sartre began showing his antagonism to the artist. He has subsequently come to abandon the writing of plays, novels, and short stories, genres in which a large part of his early output is cast. But beginning in the late 1940's the artist was criticized as helpless (the artist is the negative evildoer, the spiritual man presented above in chap. 6). As an artist deeply aware of his own subjectivity, Sartre had despised the bourgeoisie but was not politically active.

Subsequently, Sartre has turned his attention toward effecting social change. He has abandoned his more or less negative subjectivity to involve himself in creative activity in the objective world, in short to do work. This is the third stage. The three stages of man's development might be characterized by the bourgeois, the artist, and the worker. Each of the stages is characterized by a different ideal: the bourgeois by the ideal of being — he desires to be an absolute object; the artist by the ideal of nothingness — he seeks to retain the purity of his negative freedom; the worker by the ideal of doing — he sets out to change the world creatively. Being, nothingness, and doing — the sequence is that of Sartre's own development. As a bourgeois child he longed to be a pure object. As a young writer he rejected his objective being and emphasized the opposition between being and nothingness; he spoke with feeling of the nothingness he was experiencing. In his maturity he has come to deny the significance of the opposition between being and nothingness; both are rejected equally, for both are opposed to doing. Now creative action is the measure of a man. Subjectivity and objectivity are contemplative ideals that leave man with a pointless idealism:

There are two ways to fall into idealism: The one consists of dissolving the real in subjectivity; the other in denying all real subjectivity in the interests of objectivity (*SM*,33).

It is the artist who dissolves the real in subjectivity, while it is the bourgeois who denies all real subjectivity. Both have fallen into idealism. The "spirituality" of the artist is opposed to the "religion" of the bourgeois, yet Sartre feels that both the artist and the bourgeois get along fairly well together for neither one is interested in real social change. In fact the two attitudes can well coexist in the same mind. Each attitude involves an absolute: all or nothing. "Being is holy, so it must all be accepted," or "Being is profane, so it must all be rejected." The difference is only a matter of words; in practice they come down to the same thing — a refusal of the creative freedom that can act and produce real change in the real world.

For Sartre, effective action in the world has come to be the true measure of freedom. This is why he has increasingly regarded himself as a Marxist. His Marxism grows out of his commitment to the freedom of action, a freedom that can only be found in the man who works. Sartre acknowledges that most of the workers of today are not really free. This is because they still retain a longing for the ideal of pure being—or perhaps for pure nothingness. Longing for the absolute they regard their own work as a curse to be endured instead of finding in it their true liberation. The creative freedom that Sartre envisions is something he feels cannot even be understood in the present condition of society. But Sartre does indicate the step men must take in order to find the new freedom.

Crime and the Problem of Action

The freedom of the spiritual man involves a total refusal of the world, a refusal that leaves him incapable of acting. He is affected by a sort of psychic paralysis that has become a recurrent theme in the fiction of Sartre. It is first evident in the nausea of Antoine Roquentin: "I know very well that I don't want to do anything: to do something is to create existence" (N,173). This paralysis becomes the central theme in Sartre's trilogy *The Roads to Freedom*. The trilogy presents Mathieu Delarue, a professor of philosophy who views the world from the remoteness of his own intellect. At times Mathieu prides himself on his freedom and exults in his total independence; at other times he knows that his precious freedom involves a total incapacity for action. Mathieu becomes painfully aware of his helplessness when he comes upon an unexpected financial need. He decides to steal some easy money and sets about committing the theft. But in the critical moment he finds that he is incapable of stealing. It is not that he fears being caught; what he fears is any decisive action whatsoever. He concludes: "I couldn't take the money; my freedom is a myth" (AR,244). He has suddenly realized that the freedom of which he was so proud is not really freedom at all. It is the freedom of subjectivity. This freedom is a myth, for he is not able to do what he himself wants to do. It might be said that Mathieu is like Hamlet; he is paralyzed by the reflexive lucidity of his own thought and cannot make a decisive act.

Later in the trilogy Mathieu considers either marrying or throwing over his long-time mistress. Again it is a question of the decisive act. As Mathieu considers marriage, he becomes aware of a freedom that is very different than the freedom he has known hitherto:

Only for an instant; he caught a glimpse of this inexplicable freedom that wore the aspect of a crime; indeed, it frightened him and it was so remote (*AR*,245).

The inexplicable freedom is beyond his present paralysis; it involves a decisive act, and wears the aspect of a crime. Sartre never defines what he means by a crime, but the term occurs so often in his fiction that its meaning is clear. A crime is a destructive act by which being is irrevocably soiled with nothingness, and nothingness is irrevocably soiled with being. The spell of the absolutes is broken, and this is the crime. Consider other passages where Sartre speaks of crime. In *The Devil and the Good Lord*, Goetz is an idealist who alternates in his devotion to two absolutes: absolute good and absolute evil. Finally he disavows both of them and announces that in order to begin living he must commit a crime: he kills a man. In *The Flies* Orestes feels as light as air (spirituality) and looks forward to some sort of crime as his deliverance; he commits a double murder. In *The Roads to Freedom* Mathieu ultimately attains salvation by committing a crime; he fires on some advancing German soldiers. The act is destructive of being and the good; its theological context is evident.

He fired, and the tables of the law crushed about him—Thou shalt love thy neighbor as thyself—bang! in that bastard's face.... He was firing on his fellow men, on Virtue, on the whole world (*TS*,200).

It is this crime that finally delivers Mathieu from his negative freedom and gives him the ability to act. By this deed being is stained with *his* negativity and he has finally become some*thing*. His subjectivity is finally objectified in what he has done.

For years he had tried in vain to act; one after another he had been robbed of action as fast as he had determined to act; he had been about as firm as a pat of butter. But this time no one had cheated him. He had pressed a trigger, and, for once, something had happened, something definite....*His* dead man, *his* handiwork, something to mark *his* passage on the earth (*TS*, 193).

In all of the above cases the crime involves an irrevocable act. By this act, consciousness became committed to something, to its own deed. Consciousness becomes defined; it is defined the only way that Sartre will allow — by *what it has done*. By an irrevocable deed, consciousness loses its airy lightness and incurs an irrevocable guilt. Consciousness *must incur guilt* in order to overcome its paralysis. Before he committed his crime, Mathieu was even reproached *because he was to blame for nothing* (*AR*,312). In a similar way Orestes had blamed himself only for his *innocence*. He feels obliged to incur guilt in order to overcome his spirituality: "I must take a burden on my shoulders, a load of guilt so heavy as to drag me down" (*NE*,93). His innocence is the reason *why* he must commit the crime. When consciousness is bound by the guilt of crime, it has assumed a burden that is irrevocably its own. It becomes anchored in time and place, it has surrendered its purity. Consciousness is no longer wholly transcendent, it has entered the finite and has *made history*. It is by committing a crime that one is situated in time and place, and being situated in time and place is necessary for the freedom which acts. "*Being situated* is an essential and necessary characteristic of freedom" (*WL*,144; see also *KV*,50). By his crime, Mathieu has something "to mark *his* passage on the earth," and from now on he must bear the weight of his own deed.

This responsibility is what the man who exults in his negative freedom tries to avoid: he wants to retain his transcendental purity; he wants to keep all of his options open. He knows that after the crime he can no longer make the instant and total reversal that characterizes pure consciousness. It is crime that finally bars the hope of any return to the rear (*KV*,48). Through crime a history has been made that cannot be erased. The man who can always "return to the rear" is the man who can take back all that he has done by changing his mind. But if he wants to remain that way he will be powerless to act. He will watch his own life from a distance. He places himself in a dream world outside of reality and outside of history in order to guard his infinite freedom. This is the freedom that turns out to be a myth. Mathieu has infinite freedom, but he is unable to steal and unable to marry. Any definitive act will sully his nothingness. The crime is the marriage, the theft, or anything at all by which he would dirty his hands with the finite and the real.

In 1948 Sartre again considered the meaning of crime in a play called *Dirty Hands*. The play deals with members of the Communist Party in an East European country in the closing years of World War II. The two principal characters embody the two opposing forms of Cartesian freedom: Hoederer, an older man with the freedom that acts in the real world, and Hugo, the young idealist with the negative freedom of pure consciousness. Hoederer explains to Hugo the difference that separates them:

Purity is an idea for a yogi or a monk. You intellectuals and bourgeois anarchists use it as a pretext for doing nothing. To do nothing, to remain motionless, arms at your sides, wearing kid gloves. Well, I have dirty hands. Right up to the elbows. I've plunged them in filth and blood....Your purity resembles death. The revolution you dream of is not ours. You don't want to change the world, you want to blow it up (*NE*,224-25).

Hugo is the intellectual who retains a reflective purity outside of history. Like a yogi or monk, he has found the infinite freedom of consciousness and cannot reconcile himself to the finite. His conciousness has attained pure nothingness, and in order to maintain that purity all that is positive must be refused—or blown up. He is an anarchist, a nihilist who knows only the freedom of revolt. If he were to accept anything at all he would compromise himself, for "only revolt is pure." But the freedom that creates requires that one dirty his hands, that he lose his purity. This is the crime. The crime is to step out of the infinite purity of thought and dirty oneself with the finite. The monk, the yogi, the anarchist, the intellectual, the artist—in short, the spiritual man—stands apart and refuses to contaminate himself. He regards the world from a distance with a mixture of dread and disdain. Eventually this asceticism produces its effect; all of being assumes the strange insubstantiality that was described above in chapter 6: "As a result of not testing the real by action, one does not know its consistency; the world becomes merely a flat, kaleidoscopic multiplicity" (*G*,260). Hugo is paralyzed by his reflexive lucidity. He complains that his life has become artificial: "Nothing seems to be entirely real." "I live in a stage set." He becomes envious of Hoederer, the man of action, for Hugo knows that Hoederer's world is very different:

Everything he touches seems real. He pours the coffee in the cups. I drink. I watch him drinking and I feel that the taste of the coffee in his mouth is real (*NE*,187).

Hoederer points out that "All intellectuals dream of doing something," but with Hugo it is only a dream; he is unable to act, his acts are only gestures.

As the play continues, Hugo is holding a pistol when unexpectedly he is angered by Hoederer. He fires three times and Hoederer dies. It would seem that Hugo has finally committed a crime and is thereby delivered from his insubstantiality. But the matter is not that simple. Hugo's feelings about what has happened are very ambiguous:

Did I even do it? It wasn't I who killed — it was chance....Chance fired three shots, just as in cheap detective stories....Where does that put me in the thing? It was an assassination without an assassin (*NE*,240).

Hugo wanted to escape from the artificial world of the artist and the mystic. He wanted to assume the heaviness of crime. He has killed a man but still he has gotten nowhere.

I wanted to hang a crime round my neck, like a stone. And I feared it would be too heavy for me to carry. How wrong I was! It's light, horribly light. It has no weight at all. . . . It has become my destiny, do you understand? It controls my life from the outside, but I can't see it or touch it, it's not mine (*NE*,241–42).

The killing is irrevocable, but it has not brought Hugo into history. He does not feel *he* has acted. He is still horribly light. Killing Hoederer is something that "happened" to Hugo rather than something he has done. It was an act outside of his control; it was his destiny rather than his deed. He does not feel responsible, he does not feel "a load of guilt" heavy enough to drag him down to the real.

Sartre explains what is lacking in Hugo's crime when he considers an incident in Baudelaire's *l'Ivrogne*. In *l'Ivrogne* a man wants to get rid of his wife, but he does not want to kill her *directly*. On a dark night he sends her to the end of a road where he knows there is an uncovered well. As she walks up the road he muses to himself: "If she escapes, so much the better. If she falls in, it's God who condemns her" (*B*,130). Sartre explains that the man himself "does not possess the necessary strength for direct action, he puts the burden of getting rid of her on chance and magic" (*B*,131). The man wants to remain apart from his act, he does not want to see it as *his*, he does not want to dirty his hands. He merely says words and then the deed seems to happen *on its own*. When the deed is done, he still retains his transcendent purity. There has been no *crime*, only an accident. There is no experience of human causality and consequently no human guilt. A woman has accidentally fallen in a well; it is God or chance that is responsible! Consciousness is still pure spirit, it has not compromised itself with action, it has touched nothing. This is simply the magic-sacred mentality: deeds happen on their own, independently of men, while men make only idle and impotent gestures. Man is helpless, he is not responsible for all that takes place; he is stranded in the impotent and empty freedom of spirituality. He cannot really create, for nothing he does is his. This alienation of man from his deeds is what Sartre considers the meaning of the sacred. It is present whenever human deeds appear to be the result of some nonhuman agent. The sacred is the alienation of man from his own work; it is a man's free activity coming back to him as though it proceeded from someone else, as though a superhuman power were responsible for it all. It is the estrangement of spirituality.

Creative work is alienated; man does not recognize himself in his own product, and his exhausting labor appears to him as a hostile force (*SM*,13).

When a man lives in the sacred world of either being or nothingness, work appears distant and threatening; it seems to be the condemnation for a fault he can no longer remember. Longing to return to the world of being, man feels estranged from the world of his own doing. Sartre finds this estrangement to be almost universal. He points to it in Kierkegaard, who felt that he could not influence men directly and therefore devised his "indirect method." It is a similar indirect method that characterizes the work of the artist. The artist claims to serve only beauty or truth or some other nonworldly ideal and thus refuses to accept the responsibility for the real results that his art might have on real men. In *Dirty Hands* Hugo acknowledges that he has "never taken part in any direct action." Even after he has fired three bullets into Hoederer he protests that he was not the one who killed him; it was chance that fired three shots just as it happens "in cheap detective stories."[1] "In cheap detective stories" the killer does not feel guilty after the crime is committed. He is bewildered by his own act. The victim lies dead and the killer feebly protests that the deed was not really his: "forces arose within me and it was they...," "it was a crime of passion." But passions or emotions or "forces within" are only indications of man's estrangement from what he himself is doing. This was presented in chapter 3. Emotions come over a man and seem to raise him above himself, accomplishing either great or horrendous deeds *for* him. They are experienced as magic or sacred presences which replace the man himself. They are like divinities. Socrates is told by Diotima that "Love is a mighty daemon." Love is like a goddess, for it accomplishes for consciousness that which consciousness will not claim as its own. A character in Sartre's fiction explains the sacred feelings she once had in times of emotion:

I used to think that hate or love or death descended on us like tongues of fire on Good Friday [sic; the reference should be to Pentecost]....Yes, I really thought that "Hate" existed, that it came over people and raised them above themselves. Naturally, I am the only one. I am the one who hates, who loves (*N*, 150).

This is why Sartre considers the emotions sacred. The sacred mentality is basically consciousness refusing to place itself behind its deeds and acknowledge: "I am the only one"; it is consciousness alienated from its own products and ascribing them to God, or to chance, or to the "passions." The sacred is the for-itself refusing to dirty its hands with the real. Man's life then becomes only the appearance of living. The result has been decided elsewhere. Man fires guns and dead bodies fall about him, but

1. It could be said that this sentiment is not limited to cheap detective stories. In *The Iliad*, Pandaros is slain by the spear of Diomede. Homer explains that the spear was guided to its mark by the goddess Athena. Thus there is only indirect action; the deed is stolen from Diomede, who actually aimed and threw the spear. Sartre would seem justified in seeing this indirect action as characteristic of the sacred. Endless mythologies testify to gods granting victory in battle, success in the hunt, or conquests in love. In each case men are separated from their own deed; their acts appear to be only inefficacious gestures that have nothing to do with the result, or else bring it about indirectly. This is the estrangement of the sacred.

none of the deeds are his. Great events appear to take place, but it all has the unreality of acting in a play or living in a dream. The characters do not control the situation, the action is only a matter of appearance. The outcome of the Great Play has been determined in advance and long before the events began to unfold. This is the estrangement of the sacred. "Creative work is alienated; man does not recognize himself in his own product."

Several years after Hoederer's death, the Communist Party decides to change its political course. It is purely a matter of expediency, but thereby Hoederer becomes a martyred hero. This new situation puts Hugo in a difficult position for he wants to continue as a member of the Party. He explains to a Party official that the death of Hoederer was really an accident for which he should not be held responsible. Eventually the Party official agrees to accept Hugo's explanation, and he is given a new chance: the death of Hoederer is to be officially written off as an accident. However, because of the bad publicity connected with Hoederer's death, Hugo is advised to change his name. At this point Hugo unexpectedly refuses. He announces that he will not accept the type of salvation wherein he must change his name and present himself as a no one, "naked, without bag or baggage." He suddenly accepts the heavy baggage of his own past; he reverses his protestations of innocence and claims that the death of Hoederer was no accident at all. It was a crime and the crime was his; he has finally decided to dirty his hands — after the deed. Now he stubbornly refuses to disown what he has done, even though it means his death. But he goes to death in triumph for he has gained the heaviness of guilt, he has delivered himself from the insubstantiality of the intellectual. The accident has become *his* crime, and he has passed from the negative freedom of pure revolt to the freedom that is capable of acting.

The crime that Hugo assumes must ultimately extend beyond his deed as an individual, for his act has involved him in the whole ambiguous stream of human events. When Hoederer had claimed to have dirtied his hands, the dirt of which he spoke was not the dirt of a single deed, it was the dirt of all of the history in which he had lived and taken an active part. Hoederer had ideals, but he had been willing to compromise those ideals even to the extent of trying to bring the Party into a coalition with fascist and bourgeois powers. Hugo, horrified at such a coalition, had proclaimed, "Under no circumstances will I compromise"; he had absolute values which kept him apart from men, he lived in a theological world. To enter the real historical world (that is, to acknowledge the world that he is in, like it or not) he must dirty his ideals and assume guilt for all the ambiguous results his actions will have. And these results are not altogether in his control. If he chooses to work with other men, their common achievement will involve him in crimes he never intended.

Dirty Hands ends with Hugo accepting his guilt, but the communal nature of this guilt does not become a significant theme until later in Sartrean theater. In 1951 Sartre wrote *The Devil and the Good Lord*, in which Goetz is involved alternately in the idealism of good and the idealism of evil. Finally he renounces both in order to live among men and says that he must begin by crime. He kills a man, but the crime he refers to does not end there; it includes the crimes of injustice of all those whose enterprise will succeed because of the help he has given them. To become one with men he must share their guilt:

Men of the present day are born criminals. I must demand my share of their crime if I want to have my share of their love and virtue. I wanted pure love; ridiculous nonsense. To love anyone is to share the same enemy....On this earth at present Good and Evil are inseparable (*DGL*,145).

In a similar way Sartre will argue that all men are responsible for the colonialist crimes committed in Algeria and all men are responsible for the "hooligans" that populate our cities, for it is by our deeds that the unjust world continues to be possible; our mental reservations or our different intentions count for little. We would all like to cast in our lot "with the angels" but the difficulty is that angels are not to be found. We have only conflicting groups of men to choose among; criminals make up both sides. Such is the world "at present," and "pure love" and other such virtues are pure only by remaining apart from what is historical and what is real. Sartre's last work of fiction, *The Condemned of Altona* (1959), concerns the guilt that remains in the family of a German industrialist long after the war is over. The family had reluctantly supported the Nazis, and years later, Franz, the older son, remains a guilt-ridden recluse. Like other Sartrean heroes, Franz explains that he always had the desire to do something, to act. When he finally did act (a killing) he found that his act became part of a sordid history that was given to him and over which he had only minimal control. His act became part of a *sordid* history because there was no other. He explains that to act means to inscribe one's name on *what is already there*. "I'll take responsibility for the war as though I were carrying it on alone" (*CA*,145). That he might have had mental reservations about what he was doing or had different intentions than the other Nazis counts for nothing; only the deed counts. As the play ends, he has gone to his death but his recorded voice continues to speak to an empty stage: "I...have taken the century upon my shoulders and have said: 'I will answer for it. This day and forever.' What do you say?" (*CA*,178). This is the crime of which Sartre would accuse all men of today, and the crime that all must acknowledge. It is the guilt of the present human condition: "Men of the present day are born criminals." Willingly or not, our life has been part of man's vast inhumanity to man. All of the carefully worded proofs of our innocence are explanations for no one. It is our deeds that make us guilty, but — *felix culpa* — it is our deeds that set us free.

History as Salvation

In *Being and Nothingness* Sartre had presented man as a useless passion. There he outlined a reflective method (existential psychoanalysis) by which a man might come to an awareness of his useless condition. In the years since *Being and Nothingness* Sartre has abandoned this absolute pessimism. He acknowledges this significant development in his own thought and speaks of the "enlightenment" that he received from Merleau-Ponty in 1950. This enlightenment consists in the recognition that whether a man acknowledges it or not, he is in fact *making history* (*S4*,161,176). Through this acknowledgment of the essential historicity of man, Sartre has come to speak of salvation. The salvation of which he speaks does not take place by the reflective method that he had proposed in 1943, but by action: man working together with his fellow men will be able to deliver himself by his *praxis*.[2]

2. For a fuller understanding of the influence of Merleau-Ponty on Sartre, see Merleau-Ponty's extended analysis of Sartre in *Les aventures de la dialectique*.

Sartre refers to his enlightenment as an event that occurred in 1950, but as psychologists (and Sartre [*IF*,177]) are wont to remind us, every enlightenment announces itself long in advance. This would be more than true in the case of Sartre. Consider history and salvation as they are found in his early fiction. In *Nausea*, written more than a decade before the enlightenment, Antoine complains that he sometimes feels that his present deeds have been determined by his past. As *determined* by his history, he has not fully realized his negative freedom: his fixed being still appears to determine what he does. Over a period of time Antoine liberates himself from this feeling by a type of existential psychoanalysis. He gradually divorces himself from all of his own past deeds. He withdraws from the immediate activities of living in order to attain a reflective purity. He speaks of washing himself clean by abstract thoughts (*N*,56). He reflects on his own past history and considers it no longer his. "I am cast out, forsaken in the present: I vainly try to rejoin the past" (*N*,33). He gives away all of the souvenirs he has collected and finally denies that the past has any reality whatsoever. It is this total denial of his own history that provokes the full intensity of his nausea; it brings him the realization of his infinite, aimless, and negative freedom. In denying the past, he has apparently broken some sacred taboo: "I had spoken the only words I should not have said: I had said the past did not exist" (*N*,96). Antoine had been engaged in writing an historical study, but with the realization that the past does not exist "anywhere at all," he abandons the project, for now there is no such thing as history. In freeing himself from the past, his life is no longer controlled from the outside. Consciousness is finally free of the spell of the Ego, for the Ego (as explained above in chap. 4) refers only to the past:

A pale reflection of myself wavers in my consciousness. Antoine Roquentin...and suddenly the "I" pales, and fades out. Lucid, static, forlorn, consciousness....Nobody lives there anymore.... Small fugitive presences populate it like birds in the branches. Populate it and disappear (*N*,170).

Many of the objections of Merleau-Ponty have affected the subsequent course of Sartre's writing. Simone de Beauvoir explains that since 1945 Sartre "worked to repudiate idealism, to tear himself from his original idealism, to live history." She sees his evolution ending around 1950-52.

Shortly after Antoine has attained this emptiness and despair, a hint of salvation begins to suggest itself. It seems to touch him like a warm presence. The warm presence refers to his past, but a past that will someday be transformed. "And I might succeed—in the past, nothing but the past—in accepting myself" (N,178). The novel ends with this mysterious hint that he might be able to assume his own past history.

The next fictional character that Sartre presented was Orestes (*The Flies*,1943). The play opens with Orestes already feeling much like Antoine had felt towards the end of *Nausea*. He has already been purified by a long education; he feels unsatisfied and compares his airy lightness to that of a spider web floating ten feet above the ground. He is "free as air" and finds his freedom as empty as air. Orestes complains at length because he has no memories, he has no home on earth, he has no city to call his own, and he is rooted in no past. These are the very things that Antoine had made such a point of rejecting. When Orestes first considers committing a crime, he sees it as a means of gaining memories. A crime is the means by which one gains a past and a native city and thereby renounces his transcendent freedom. Orestes aspires to the heaviness of stone, and crime is his means. The goal of Orestes is in sharp contrast with the purification and progressive *disengagement* practiced by Antoine. It is from the heaviness of stone that existential psychoanalysis is supposed to liberate consciousness; but this heaviness is what both Orestes and Hugo are seeking, and Sartre presents them as heroes for doing so. The list of memories that Orestes desires is a list of the very things for which Antoine had so despised the bourgeoisie (NE,60-64).

It might seem that Sartre is simply reversing himself, but this is not really the case. To explain the transition, I would refer to the successive stages proposed earlier in this chapter. The negative freedom must totally intervene before the final freedom can make its appearance. Antoine was reaching for the negative freedom while subsequent Sartrean heroes have the negative freedom and are trying to regain the power to act. Sartre would seem to be offering a parallel to what Kierkegaard outlined in *Fear and Trembling*. There the knight of faith is the one who grasps the finite and the temporal *after having given them up* (pp.33,60). Before the knight can grasp the temporal he must renounce it by the act of "infinite resignation"; this resignation strongly resembles the negative freedom described by Sartre and practiced by Antoine. The final stage (which both Kierkegaard and Sartre would consider salvation) strongly resembles the life of the bourgeoisie, but actually it is radically different because a total disengagement has intervened (see *Fear and Trembling,* p.50).

Sartre's heroes desire to take on the heaviness of stone and Sartre approves. This can appear to be the denial of all that he has said about the insubstantial nature of consciousness, but there is a difference: now men freely make themselves rocks. They assume the inertia, the inertia does not assume them. The difference goes back to what Sartre regards as the basic axiom of existentialism: *existence precedes essence.* This does not mean that man is pure existence (negative freedom) and without essence altogether. Rather it means that man *gives himself* his essence. Man's definition does not come from what he is, rather man defines himself by what he *has done.* Essence, therefore, refers only to one's past: "Essence is all that human reality apprehends itself as *having been*" (*BN*,42; see also *BN*,145). Thus man is not simply without an essence, rather each man forms his own essence and assumes it subsequent to his action. The action or the existence comes first; it precedes the essence. Sartre explains that men can share a common essence only if they share a common past. If men rise up in the same revolution and bind themselves together by an oath, "this is the beginning of humanity" (*CRD*,453). These men have the same essence because they share the same past; they have risen from the mire of necessity in the same historical action. The common essence becomes their own only when they assume it after the deed and bind themselves together by a common oath.

The child was said to perceive himself as an absolute object. This means that the child regards what he *is* as wholly determinate of what he *does.* His deeds seem to be the acts of his being, he is controlled by his destiny. In philosophical terms his essence seems to precede his existence; his *agere* seems to be determined by his *esse*, or as the scholastic phrase would have it, *agere sequitur esse.* This is the fundamental belief of bourgeois man and the belief that Sartre is so vehement in opposing. The purpose of existential psychoanalysis is to purify oneself of every remnant of this belief. It is this belief that inhibits all creative action and gives rise to the contemplative life; it causes the world to appear as a magic garden where actions proceed out of fixed beings: things appear to be acting, and human freedom is paralyzed. Man must choose for himself if his world is to be magical or technical (*BN*,544), that is, whether essence precedes existence or existence precedes essence; and the beginning of one's choice of the technical world is the painful process of existential psychoanalysis. By existential psychoanalysis a man divorces himself completely from his past (his essence) and attains that infinite, dreaded, and aimless freedom that Sartre has presented in *Nausea*. Essence, past, and ego have vanished and man attains the purity of existence. Existence is totally freed from essence, nothingness is totally distinct from being. Then comes the final stage: essence must be assumed.

Existence has now affirmed its primacy, and man acquires his past (his Ego or his essence) as something that is secondary. The final stage will thus involve both existence and essence, but the order has been reversed. Because the final stage involves the same two elements as the primary stage (when essence appeared to precede existence), it may appear to be the same, but actually it is radically different. This is the salvation envisioned by Antoine at the end of *Nausea*: "And I might succeed — in the past, nothing but in the past — in accepting myself." That is, he might succeed in accepting his essence-ego-past, all of which first had to be rejected. Again, the process can recall Kierkegaard's description of the man who holds onto the finite and the temporal *after having given them up*.

In 1960 Sartre published the first volume of a massive study (755 pages) of man as the maker of history: the *Critique de la raison dialectique*. The second volume was to appear soon afterwards, but it has not appeared and Sartre has put the matter aside. The first volume of the *Critique* offers a theory of knowledge that is difficult to reconcile with the fundamental concepts of *Being and Nothingness*. This difficulty indicates the fundamental change in Sartre's thinking. In *Being and Nothingness* he wrote of spontaneity (the for-itself) and its radical separation from any determinism. For example, in writing of the passions as determined, Sartre explained:

A priori this spontaneity would be capable of no action on a determinism already *constituted*....Moreover, what instrument would this spontaneity have at its disposal? If the hand can clasp, it is because it can be clasped. Spontaneity, since by definition it is *beyond reach*, can not in turn *reach*; it can produce only itself. And if it could dispose of a special instrument, it would then be necessary to conceive of this as of an intermediary between free will and determined passions — which is not admissible....Indeed it is impossible for a determined process to act upon spontaneity, exactly as it is impossible for objects to act upon consciousness. Thus any synthesis of two types of existence [the spontaneity of the for-itself, and the determinism of the passions] is impossible; they are not homogeneous; they will remain each one in its incommunicable solitude (*BN*, 540).

This paragraph explains well why a series of heroes in the fiction of Sartre has had difficulty with action in the real world. Spontaneity "can produce only itself"! Consciousness turns out to be the *causa sui* but the cause of nothing else! This is precisely the difficulty encountered by the Sartrean heroes, and it is also the difficulty encountered by Sartre himself in the *Critique* when he sets out to present a philosophy of man as the maker of history. The whole point of the *Critique* is that history is made by men. Therefore the *Critique* must abandon the incommunicable solitudes that were fundamental to *Being and Nothingness*. In the *Critique* the in-itself and the for-itself are hardly mentioned. In place of the for-itself the *Critique* offers a double form of reason: dialectical reason and analytical reason. The dialectical reason bears some resemblance to the for-itself: it is always a withdrawal from that which is, into that which is not. Thus it is the source of novelty and change. The analytical reason is of more interest. It is said to be "a synthetic transformation with which thought intentionally effects itself: this thought must make itself a thing and govern its very own self in exteriority...." Thought "makes itself a directed inertia in order to act on the inert" (*CRD*, 148). There is a basic change in Sartre's ontology: now thought is said to "make itself a thing" and to make itself "a directed inertia." This is exactly what had constituted a "relaxation of the bonds of being"; thought-as-thing or thought-as-inert is the way Sartre had defined "magic" or "the sacred." They were dismissed. Now the thought-thing is not dismissed, rather it is the key to Sartre's whole philosophy of action. The thought-thing is the special mediator that Sartre has had to introduce so that consciousness can produce something other than itself and man can be a maker of history.

In presenting his new epistemology Sartre explains that analytical reason is "only a certain practical moment of dialectical Reason....dialectical Reason sustains, directs and reinvents without cease the practical (analytical) Reason as its rapport of exteriority with natural exteriority" (*CRD*,148;see also *CRD*,176). In this passage and in his whole presentation of the two forms of reason, Sartre has abandoned the radical dualism of *Being and Nothingness* and offers instead a Bergsonian model. The dialectical reason resembles nothing so much as the familiar *élan vital*: dialectical reason is sum of the old and source of the new. It casts out successive inert forms (analytical reason) in the course of its own creative and upward advance through matter; the inert form is produced by dialectical reason so that it might gain a foothold in and thus act upon the inert material world. Even Bergson's phraseology is echoed as Sartre explains that analytical reason is "produced like the chitinous carapaces of certain insects."[3]

Being and Nothingness has spoken of the "incommunicable solitude" of both consciousness and the world; they could not act on one another as they were "not homogeneous." Now it is different: thought reaches the world; in the name of action it has made itself "inert." Analytical reason turns out to be homogeneous with both spontaneity and inertia ! The ontological character of spontaneous inertia is not treated, but it is precisely this dual character of analytical reason that enables consciousness to act outside of itself and thus enables man to be the maker of history. Analytical reason mediates between the two absolutes of *Being and Nothingness* and thereby man is delivered from his helplessness. The significance of human action is that, in order to work, man reduces himself to inorganic materiality in order to act upon matter (*CRD*,246). This is the crime. Transcendence dirties its hands; it intentionally infects itself with inertia and becomes stone; its purity as transcendence is gone. At the same time Sartre

3. Bergson had considerable influence on the early Sartre. Sartre's analysis of nothingness and consciousness, as presented above in chapter 2, resembles Bergson's treatment in *Creative Evolution* (pp.275ff.). Compare Sartre's analysis of automated man with Bergson's *Laughter* (see *IF*,811,817).

would still insist that since thought infects itself with inertia and not vice versa; its freedom is antecedent to its inertia. It adopts the inert only *after having given it up*. Adopting inertia and then breaking anew into freedom is an ongoing process: dialectical reason ceaselessly negates its own inert form and the inert world that it has shaped, and in that negation it ceaselessly invents the new. This is the dialectic with all of its Bergsonian overtones.

The starting point for the *Critique* is that man is first of all *action*; any other starting point is said to only maintain or increase man's alienation (*CRD*,248). With this starting point, subjectivity is redefined and turns out to be no longer nothingness; rather it is a moment in the dialectic (*SM*,33; *CRD*,31). As for pure matter—that is, being totally devoid of any signification—it is said to be found nowhere in human experience. Sartre repeatedly rejects the extremes of pure gaze (now referred to as God!) and pure matter. "Matter could be matter only for God or for pure matter, which would be absurd" (*CRD*,247). Brute matter would exist for man only if "he were a god or a pebble" (*CRD*,248). Sartre argues that as pure gaze, that is, as god, man would not truly act, rather he would produce by lightning intuitions; as a pebble he would not act either, as he would be totally part of the given. In neither case could he act or be acted upon. But man finds that he does act and that he acts in a humanized world, a world that is part matter and part meaning; man himself is also part matter and part meaning. The world man encounters is already partially humanized. Any situation he deals with comes to him with a human meaning. For example, an economic crisis has a human meaning and has no meaning at all apart from man; it would mean nothing, for either "the block of stone in the mountain, nor for God" (*CRD*,288). In all of these phrases contrasting God and the rock, the emphasis is on the middle ground between the pure opacity of stone and the pure transcendence of God, between pure object and pure gaze. Throughout the *Critique* Sartre tries to steer a middle course between the two extremes, between the alternative alienations of deterministic materialism (stone) and transcendent idealism (God) (*CRD*,29,31,157,248,688). Sartre regards both philosophies as forms of idealism; one is the idealism of the Right (the bourgeois man as pure object) and the other is the idealism of the

Left (the nihilist as pure revolt) (*CRD*,29;*SM*,29). Both are idealisms because they destroy the possibility of any creative human action in the real world. In basing the *Critique* on the reality of human action, Sartre is trying to steer a middle course between the two extremes that destroy the possibility of action. But the two extremes that he is trying to avoid resemble nothing so much as the in-itself (pure object) and the for-itself (pure transcendent gaze)—the all and the nothing, the fullness and the lack, the "two absolutely separated regions of being," "two regions without communication" (*BN*,lxxvi), that dominated *Being and Nothingness*. Sartre's fictional heroes found their attempted actions reduced to ineffective gestures because Sartre himself had once maintained that consciousness "can produce only itself" (*BN*,540). The middle course that Sartre is trying to steer in the *Critique* lies between the absolute opposites that he himself had established in *Being and Nothingness*.

With this different orientation, Sartre's atheism has come to have a different meaning: now it is not the absolute opposition that prevents there being a God, rather it is the absolute opposition itself that constitutes the theological world. Now God is not so much identified with the impossible synthesis of the in-itself and the for-itself, but with either one of the terms set in radical opposition to the other. God is now the human dialectical situation pushed to either one of its two inhuman, nondialectical extremes. So in the above passage from the *Critique* God is identified with pure gaze, but the whole point of the passages is that gaze is not pure; to think it is, is only to extrapolate into helpless idealism (the monkish purity of Hugo). When Sartre finds implicit theology in various literary figures, it is only because they have presented the absolute character of the opposition: either in trying to maintain the purity of evil in opposition to God's world of pure good,or in trying to maintain the purity of their virtue in opposition to Satan's world that is pure evil. It is the purity to which Sartre objects. He finds an implicit theology in these authors because of the extremity of their respective positions. The old opposition is now dismissed as "Megarian austerity" and a pre-Socratic use of the principle of the excluded middle that refuses to make use of the synthetic judgment (*IF*,552). In *Being and Nothingness* Sartre had based his atheism on the irreconcilable opposition of the in-itself and the for-itself; later, the irreconcilable opposition itself is seen to contain an implicit theology. Currently, it would seem that Sartre regards absolutes reconciled or absolutes opposed as equally a matter of absolutes and therefore equally irrelevant to the *present* human condition.

If the two regions of being are to be found at all in the *Critique*, they are only moments in the interplay of the dialectic, and whatever separation they have is continually mediated by thought repeatedly making itself a thing. In the dialectic, human spontaneity acts on matter in order to introduce the new, and matter reacts on man with the rigidity of the old. Tools are manufactured by man, but then they turn out to have a finality that opposes the finality that man would give them; man's freedom then becomes subject to them. They impose a destiny on man, but man reacts and imposes a freedom and a meaning on them. Thus the dialectic: man is continually being caught by, and continually escaping, the destiny imposed on him by matter. Since the process is continuous, it might be asked what difference it makes if consciousness is said to assume inertia or inertia is said to assume consciousness (existence preceding essence or vice versa). However this might be answered, it still remains clear that consciousness is said to assume the inertia, and existence precedes essence (*CRD*,148,291).

This precedence is further qualified by Sartre's present understanding of human interrelations. In the earlier writings of Sartre, truth is found in the purity of the *cogito*, and the influence of others draws me away from the certainty that I have into an essence that is only hearsay. But increasingly it is not the *cogito*, but the give-and-take of human reciprocity that is the measure of truth (*le gage du Vrai*) (*IF*,622,159; see *G*,41). If various Sartrean heroes are reflective loners (Antoine, Orestes, Hugo, Goetz, Franz), experiencing much difficulty in trying to work together with their fellow men, perhaps it is because the purity of the Sartrean *cogito* still recalls that Hell is other people. The *cogito* is reluctant to come out of its solitary truth and accept a different truth, one that is partially elsewhere — in reciprocity with others. The change is part of the enlightenment. Now there is a tension between the old understanding and the new. In the present world situation this tension must remain; this is the dialectic. It is the tension between what I am told and what I see. In order to see anything for myself I must partially rebel against what I am told. This rebellion isolates me from others; but it is only the rebellion that allows me to make *my* contribution to history and thus come together with others in work. Thus the dialectic continues.

In the present phase of the dialectic, we are all more or less estranged from our deeds. We all find ourselves caught on the whirligig of helplessness: we set out to do one thing but it all turns out differently than we had intended. We perform an action and find that it passes beyond our control; it is misunderstood many times over and when it finally comes back to us we cannot believe that we ourselves are the doers. The result is staggering; beside it, our act appears to be only a helpless gesture. We protest that it was an accident and claim that we are the victims of chance — and we are. We are the victims of what the French call *la force des choses*, that which Sartre defines as "the inhuman power which steals our acts and our thoughts" (*S4*,161-62). By such inhuman powers we feel alienated from our deeds. We all find ourselves more or less in the position of Mathieu or Hugo: our deeds are stolen from us one by one as if by a magic power. We cannot recognize our deeds as our own, our acts become so many helpless gestures before a fate that all but overtakes us.

This inhuman power is part of the present atomized condition of society, but Sartre sees history moving with a forward evolution to an age wherein alien necessities will be removed and a period of freedom will begin that we cannot even understand at the present (*SM*,34; *CRD*,32,249). When Goetz joined with his fellow men he announced that "men of the present day are born criminals" and "On this earth at present Good and Evil are inseparable." One day it will all be different, but at the present our own history and our own truth elude our grasp; the heroic act we think we are doing turns out to be cowardice to those who look back upon it. We are powerless to determine its truth. In the socialist state of the future there will be only *one* history and *one* truth for all men (this is to be explained in the second volume of the *Critique* [*CRD*,10,156]). Then both Marxism and existentialism will have outlived their time, for both speak of the alienation of man. Sartre, like Marx himself, looks forward to that future and the freedom that is beyond our present state of comprehension in a state beyond the sphere of material production (*SM*,34; *CRD*,32). Sartre often reverts to Marxist terms to characterize that future unity of man: man will no longer be the product of his product, he will be his own product (*CRD*,360,639); then men will say, "we are *our own sons,* our common invention" (*CRD*,453). As for the present age, wherein this is not the case, Sartre sees great wisdom in Marx's vision and in his desire "to transcend the oppositions of externality and internality, of multiplicity and unity, of analysis and synthesis, of nature and anti-nature" (*SM*,87 n; *CRD*,61 n).

When Sartre defines what he means by work, he sets it in opposition to the "purity" of the yogi or the monk. There is a way that Sartre's objection may seem to be unfounded: Christian monasticism has repeatedly renounced the passivity of various quietist tendencies. At the beginning of Western monasticism, St. Benedict proposed an ideal that included physical work: *Orare et laborare*; he warned that idleness is the enemy of the soul. The monastic movement was even influential in changing Western man's attitude towards physical labor. Lewis Mumford writes that the Benedictine Rule "certainly took the curse off work." Still Sartre's objection is not unfounded. The monks had a commitment to action, but the action is not the same as Sartre would recommend in speaking of "dirty hands." The difference would ultimately be found in the monastic vow of obedience. By obedience, the entire day of the monk was regulated from the outside: his *laborare* was not really his own; he was only doing what he was commanded to do. The responsibility for the deed did not refer back to him; the abbot's will was the source of the deed. The monk was only the agent; he worked, but he was not defined by the work. He tried to be indifferent to the type of the work that he did, as well as to the actual result. This is what allowed the monk his inner freedom and his peace of soul. It is this unencumbered freedom that Sartre rejects as characterizing the yogi and the monk. The monastic indifference is expressed in the old story of a monk who wove a basket one day and unwove it the next. He was not defined by his deed, which could be reversed. The monk was active, but the outcome was unimportant. If he would succeed, he would not see himself in the success, but only God's doing. As St. Paul wrote: "So neither he who plants nor he who waters is anything, but only God who gives the growth" (1 Cor.3: 8). (However, several verses later Paul does refer to himself as "God's fellow *worker*.") The belief that all growth or all real action comes from God is what Sartre means by the sacred: man works, but it all takes place indirectly, for the result is not seen as the outcome of what man does, but something bestowed on man by God. Man is not the doer; he only makes the gesture, and God makes the increase.

The separation between man and his deeds is even more systematically sought in the mysticism of the yogi. The *Isa Upanishad* states with precision what Sartre objects to: "Only actions done in God bind not the soul of man." This is the sacred: there is a way of acting in which man is not bound by his own deeds. This type of action is treated at length in the *Bhagavad Gita,* and there as in the fiction of Sartre it centers around a possible crime. A battle is about to begin and Arjuna, one of the warriors, faints with grief at the thought that soon he will be killing his relatives and friends. The god Krishna appears to Arjuna and bids him to have courage, for killing the opposing warriors will not be Arjuna's deed at all: "I have doomed them to die; be thou merely the means of my work." Thus the divine Krishna assumes full responsibility for Arjuna's action. Krishna praises the man of inner freedom who stands apart from his deeds: "even if he kills all of these warriors, he kills them not and is free." When a man has obtained this type of freedom, "only his body works: he is free from sin...his works bind him not" (*Bhagavad Gita*,pp.92,116,63). This is what Hugo and Mathieu experienced. The man who is free is not the doer of his own deeds, his deeds merely take place as the outcome of divinely established natural forces. The *Gita* explains.

All actions take place in time by the interweaving of the forces of Nature; but the man lost in selfish delusion thinks that he himself is the actor [the doer] (p.58).

The yogi has purified himself of the belief that he is the doer; he has attained to *naishkarmya karma* or actionless action. Everything has become a matter of duty, there is no further personal responsibility. The yogi is indifferent to the outcome of his actions; he is free. He still goes about the ordinary routines of walking, sleeping, or talking, but even in such insignificant acts as opening or closing his eyes he remembers that *he* does nothing: "It is the servants of my soul who are working" (*Bhagavad Gita*,p.67). This is the purity of the yogi, but it is not limited to the holy men of India. In Chinese Taoism it is found in the ideal of *wei wu wei*, the "doing without doing" that characterizes the true wise man. In medieval Europe the phrase of St. Gregory the Great was often quoted, *quies in labore*; in modern Europe the ideal was proposed by Simone Weil: good consists in "action not active [*action non agissante*]," and Martin Buber recommended that type of action which is "as if it were non-action [*Tun... wie wenn es Nichttun wäre*]." But whether it is the obedience of the monk, or *naishkarmya karma*, or *wei wu wei*, or *quies in labore*, or *action non agissante*, or *Tun...wie wenn es Nichttun ware*, it is the same state of passivity in action. It is the purity of the yogi or monk; it is the passive freedom experienced by Antoine at the end of *Nausea* (*N*,156 ff.); and it is the fundamental philosophy that Sartre has come to reject.

Can Sartre justify this rejection? Consider again the comparison already made in this chapter between Kierkegaard and Sartre. Kierkegaard spoke of the knight of infinite resignation who purified himself of all desire for the finite and the temporal. When he was writing this passage, Kierkegaard renounced his beloved fiancée and spoke of living as a dead man in the isolation of his own reflective thought. It is in a very similar reflective isolation that Orestes, Mathieu, Goetz, and Hugo find themselves. It was in this context that each of the Sartrean heroes considered committing a crime to achieve true freedom. But unlike Kierkegaard's hero, Sartre's heroes would have a particular difficulty at this point, for they are provided with no context of objective good in which they can be bad. They seek a load of guilt which alone can drag them into the real; but without an objective right and wrong guilt is hard to come by. For Sartre deliverance comes through crime, but because he denies any objective morality there would remain no possibility of a crime, hence no salvation. After Kierkegaard spoke of infinite resignation, he suggested a second movement that might follow that act; the second movement was faith. Faith turns out to be philosophically absurd, but Kierkegaard admired it nonetheless. It was by virtue of this absurdity that the infinitely resigned man would regrasp the temporal and the finite that he had renounced. Orestes, Mathieu, Goetz, and Hugo have each renounced the temporal and the finite. Then, suddenly, each of them is doing what Kierkegaard had considered as the absurd movement of faith: they are reentering the historical. The dramatic moments in which Goetz, Orestes, and Hugo unexpectedly assume historicity and guilt are among the most unconvincing moments in Sartrean theater. ("You can't have understood" [*NE*,246]; "Your eyes are shining, you are no longer the same" [*DGL*,134]; "Oh, how you've changed! Your eyes have lost their glow; they're dull and smoldering" [*NE*,93]; and so on.) In each case the moment has an element of the deus ex machina about it. Kierkegaard would be the first to acknowledge that faith *is* a deus ex machina and therefore both dramatically and philosophically unconvincing. But the difficulty with Sartre is that he is unwilling to make any such acknowledgment. He introduces the same incomprehensible movement that Kierkegaard saw as the absurd movement of faith and tries to pass it off as good drama or good philosophy. But because of the unjustifiability of the movement—the movement from negative freedom to creative freedom—it is neither. The crime to which Sartre often refers turns out to be both a theatrical and a philosophical one: a leap has been made from the purity of the *cogito* into the process of history; it has not been justified. An infinite and distant reflecting consciousness has suddenly assumed the finitude of history. Spirit has taken on flesh; it has become incarnate; the for-itself has assumed the in-itself. It was a very similar leap into the finite historical world that Kierkegaard had presented as the leap of faith (*Concluding Unscientific Postscript*,pp.343,345ff.).

Sartre and Merleau-Ponty had a long debate over the meaning of freedom in the course of which Sartre seems to have acknowledged the double aspect in his understanding of freedom:

One must not say that if man is free, then his liberation makes no sense; rather this liberation could not be understood if man was not free to begin with. Only a being essentially free [*libre par essence*] can aspire to liberate himself (in Jeanson, *Le problème moral*,p.253).

The need of being essentially free in order to liberate oneself seems to put essence before existence. This gives rise to basic difficulties in trying to explain how the transition (the leap) from essential freedom to actual freedom is effected. Because Aristotle had implied the transition from essence to act, Sartre had called him the magician of logic. To explain this "leap," scholastic philosophers spoke of the divine concordance. Sartre's associate, Francis Jeanson, likewise implies a divine concordance to explain the transition: "il faudrait concevoir quelque conversion passive du sujet par une sorte de grâce divine" (*Le problème moral*, p.253). Sartre has written a laudatory introduction to Jeanson's book, but there or subsequently he has not tried to explain the "grâce divine" involved in the transition. When he finds Flaubert making this same transition (from the freedom of pure refusal to the freedom that acts) he likewise postulates a concealed theology and implicit grace, though Flaubert did not.

If Sartre does not really acknowledge the leap that he has made, both the extent and the character of the leap can become clear if a comparison is made betwen the basic supposition of *Being and Nothingness* and the basic supposition of the *Critique de la raison dialectique*. The fundamental starting point for *Being and Nothingness* is the transcendent *cogito* as set forth by Descartes and developed with great precision by Sartre and the phenomenologists. The starting point for the *Critique* is radically different: it is the reality of human action as the maker of history. That is, in the *Critique* Sartre *begins* with the *belief* that man is the creative maker of history; it is in terms of this belief that Sartre rejects various opposing alternatives, and it is in terms of this belief that he explains man, matter, and society. In Sartre's early philosophy the *self*-validating *cogito* served as foundation for his certitude. Now his original certitude is not founded on the self-validating *cogito* at all, rather it is founded on the enlightenment that he received from Merleau-Ponty in 1950. This transition from one starting point to the other (from the *cogito* to an enlightenment) is made many times in the fiction of Sartre, and the crime that is involved is that the purity of the self-validating *cogito* has given way before a nonvalidated enlightenment. Sartrean theater and Sartrean philosophy enact the same unjustified leap.

When Sartre analyzed the two forms of Cartesian freedom, he objected to the intrusion of Descartes' Christian faith. He found it scandalous that the autonomous and infinite freedom of Descartes' *cogito* should suddenly be disposed by grace to accept the Christian faith. It would seem to be a similar scandal that the autonomous and infinite freedom of the Sartrean *cogito* should suddenly be disposed to receive an objective enlightenment. But Sartre has found the change to be for the better. In 1963 he reflected on a number of the basic points that he had presented twenty years earlier in *Being and Nothingness* and concluded: "For the last ten years or so I've been a man waking up, cured of a long, bitter-sweet madness" (*W*,158).

The enlightenment and the waking-up of which Sartre speaks can be considered in terms of one of the more significant passages from *Being and Nothingness*:

The for-itself arises as the nihilation of the in-itself and this nihilation is defined as the project toward the in-itself. Between the nihilated in-itself and the projected in-itself the for-itself is nothingness.

Sartre goes on to explain that since the for-itself is the negation of the in-itself, and that, though the for-itself desires the in-itself, it does not desire a return to the in-itself, which it negates; rather, its project is to be an in-itself that would be its own foundation, its own cause; this would be the in-itself-for-itself.

The fundamental value which presides over this project is exactly the in-itself-for-itself; that is the ideal of a consciousness which would be the foundation of its own being-in-itself by the pure consciousness which it would have of itself. It is this ideal which can be called God (*BN*,693–94).

This passage tells of the three-phase sequence (in-itself, for-itself, and in-itself-for-itself) considered above in chapter 2 and at the end of chapter 6, but this sequence also resembles the three stages outlined at the beginning of the present chapter: the in-itself which is nihilated recalls the first stage, that of the bourgeois; the for-itself which rises out of the in-itself as the negation of the in-itself is the second stage, that of the artist in revolt. Then comes the third stage: the for-itself longs to be something, but it does not want to be simply the in-itself that it has renounced; it wants to be the in-itself-for-itself—God, the synthesis Sartre had rejected as impossible. This stage was not attained; it was found to be a contradiction, and this was the reason that all of man's actions necessarily became failures. Man was a useless passion (*BN*,754). But subsequent to *Being and Nothingness* (1943) the whole critique that Sartre has brought against the spirituality of the artist would have no point unless there is a third stage beyond the nothingness of the for-itself. The whole defense that Sartre has made of the freedom that acts, would have no point unless man would be able to succeed in some of his acts. The only way that this would be possible is through the reality of the third stage, the in-itself-for-itself. There are texts of Sartre that imply the possibility of the third stage. For example, he writes of his student days: "The total concrete was what we wanted to leave behind, the absolute concrete was what we wanted to achieve" (*SM*,19). The "we" is a for-itself between two concretes, and the whole import of the passage is that "we" should have been taught this third stage, "the absolute concrete." For this third stage to be realized, the for-itself would have to be the foundation of its own being, not only of its own nothingness. There are even texts of Sartre indicating that this will be possible at some future date: he tells of the new humanity claiming "we are *our own sons*, our common invention" (*CRD*,453). Are they not claiming to be the cause of their own *being* (*causa-sui*)? Does not Sartre allow that man might also become the cause of his own being when he envisions a transformation through which man will become *his own project*? (*CRD*,639).[4] In the future that Sartre envisions, the opposites are to be reconciled; good and evil, being and nothingness will be re-welded together (See the end of chap. 5 above, and *G*,186); a whole series of opposites can be transcended (interiority and exteriority, multiplicity and unity, and so on [*SM*,87 n; *CRD*, 61 n]); and even freedom will be one with necessity (*liberté et nécessité ne font plus qu'un*)! (*CRD*,377).

Is not the future that Sartre envisions really the third stage, the

4. In speaking of man as his own project Sartre is adapting a text from Karl Marx, who also implied self-causation in man's ultimate achievement. Similarly, Kierkegaard would have it that the knight of faith "gives birth to his own father" (*FT*,38). Simon Magus tells of the divine force that is in man: "it generates itself...it is its own son, mother, father." Sartre writes of Achille Flaubert that he had only one passion: "to reproduce his generator in producing himself" (*IF*,1,137). The Sartrean preference is for becoming our own son, not our own father; the difference would probably go back to existence preceding essence.

in-itself-for-itself? The nothingness of consciousness has been transcended; man's actions are no longer essentially failures; man will be his own maker, and the opposites will be welded together. Sartre's references to this future state are brief and indirect, but it seems that his understanding of this future coincides with the definition of God that he had offered in *Being and Nothingness* and rejected as impossible. Sartre has been widely known as an atheist, but perhaps today he could be better understood as a religious prophet preaching a process theology; in the manner of Renan or H. F. Alexander, he seems to be looking forward to a god who is coming to be.

Sartre envisions both a corporate salvation for man and the experience of a new kind of freedom that is beyond our present ability to comprehend. Since both corporate salvation and a new freedom are also claimed by Christianity, it might be worth comparing Christian salvation with the salvation that Sartre anticipates.[5] Sartre sees contemporary man living in a state of slavery — "Men of the present day are born criminals" — and in this he is not far from the tradition of St. Paul. For Sartre this slavery is universal and long-lasting; it is like original sin, for it is passed on to each new generation by one's parents (it is their look that leaves the child in bondage to the other). Sartre speaks of men having the "feeling of an original fall" a vague all-inclusive sense of guilt that transcends the guilt that one feels because of any particular fault (*BN*,354). To explain this sense of guilt, both

5. A more ambitious attempt at showing parallels between Sartre and Christian faith, with references to trinitarian theology, has been attempted by Francis Jeanson, an associate of Sartre and Sartre's favorite expositor of Sartre (in *Sartre: Les écrivains devant Dieu*). Sartre takes up similar trinitarian themes in *IF*,112-14. A sustained effort at presenting Christianity in the context of Sartrean philosophy was undertaken by Daniel Patte in *L'athéisme d'un chrétien; ou un chrétien a l'écoute de Sartre*. Patte argues that the God Sartre rejects is only an idol and then tries to show how Jesus reveals what an authentic life is and thus breaks the circle of bad faith; he similarly treats other New Testament themes. Sartre would seem to acknowledge an element of Christianity in his thought when he writes, "And we are all still Christians today; the most radical unbelief is a Christian atheism; that is, it preserves in spite of its destructive power certain directive patterns — not much for the thought, more for the imagination, much for the sensibility — whose origins must be sought in the Christian centuries of which all of us are the inheritors, like it or not" (*IF*,2,124).

Sartre and St. Paul refer to the story of Adam and Eve.[6] But the ancestral guilt is passed on to Adam's descendants, and men find they dwell in a common hell, a hell that is other people.

Since Sartre judges that the nature of man's perdition is essentially social, the salvation that he anticipates requires a transformation of all human relationships from strife into brotherhood. In order that this brotherhood, or the new humanity, be achieved, men must rise up from their slavery in a common experience. Brotherhood is possible only if men share together in a *common past*. Sartre argues that the brotherhood of man can never be based on the common nature shared by all man; canned peas have a common nature but this gives them no basis for brotherhood! Brotherhood can come only when men share in a common historical experience. Only by sharing a common past will men acquire a common being and thus be united. Brothers are those who have been liberated together. "We have come out of the mire on the same date" (*CRD*,453).

In a similar way Christians maintain that brothers are those who have been liberated together. As in Sartre, the brotherhood of man is not founded upon man's common nature; it is founded on a liberating historical event (the Passion-Resurrection). It is by sharing in this event that men become brothers, not because men have a common nature. Like Sartre, St. Paul speaks of men rising from the mire in a common experience: we have been buried together with Christ in order that we might rise with him to the newness of life (*Col.*2:12). Paul argues that for those who share in this experience of liberation all class distinctions have been abolished ("slave and free, Jew and Greek, male and female"). Christians together form a single Being, they constitute one divine Body; for each of them, "to live is Christ." Sartre would put it that "the being-of-group is lived by each one as nature" (*CRD*,453).

The being-of-group is founded on a common liberation, but beyond the liberation itself Sartre intends that the liberated bind themselves together by an oath. Only in the oath do the separate

6. Sartre makes several references to Adam and Eve to illustrate what he is saying. Shame is explained thus in *BN*,354; temporality is explained thus in *KV*,50; even Sartre's basic "existence precedes essence" is seen as illustrated in the story of the Fall. Since Adam has a *fallen* nature, his deeds are not determined by his nature. Thus Adam is what he is because of what he has done (see *IF*,210).

individuals become a group. Through the oath a man definitely enters into history; he is not able "to return back beyond a specific date" (*CRD*,453). This also presents a parallel with Christian spirituality, for Christianity has required irrevocable oaths at baptism, marriage, and the entrance into monastic life. In each case a person becomes bound by his act so that the possibility of return is denied. The permanent vows of baptism, marriage, and monasticism are made in the face of what is necessarily an uncertain future; any vow of this kind has always been regarded as a *crime* by those who consider themselves to be "free spirits." Such people do not want to be bound by any tie, they drift uncommitted like the wind and this gives them their sense of spirituality and freedom. Currently the term "free spirits" is used by many hippies to describe themselves; it refers primarily to the fact that their spirit is not bound to a single sexual partner. Many hippies could also identify with the spirituality that was presented above in chapter 6: they too disdain the material world and its values, their interest is in the theater, the occult, and psychedelic art; they prefer not to work and their political sympathies lean towards anarchy or nihilism — "only revolt is pure." Sartre's analysis of spirituality would seem to be a perceptive study of the "free spirit." In the first centuries of Christianity there was a similar spirituality espoused by various gnostic sects. The gnostics were often free spirits who disdained the material world. Their sexual practices were liberal and uncommitted, and their ideas were propounded in a striking form of psychedelic prose; but their doctrines were rejected by orthodox Christianity. Sartre has shown himself sympathetic with individuals of this type, and the analysis that he makes of their mentality shows how deeply it is part of his own; but ultimately he does not agree with them. He calls for an end to psychedelic fantasies by the only way possible: committed historical action. Spirit takes on flesh only by making an irrevocable commitment, the one thing that the "free spirit" is not free to do. Afterwards, spirit is rooted in reality and cannot turn back beyond a specific date; it has become incarnate.

When Sartre urges an *entrance* into history and one from which there is no return, he touches again on a basic theme in Christian spirituality. The mysticisms of the East are oriented in a very different direction: they offer disciplines to *detach* their followers from history. The yogi did not want a definitive entrance into the historical world; he tried to work his way free of this world with its cycle of births and deaths. A series of incarnations had to be endured until he could attain a definitive *disincarnation*. All of his acts were capable of being reversed; in fact, liberation will ultimately come for him only when every one of his historical deeds is undone and he is free of his karma. Hindu Gods are like Hindu men: they assume a number of incarnations, but none of them is really definitive. In contrast, Christianity could be defined as the religion of definitive incarnation. Both the God of Christianity and Christian men become incarnate (enter history) only once; incarnation is so definitive that it will not be repeated, and therefore Christian history is not an ever-recurring cycle. A cyclic understanding of history is found in many forms of non-Christian thought; it has had a particular appeal to "spiritual men" in both the East and the West (Plato, Melville, Nietzsche, and others). But the noncyclic character of history was strongly affirmed by the early Church in opposition to the gnostic spiritualities of the times: Christ's incarnation would not repeat itself and neither would individual men be reincarnated; history is definitive and there is no turning back; men lead only one life and everything counts; even man's present body would always be his. This affirmation of the reality of history has dominated the Western mind ever since; it is the belief repeatedly appealed to in Sartre's recent study of Flaubert and that serves as the starting point for the *Critique de la raison dialectique*.

Sartre was probably the first to recognize the parallels between Christian salvation and his own theory of salvation. In 1940, shortly after the German invasion of France, Sartre became a prisoner of war. The following December he tried to bring believing and nonbelieving prisoners together by writing a Christmas play: *Bariona*. Some twenty years later he allowed it to be published in a limited edition, but explained that his use of the Christian myth did not represent a lapse from his more familiar position.

Bariona is a leader of the Jewish people at the time of the birth of Christ; he has been urging his people to stop bearing children in order that the Jewish people might die out rather than continue to live in misery under the Roman occupation. Bariona's heart is "clenched in refusal" and he argues that "the dignity of man is in his despair." When Bariona hears of the birth of Christ, he sets out for the stable at Bethlehem with the intention of killing the child. But on the way he meets Balthazar, one of the magi, who explains to Bariona the meaning of the birth of Christ:

Christ will suffer in his flesh, for he is man. But he is also God, and with all of his divinity he is beyond this suffering. And the rest of us, men made to the image of God, we are beyond all suffering in the measure that we resemble God....Bariona, you would be a man of the old law. You have considered your misfortune with bitterness and you said, "I am fatally wounded," and you wanted to lie on your side and consume the rest of your life meditating on the injustice done to you. But Christ has come to redeem us; he came to suffer and to show us how to deal with suffering (*Bar.*, 101-2).

Upon hearing this explanation, Bariona is deeply moved and undergoes a change of heart. He enters the stable devoutly. Soon he comes to learn that Herod has threatened the life of the Child, so he assumes his former powers of leadership and organizes the peasants to take militant action to protect the Christ. As the play ends, Bariona urges the peasants to advance into battle in joy, for the Christ is born.

Bariona makes the same unexpected transition that became central to Sartrean theater: the transition from the negative freedom of pure refusal to the positive freedom which acts creatively in union with other men. This is the Sartrean salvation that would take many forms; it is the transition that Jeanson sees as involving "une sorte de grâce divine." The only time Sartre tried to explain it (in *Bariona*), he used Christian images. When someone in Sartrean theater first renounced the sterility of pure refusal to assume creative action in the world, it was Bariona passing from the "old law" to the new.

Sartre should be taken at his word: *Bariona* was not a profession of faith. There is no point in calling him a believer or an anonymous Christian, when he is so abundantly capable of speaking for himself. He acknowledges that there is a Christian orientation in much of his writing and ends his autobiography with the following explanation:

I was taught Sacred History, the Gospel, and the catechism without being given the means for believing. The result was a disorder which became my own particular order. There were twists and turns, a considerable transfer; removed from Catholicism, the sacred was deposited in belles-lettres and the penman appeared, an *ersatz* of the Christian I was unable to be....a tremendous collective power had entered me. Lodged in my heart it lay in wait. It was the faith of others. All that was necessary was to rename its customary object and to modify it superficially....I grew like a weed on the compost of Catholicity; my roots sucked up its juices and I changed them into sap.

Other Works
Cited in
the Text

Aquinas, Thomas. *Scriptum super libros sententiarum magistri Petri Lombardi,* edited by R. P. Mandonnet, O. P. Paris: Lethieleux, 1929.

_____. *Summa Theologiae,* general editor Thomas Gilby, O. P. New York: Doubleday Image Book, 1969.

Aron, Raymond. *Marxism and the Existentialists,* translated by Helen Weaver and Robert Addis and John Weightman. New York: Harper and Row, 1969.

Augustine. *The Confessions of St. Augustine,* translated by Rex Warner. New York: New American Library, 1963.

Beauvoir, Simone de. *The Prime of Life,* translated by Peter Green. Cleveland: World Publishing, Meridian Book, 1966.

Bergson, Henri. *Creative Evolution,* translated by Arthur Miller. New York: Henry Holt, 1913.

The Bhagavad Gita, translated by Juan Mascaro. Baltimore: Penguin Books, 1962.

Buber, Martin. *Eclipse of God,* New York: Harper Torchbooks, 1957.

_____. *I and Thou,* 2d edition. New York: Charles Scribner's Sons, 1958.

The Cloud of Unknowing, translated by Clifton Wolters. Baltimore: Penguin Books, 1961.

Collins, James. *The Existentialists.* Chicago: Regnery Gateway Edition, 1964.

Coomaraswamy, Ananda. *Hinduism and Buddhism.* New York: Philosophical Library, 1943.

Denzinger, H., and Schonmetzer, A. *Enchiridion Symbolorum, Definitionum, et Declarationum.* New York: Herder, 1963.

Desan, Wilfrid. *The Marxism of Jean-Paul Sartre.* New York: Doubleday Anchor Book, 1966.

_____. *The Tragic Finale.* New York: Harper Torchbooks, 1960.

Eckhart. *Meister Eckhart,* translated by Raymond B. Blackney. New York: Harper Torchbook, 1941.

Greene, Norman. *Jean-Paul Sartre, The Existentialist Ethic.* Ann Arbor: The University of Michigan Press, Ann Arbor Paperback, 1963.

Hammarskjold, Dag. *Markings,* translated by W. H. Auden and Leif Sjoberg. London: Faber and Faber, 1966.

Happold, F. C. *Mysticism, A Study and an Anthology.* Baltimore: Penguin Books, 1970.

Hartmann, Klaus. *Sartre's Ontology.* Evanston, Ill.: Northwestern University Press, 1966.

James, William. *Varieties of Religious Experience,* New York: New American Library, 1958.

Jeanson, Francis. *Sartre: Les écrivains devant Dieu.* Paris: Désclée de Brouwer, 1966.

_____. *Le problème moral et la pensée de Sartre.* Paris: Editions du Seuil, 1965.

John of the Cross. *Ascent of Mount Carmel,* translated by E. Allison Peers. New York: Doubleday Image Book, 1959.

Jolivet, Regis. *The Theology of the Absurd,* translated by Wesley C. Piersol. Westminster, Md.: Newman, 1967.

Julian of Norwich. *Revelations of Divine Love,* translated into modern English by Clifton Wolters. Baltimore: Penguin Books, 1966.

Jung, C. G. *Psychology and Alchemy,* translated by R. F. C. Hull, Princeton: Princeton University Press, 1968.

Kierkegaard, Soren. *Concluding Unscientific Postscript,* translated by David Swenson and Walter Lowrie. Princeton: Princeton University Press, 1941.

_____. *Fear and Trembling,* translated by Walter Lowrie. Princeton: Princeton University Press, 1968.

_____. *The Journals,* translated by Alexander Dru. New York: Harper Torchbooks, 1959.

Lovejoy, Arthur. *The Great Chain of Being.* Cambridge: Harvard University Press, 1957.

Merleau-Ponty, Maurice. *Les aventures de la dialectique,* Paris: Gallimard, 1955.

Merton, Thomas. *New Seeds of Contemplation.* New York: New Directions, 1972.

_____. *No Man Is an Island.* New York: Doubleday Image Book, 1967.

_____. *Mystics and Zen Masters.* New York: Dell, 1969.

Murray, John Courtney. *The Problem of God,* New Haven: Yale University Press, 1964.

O'Brien, Elmer. *Varieties of Mystical Experience.* New York: New American Library, 1965.

Patte, Daniel. *L'athéisme d'un chrétien; ou un chrétien à l'écoute de Sartre.* Paris: Nouvelles Editions Latines, 1964.

Plato. *Theaetetus, Sophist,* translated by Harold North Fowler. Cambridge: Harvard University Press. 1942.

Plotinus. *The Enneads of Plotinus,* translated from the Greek by Stephen MacKenna. Boston: Charles Branford Co., 1916.

Reinhardt, K. *The Existentialist Revolt.* Milwaukee: Bruce Publishing Co., 1952.

Rideau, Emile. *The Thought of Teilhard de Chardin,* translated by René Hague. New York: Harper and Row, 1967.

Scripture quotations are taken from the Revised Standard Version.

The Secret of the Golden Flower, translated by Richard Wilhelm. New York: Harcourt, Brace and World, 1962.

Smith, Huston. *The Religions of Man.* New York: Harper and Row, 1965.

Teilhard de Chardin, Pierre. *The Divine Milieu,* New York: Harper Torchbook, 1968.

_____. *Writings in Time of War.* New York: Harper and Row, 1965.

Teresa of Avila. *Interior Castle,* translated by E. Allison Peers. New York: Doubleday Image Book, 1961.

Troisfontaines, Roger. *Le choix de Jean-Paul Sartre.* Paris: Aubier, 1945.

Underhill, Evelyn. *Practical Mysticism*. New York: Dutton, n. d.

Weil, Simone. *Gravity and Grace,* translated by Emma Crawford. London: Routledge and Kegan Paul, 1953.

Whitehead, A. N. *Science and the Modern World*. New York: New American Library, 1948.

Index